Green Business – the Billion Dollar Deal

The Dot-Coms Make an Exit – Showtime for the Dot-Greens

Dietrich Walther

icet

International Center for Education
and Technology, LLC

Green Business—The Billion Dollar Deal: The Dot-Coms Make an Exit—Showtime for the Dot-Greens

Originally published in German:
Title: Green Business das Milliardengeschäft. Nach den Dot-coms kommen jetzt die Dot-greens Publisher: Gabler Verlag Wiesbaden Germany 2008

icet

International Center for Education and Technology, 109 E Lamme Sreet, Bozeman, MT 59715

Printed in the United States of America

ISBN 13: 978-0-9856672-0-7

Table of Contents

Introduction

The breathtaking speed of development of the Internet-supported economy during the last 15 years, and the worldwide emergence of dot-coms—almost out of the blue—showed an entrepreneurial degree of activity that is urgently needed today for environmental and climate protection activities.

Beyond that, there are further reasons why particularly the dot-coms are referred to as connecting factors in this book. The most important thing is: Never before, not even in the founding years of the 19th century, or in the years of the economic miracle in the middle of the 20th century, was there such a tackle-mentality present: so many people who dared to set up their own business relying upon their own performance. But at the same time, rarely were so many mistakes made, so many tricky fraudulences invented, and a number of new shareholders just discovering the stock market were disappointed.

What does it mean to enforce new incorporations of environmental companies with at least the same speed and acceleration as the dot-coms, and yet to practice high-technology-based environmental protection from the beginning? What is the difference between growth-oriented politics for all states and the abdication politics that some environment protectors are delighted to preach to developing countries? Meanwhile, more and more "green" companies have understood how negative the consequences of the excessively nourished animosity towards technology are. This technology abstinence can be compared with the widespread lack of competence in mathematics as a school subject or field of study. In a remarkable leading article in the daily newspaper "Welt" called "Alles ist Zahl" ("It's all figures"), Norbert Lossau wrote: "It is still trendy to boast at parties that one had bad marks in math." Lossau's arguments are convincing as he writes: "The big challenges for humanity, be it the battle against dangerous pathogens, the exploitation of new energy sources, or the development of innovative technologies for climate protection, can only be mastered with the help of computers and mathematics." [1] Furthermore, being able to calculate correctly and assess soundly is always and everywhere important. Finally, we can also note the miscalculations in the environmental sector: let us just think of the

---

[1] Die Welt, March 25, 2008

i

climate prognoses that were equipped with new figures only recently, as well as the false speculations of the "New Economy" on the Internet that, unfortunately, often were revealed too late. These examples have clearly proven that nothing works through whitewashing or manipulating figures, and nothing innovative has sustainable chances for the future without mathematics, which is indispensable in the digital and economic world. You have to calculate precisely, and then recalculate again—argue with undeniable figures and then evaluate qualitatively. This applies if you want to get others to put their own money into environmental projects. Of course, figures are not everything, but nonetheless they are a very, very important part. Especially in the environmental sector, there are many facts that, up until the present, have not been sufficiently evaluated. For example we can site the warming and pollution of our atmosphere. Up until now, "natural capital" has not sufficiently been included in the calculations of the national economy and the world. But is clean air worthless? Environmental protection is also always health protection, and many new environmental products and services are political products: catalytic converters or fine particle filters are just two examples. The new green multi-billion dollar business has evolved from the sheer will to survive and a worldwide paradigm shift in environmental and energy politics. In the ongoing US presidential election campaign, Barack Obama proposed $150 billion of public research funds for alternative energies alone.

In this sense, new considerations will be made in this book that are indispensable as success factors for green business entrepreneurship, paired with the basic and further training required for such entrepreneurial pursuits.

The starting point was the rise of the New Economy, the up until now unique entrepreneurial activity connected therewith, and the high interest in marked-based share transactions in Internet companies leading up to the bursting of the dot-com bubble. The deeper question is whether the green revolution is a similar phenomenon, or a sustainable, long-term trend. My answer is: The new environment-oriented start-ups, I call them "dot-greens," will bring with them multi-billion dollar business.

The doctrines of this issue create the basis for the 2nd chapter and the new gold rush in California of green business innovations. As a result of innovative theoretical findings, the propagation paths of clean technologies, and the paradigm changes in ecological thinking connected therewith, all sectors in the industry will be forced to reroute. Above all, the newly defined five main directions of the eco-influence on the economy show that beneath the current trend of the US economy there lays hard economic constraints and not just eco-emotions.

Referring to well-known Silicon Valley companies, the 3rd chapter deals with the way green IT company strategies are enforced, and the way the race to catch up with going-green takes place in the USA in practice. I call the simple formula of success derived from that evaluation "IMEAS": Ideas + Money + Experience + Activity = Sustainable Success. According to my experience, in times of upswing, not only courage and energy are required if you want to be successful, but also the ability to persevere if things are not going well or even going downhill. Practical tips emphasize that.

The 4th chapter explains which role the early formation of a knowledge-based new entrepreneurship plays for the future. This section explains the close interdependence of economy and academic research in the Stanford environment and other private academies, and shows how profitably this long-time tradition moves to sustainability.

Finally, conclusions for a lasting, sustainable academic education resulting in a long-term advance in innovation are derived. Without radical reconstruction of our basic and advanced training systems, a sustainable, green, multi-billion dollar business will be of no avail. Thus, corporations in new fields of green business have to emerge.

Globally, a turnover of about 50 billion euros is produced in the environment industry in 2008. At present, Germany holds about 25% of the export of environment technology worldwide. In order to maintain and extend this share, concentrated efforts have to be made, because the great number of start-up companies in the USA and other regions of growth are just now entering the competition. The August 2008 edition of the solar power magazine "Photon" lists 50 start-up companies in the USA alone, 25 of which are from the region around San Francisco. This outlines once again why this technology center receives special attention in this book.

Since we are living in a global world where everyone is similarly affected by the topic of environment and climate change, as well as the entrepreneurial chances of the resulting multi-billion dollar business, this book is simultaneously published in English, Spanish and Russian.

Dietrich Walther, Iserlohn, Fall of 2008

1. How the Dot-Coms changed the World

Silicon Valley – The Birthplace of Cyberspace

There is only one region in the whole world that managed to advance from an area of apricot and plum cultivation to the professional metropolis for high technology: the "Silicon Valley". Regarding the degree of popularity, this digital dream factory can be compared with Hollywood, and it has already produced more millionaires than has Hollywood's well-known actors. Insiders are of the opinion that during the golden age of the Silicon Valley, 64 founders per day succeeded in becoming millionaires.[2]

The valley got its name from silicon, the most important raw material of microelectronics and the chip industry in the 1970s. The nickname was invented by the journalist Don C. Hoefler, and many other regions have tried to appropriate it. Today, the term "Silicon Valley" stands as one of the most important industry settlements in the world, especially in the high-tech sector. However, it also represents a unique entrepreneurial spirit and a blooming founder landscape. The valley is located in southern San Francisco in the American state of California and enjoys international fame. There is no place-name sign and no border, no particularly remarkable natural environment, but there are numerous highways and broad roads of communication between the residential and industrial areas. The string of companies in the technology parks reads like a Who is Who of the computer age. Companies like Apple, HP, Xerox, Google, Oracle, Sun Microsystems and Yahoo – they all are based in the Silicon Valley.

Research and development centers of space and air navigation operate besides these pillars of the computer industry, as well as world-renowned universities, from Stanford to Berkeley, as well as the city of San Jose, the uncrowned capital of the Silicon Valley with its own airport.

The latest publications on the genesis of the Silicon Valley draw comparisons with the great period of the Renaissance in Europe. The editor of the book "Silicon Valley", John R. McLaughlin, even speaks of the "110 Year Renaissance", and compares the second revolution in

---

[2] cf. David A. Kaplan, Silicon Valley, Munich, Heyne Verlag 2000, p. 32

1

information with the invention of letterpress printing by Johann Gutenberg.[3]

The superior nature of the comparison shows how the modern creators of the information revolution classify themselves. They are the Gutenbergs of the 20th century. The development and practical introduction of the Internet as a new infrastructure of the cyber world definitely justifies that. Never before had it been possible to make such an abundance of information useable in such quality, at such high speed, and to such a gigantic extent. And all of that in a practically simultaneous and global manner. Thus, the invention and practical realization of the worldwide web holds up to the comparison with Gutenberg's achievement. Of course, the parallel introduction of personal computers as counterparts to the previously dominating big computers and host systems generated the tool that was of absolute necessity for that purpose. Without the home computer and the radical extension of computer performance, combined with the simultaneously rapid downsizing of the microelectronics connected therewith, this technological change would have been impossible.

The technical innovations from Silicon Valley have cross-fertilized and, in turn, accelerated the associated information and communication forms. McLaughlin emphasizes: "The convergence of the personal computer, router technology that allows different computer platforms to communicate and the end of the Cold War, which prompted the democratization of the Internet, all were crucial to the new Information Revolution."[4] With the flourishing Internet economy in particular, the reputation of Silicon Valley as America's high-tech development center grew to an extent never experienced before. In many publications about this phenomenon, the outstanding American entrepreneurial spirit is held responsible for this above all else. But this does not go far enough. In this context it is frequently overlooked that politics also have a strongly supporting or hampering effect. In particular, this also applies to environmental protection technologies because until now, the market mechanism alone has not been able to generate the innovations needed for sustained development. Thus, it is also indisputable that the high degree of government aid for military research in Silicon Valley has to be

---

[3] cf. Silicon Valley 110 Year Renaissance, 2nd. Edition, Palo Alto 2008, Introduction

[4] Ibid

taken into account. In her book "Schöne neue Cyberwelt"[5] (Fair new Cyber World) Paulina Borsock emphasizes: "Without the state, there would be no Internet. Furthermore, there would be no chip industry; the origin of the prosperity of Silicon Valley (governmental research monies for electrical engineering) made the early computer possible." Of course, the sympathizers of techno-liberalism do not enjoy reading such unemotional opinions. Still, it is true, and ultimately it also it will play a central role in the enforcement of new environment and climate protection objectives. Many environment protection products are also political products.

The high-tech region of the Silicon Valley consists of 16 cities, including such well-known places as Fremont, Los Altos, Menlo Park, San Jose, and Santa Clara or Saratoga. The most important high-tech companies come from this region, which has acted as an impulse generator for basic innovations for decades: they have been forming the basis of common products like personal computers, mobile phones, or Internet search engines for a long time. A part or idea from Silicon Valley can be found in almost all of today's top products, even if it was just a starting idea or the basis for a patent. The Dot-Com company foundation boom also originated here.

In the middle of the 90s, a previously unseen activity hit the world economy. In the first place, it was based on the Internet that had hardly been known beyond the realm of the sciences up to then. The Internet seemed to be the ideal base to make the economy gain new momentum and to open a new economic world that labeled itself just that, the "New Economy".

The former President of the USA, Bill Clinton, and his Vice President Al Gore, who acted as more of a technological than environmental pioneer at the time, made a considerable contribution to this upswing. In February 1993, immediately after assumption of their offices, at a town meeting in Silicon Valley, they made a statement of their high-tech strategy that, in turn, emphasized the regulating power of the state.

The central focus of this speech was the future of the great number of existing networks, media and information services. What they meant was the Internet. Al Gore called upon the industry to improve their resources

---

[5] Paulina Borsock, Schöne neue Cyberwelt. Mythen, Helden und Irrwege des Hightech (Fair new Cyber World. Myths, heroes, and abberations of hightech) München dtv 2001, p. 12

3

and to make them available to the public. Already at that time, they were aware of the incredible effect of the new Internet technology, even though it was in its formative stages. The technology experts overbid each other in their flowery prognoses for the future of the new media, and thus sparked a kind of forty-niner mood amongst the companies.

Special emphasis was put on the new electronic infrastructure for education, science, health, and culture—at this time the impact on the environment and climate were not yet issues. Thus, the National Information Infrastructure Agenda for Action, the Clinton/Gore strategy paper following the speech, can definitely be called the initial spark for the real success of the Internet. Here, politics called upon the economy to act and were heard. In Europe almost nobody talked about the Internet at that time. In 1994, the EU study that became famous as the Bangemann paper, "Europa und die globale Informationsgesellschaft" (Europe and the global information society) asked which destination the train was heading for. However, this dossier was a description of the situation rather than a vision or even a call to become active. Only when the first results of this forty-niner mood spilled over into Europe was the awareness of lagging behind the USA in a crucial infrastructure key technology made, and it initiated a massive catch-up race. Despite the efforts made by Europe and also Asia, the USA is still the leader, not the least because the bulk of the servers installed in the whole world (i.e. the host systems on which the Internet services are saved) are located in the USA. A big portion of the technological developments for the global network also came from American companies like Cisco Systems.

Of course, this boom also spread to commercial usages and developments. But the first requirement for commercial development was speed. If modems had been sufficient for the worldwide access up to then, the limits of this basic data transmission technology were reached within no time. Initially, the term Internet went around the world in expert circles only. This was mainly due to the previously mentioned poor connection capabilities. The Internet did not become accessible for the general public until the end of the 90s. In the beginning, advertising was frowned upon, but when it snuck in and broke through, an enormous new global business field developed. In Germany, the first companies and different competitors from abroad—like America Online or Compuserve—offered Internet access at more and more favorable conditions all over Germany, and massively advertised these services. The speed of the modems for access to the data highway was pushed to the former physical limit. In Europe, for a start, ISDN connections followed allowing for digital transmission and bundling of the data for the first time. The HDSL technique, which was already being used in the USA in the early 90s was developed further with consideration of the possibilities of the Internet and represents the fastest data transmission method on the Internet today. Besides the rapidly rising transmission rates and the increasing amounts of data, the number of global broadband connections grew, too.

As a consequence, the Internet gained higher popularity and economic importance, so that many bigger companies started to present and advertise their products and services on homepages. Suddenly, it became very easy for young, dynamic entrepreneurs to found a company and to present themselves as shiny and brilliant. For starting a new, wonderful business idea you did not need more than an Internet address and a homepage in order to offer your goods and services to a circle of millions of interested people. More and more industries launched into the new sales and presentation field of the Internet. But hardly anybody knows that it was primarily the oldest profession in the world that was responsible for the skyrocketing expansion of the Internet: the sex industry. It disposed of enough money to develop new technologies and an enormous interest in marketing on the, at the time, still broadly anonymous Internet. Pornography considerably increased the development of faster data transfer possibilities and especially the development of image compression methods.

While presentation in the World Wide Web became easier and easier, the hunger for more business capital grew at the same time. Some of the founding entrepreneurs even went one step further, and created companies that acted only on the Internet, and offered goods and services there. With low starting capital they could realize ideas that were well accepted by the customers. In order to expand their businesses, the companies went public and, in doing so, they acquired the necessary capital. In the 90s, Internet addresses were mostly derived from the company name followed by the mandatory dot (for separation) and the ending "com". The word dot and the ending com for commercial became the term dot-com, and the boom of Internet companies going public turned into the dot-com-boom.

Investors sensed big business and distributed venture capital to Internet-oriented companies in unprecedented sums. E-commerce, i.e. electronic commerce, became the number one carrier of hope. The dot-com companies sprang up like mushrooms out of the virtual ground, and the prognoses of the self-established business plans outdid each other.

With the dot-com boom, the need for catchy Internet domain names that could be regarded like a telephone number of the respective company also started to grow. Very early it became clear that the previously favored ".com" addresses would not be sufficient. The internationalization of domain endings was achieved at considerable speed, and brought into being numerous additional endings for many different applications. One of the first novelties was the country domain. Consequently, companies in Germany used the ending ".de", companies in Holland ".nl" etc. Meanwhile, the ending ".com" that was originally exclusively reserved for US-companies, is free to be used by every company and is the preferable domain used by internationally acting companies. Die Welt reported on June 24th, 2008 that from 2009 on, any domain ending should be possible.[6] Thus, the initially explained new abbreviation dot-green also becomes possible in order to clearly distinguish between the new green-tech companies and classical firms.

An officially acknowledged definition for the new Internet company types did not exist when they developed. Theorizers had to learn to understand the digital economy themselves first before they could interpret it to its very developers as well as everyone else. Originally, "dot-coms" described those companies acting mainly or exclusively via the Internet, i.e. their entire business model was based on the world wide net.

Not only did digital startups use the Internet boom, classic enterprises also directed their offers and forms of customer communication more and more towards the Internet. The big companies invested millions in the establishment of the own network and connection to the Internet. Emails mutated to the most important time and cost saving factor, and the homepage reflected the modern company image. Internal communication also profited from the great wide network. If formerly everything was sent from office to office via post, suddenly electronic data traffic was available. The latest and poshest trend with all commercial software solutions was electronic data traffic. Data reconciliation and control via the Internet, shopping directly via the Net

---

[6] Internetadressen dürfen bald Wunschkürzel haben, (Internet addresses can soon have any ending) Die Welt, June 24, 2008, p. 15

with direct insight into the respective goods, shaped the highlights of modern web site development. Within no time, the Internet advanced to the carrier of hope for all big companies. As the design of a homepage was still very difficult and troublesome in the 90s, myriads of programmers were able to make a fortune with this business. However, it must not be kept secret that the majority of the results were horrible because a programmer is simply not a graphics designer. When the companies became aware of this, cost efforts were increased many times over because now a web designer had to connect graphics and programming with each other.

The Internet rapidly developed into a shipping platform for all goods that one did not necessarily have to handle in the shop. Preferred items were computer construction parts and books. Mail order companies saw their big chance to reach an even broader public, and companies like the German Otto-Versand or Karstadt-Quelle invested millions in the dream of the big virtual department store.

For a long period of time, smaller businesses had a rather doubtful and helpless attitude towards the Internet. The registration of a domain, the design of a company homepage, and the provision of staff with their own e-mail addresses took place significantly later with most of the smaller companies than in the big enterprises. The reasons were mostly the result of a lack of personnel that would have had to be able to monitor and assess corresponding trends in the industry and, above all else, the enormous costs that were eaten up with the installation of the new medium. Homepages at DM 50,000 and more were the norm, and for under DM 10,000 a web page was absolutely out of reach. In addition, there were serious problems with the animation of web pages, as this also had to be equipped with contents and again that meant creative work regarding text and image design. Thus, most of the medium-sized companies remained skeptical and waited while those daring to make the step into the Internet quickly and determinedly could achieve success in the form of international business transactions in the early years of the World Wide Web. These advantages arose from the fact that with a homepage, products and services could suddenly be presented to a worldwide public. Electronic trade had a first real big upswing because interactive videotext never managed to exceed the number of one million users even in the boom years of its career, and was finally turned off in 2001 after a long death period. The Internet and the World Wide Web offered completely different presentation possibilities that, as you know, already unified all media, from text to image, photo and sound.

At the end of the 90s, the fruits of Silicon Valley and many other regions also found their way into the living rooms, briefcases, and waistcoat pockets of normal citizens. The rapid distribution of home computers and mobile phones that became increasingly cheaper along with the perspective to surf the worldwide data network provided for a brilliant run at the computer markets. The Internet had its final breakthrough at the end of 2001, when Apple not only launched the iPod as a digital player for music, but at the same time also presented the first official online market for music that could be downloaded directly. In the previous years, the fame of file sharing networks like Napster was rather dodgy, as they offered the possibility, especially to youngsters, to download and swap their music favorites from the Internet more illegally that legally.

Even those who considerably contributed to its distribution were surprised by the victory lap of the Internet. Companies like IBM and Microsoft missed the jump on the bandwagon, and were able to ensure only a small place in the history of the Internet by company takeovers. The Internet, originally developed for internal communication by military and research institutions, provided for a foundation and innovation boom in a way that previously had not even happened with the introduction of the personal computer. Suddenly everything was possible, there were no more limits, and everybody could publish himself and his ideas throughout the entire world, and make money with the inexhaustible digital fortune. Here, Silicon Valley played a decisive role. Topics like environmental protection or climate collapse were not heard. Because it was a new virtual world, there basically were no guilty feelings, since it seemed that resources were also being saved. However, as the personal computer became popular people believed that paper consumption would drastically decrease now, as can be read in numerous advertisements. But exactly the contrary was the case, and this error was not the last. Today, not only the notion of climate collapse and the exhaustion of raw materials are forcing us to rethink, but also fuel prices at the petrol pumps, which calls for quick restructuring. "Going-green" is not only posh and climate protecting, but also economically profitable, because a multi-billion-dollar business attracts.

What Connects the Period of Promoterism in Germany with Silicon Valley

At a first glance, the Ruhr area and other German industry regions do not stand the comparison with the famous Silicon Valley, even if some entrepreneurs in Silicon Valley also talk about the Rhine or Ruhr Valley. If you take a closer look, however, you can definitely spot more similarities than scenic differences. Of course, it rains more frequently in the "Pott" than in sunny California, and for decades the area on the Ruhr was said to be highly polluted due to the particularly concentrated coal and steel industry located here. But this image has radically changed in the last twenty years: the Ruhr area now also flies a green flag.

From the historic point of view, there are many more parallels. Five of these parallels will be examined in detail.

At foremost position, there is the first high foundational boom period in Germany from 1848 to 1871.[7] This foundational boom gave the name still used today to the entire epoch, and created a completely new and highly modern infrastructure due to the area-wide introduction of railways, telegraphy and telephony. Never before in German history were there so many corporations with such high innovation potential. The first important transport and communication companies developed—for example, the Hamburg-America-Line in 1846, or the telegraph construction institution Siemens & Halske and the Norddeutsche Lloyd in 1847. The chemical companies Bayer, Hoechst, BASF and Kalle were founded 1863-5.[8] In parallel, after the approval of telegraphy for private use in the year 1849, the first news agency that initially published only commercial news developed as the Wolffschen telegraph office in Berlin. Germany was in a real foundation frenzy.

One of the founders from the Ruhr area especially stood out from the crowd, and essentially formed the international reputation of German industrialization: Alfred Krupp. In 1811, his father, the master forger Friedrich Krupp from Essen, had already founded a mill for the production of cast steel. In 1816, Friedrich Krupp first succeeded in

---

[7] cf. Gründerzeit 1848 -1871 (Period of Promoterism 1848 1871) (Special Exhibition of the German Historic Museum in Berlin), published by U. Laufer and H. Ottomeyer, Dresden, Sandstein-Verlag, 2008

[8] Later they became known as IG Farben, the newspaper Berliner Morgenpost published a special edition about the period of promoterism exhibition.

9

producing high amounts of steel that corresponded with the English standards at the time. In 1826, the steel works of the father that employed seven workers was assigned to the son Alfred Krupp, who was only 14 years old then. But only after the foundation of the German tariff union in 1834, which considerably improved the conditions of existence in trade and commerce, could the committed young entrepreneur realize his dreams of making his company prosper just in the style of today's Silicon Valley. In his efforts he made initial mistakes that were so grave that they seriously endangered the existence of the company. The company crisis from 1847-8 that resulted from these errors forced him to modernize and reorganize his company. After that, the most rapid rise of the period of promoterism started for Krupp. After he succeeded in producing train wheels without weld seams, which had frequently led to wheel breakages (up to then, wheel breakages counted among the most frequent causes for train accidents), he had his method registered as a patent in 1852. In addition, in the beginning of the 1860s, Krupp was especially celebrated as the "canon king". The orientation towards the production of war devices not only enabled him to stabilize his sales, but also to further expand steel production. After liquidity problems in the 1860s, Krupp was able to fall back on Prussian and French financial aid. Grudgingly, in turn, the owner of the company had to grant the broker bank consortium certain rights of influence and give in to the signs of the times.

Here, the second parallel becomes visible. In the comparison between the company foundations in Germany 150 years ago and today's Silicon Valley, the pattern of the influence of the banks is of greatest importance. From now on, the co-financing banks also had a crucial say in business matters. A considerable number of wrong decisions were the result; the consequence of the lack of foresight and non-entrepreneurial thinking of the bankers.

For the first time, the numerous newly founded banks in Europe and Germany played a decisive role for the development of shareholder companies in the period of promoterism. Between 1850 and 1870, 295 German shareholder companies developed. The previously family-owned businesses were no longer able to finance the enormous expansion, including the increased export of goods, machines, and, not the least, military equipment in Europe and the whole world. Even if shareholder companies basically did not offer novelties, the East India Company was organized as a shareholder company already in 1602 and the shareholder company as a modern legal form developed no earlier than in the 19th century. 1871-2, with the foundation of the Empire, 780 shareholder companies developed in Germany alone.[9] In contrast, there were only a total of 390 sustainable companies between 1790 and 1870 that could raise the money needed for big projects like the build-up of the railway network to the construction of locomotives or plant engineering. Today's big banks, starting with the Deutsche Bank, the Commerzbank and the Dresdner Bank, all developed in these years of promoterism. The increasing overseas trade could not be managed without banks. Until then, financial institutions from London dominated the profitable business of crediting commercial overseas businesses. The Deutsche Bank, which quickly gained strength, belonged to the pioneers for bigger share transactions as the close business relationships with AEG, BASF, Bayer, and Siemens proved. Important financial institutions founded previously, like Oppenheim, Rothschild, or Wartburg and Metzler, survived the first big bank and stock market crisis in Germany in 1873. 60 banks slipped into insolvency in Austria and Germany alone. The period of promoterism had ended.[10]

The parallels with the dot-com bubble are obvious. Like during the period of promoterism of the 19th century, when the banks had the say, the greed for money brought on the crisis in Silicon Valley. The dot-com companies needed money to develop their technologies and make their innovative ideas effective in the market in form of an incorporated foundation. There was no business expansion without the consent of the

---

[9] Berliner Morgenpost, Special Edition for the exhibition of the period of rapid industrial expansion in Germnay by the German Historic Museum Berlin, 2008, p. 7

[10] Böhme, Helmut: Bankenkonzentration und Schwerindustrie, 1873 – 1896. Bemerkungen zum Problem des "Organisierten Kapitalismus", (Concentration of banks and heavy industry, 1873 1896. Remarks about the problem of "organised capitalism") in: Sozialgeschichte heute. Memorial publication for Hans Rosenbert on his 70th birthday. Published by Hans-Ulrich Wehlen. Kritische Studien zur Geschichtswissenschaft (Critical studies about historic sciences). Volume 11, Verlag Vandenhoeck & Ruprecht, Göttingen 1974, P. 432-451; Carsten Burhop, Die Kreditbanken der Gründerzeit (The credit banks of the period of promoterism), Schriftenreihe des Instituts für Bankhistorische Forschung e. V. (Series by the institute for bank-historic research e.v.), Volume 21, Franz Steiner Verlag 2004.

11

venture capital firms. In turn, the risk capital providers were responsible towards their investors. In order to persuade them to invest, the venture capital firms preferably sold unbeatable visions that conveyed the general enthusiasm to the investors. To do that, founders of new businesses and junior entrepreneurs also had to use their imagination more and more frequently.

Analogue problems existed in the period of promoterism of the 19th century. The market was waiting for new products and services, like, for example, the idea of a worldwide telegraph network. But the entrepreneurs could not cope with the pre-financing of these new products the market called for. The banks that had always been intent on extreme safety thought they were on the safe side if they could only exert enough influence. They wanted to prevent risky wrong decisions and cater to crisis-proof growth without taking the indispensable entrepreneurial risk. These actions came back to haunt them at the first big stock market crash.

For over almost twenty years, the German national economy recovered only slowly from this crisis, and generated a phenomenon that persists yet today: a deep-rooted distrust of many investors towards shareholder companies. While this legal form of a company has gained more and more confidence in other countries, and especially in the USA, skepticism that can obviously be traced back to this stock market and bank crash persists in Germany. That is another reason why on the occasion of the 20th anniversary of the German Stock Index Dax, the Federal Minister of Finance Steinbrück called on the German citizens to acquire more shares.[11]

Still, for many people, buying shares is a speculative business and not a globally spread instrument for the participation in big industrial projects and the associated profit perspectives. Here, in the years of promoterism, the fact that many tradesmen, smaller businesses, craftsmen, and people previously working in agriculture became poor in the course of industrialization, or did not own noteworthy capital anyway, played a major role without a doubt. The people's and cooperative banks developed no earlier than the 19th century. Hermann Schulze-Delitzsch successfully developed the idea of the people's banks and Friedrich Wilhelm Raiffeisen created the cooperative banks that were

---

[11] Seibel, Karsten: Steinbrück ruft zum Aktienkurs auf, (Steinbrück calls to the stock price) Die Welt, July 2, 2008, p. 15

destined mainly for the farmers. The savings banks that had already developed at the end of the 18th century acted regionally at first and supported the so-called "little men" with retirement provisions and the allocation of small loans without the primary profit intentions of the big banks. Their progressive role throughout the entire industrialization process must not be underestimated in any way, and numerous international imitators can be found. The structure of the banks the way they were founded already in the 19th century still exists today, even if more and more virtual bank institutions have emerged due to the Internet and financial innovations are frequently connected with crashes. The latest bad speculations on the American real estate market and their impacts on internationally acting banks and national economies are just further proof for that. It goes without saying that investors' confidence was deeply shattered anew for this reason.

A third parallel between the German period of promoterism and the persisting corporation boom in Silicon Valley are the political-social effects of industrial growth, based mainly on coal and steel in Germany. This became particularly obvious in the coal regions of the Ruhr area. Besides Krupp, Heinrich Friedrich Grillo, born December 20th, 1825 in Essen, belonged to the entrepreneurs with the strongest influence in the period of promoterism. Similar to Krupp, the merchant's son had taken over his father's company and gone after the realization of great plans, exactly in the style of today's Silicon Valley. As a result, he became a shareholder in different coalmines, and gained more and more influence. At his instigation, explorative drillings were executed in the Schalker Mark near Gelsenkirchen that led to the conclusion that there were rich black coal deposits under the little town Schalke and the surrounding farms. At his initiative, in the year 1872, the "AG der chemischen Industrie", the "Schalker Gruben & Hüttenverein AG", and the "Dortmunder Union" were founded. The two latter shareholder companies were mountainous companies with smelting works and coalmines. In collaboration with banks from Cologne and Berlin, Grillo successfully managed to push through the shareholder company as a typical legal form of enterprise in the Ruhr area and to strengthen the connection between banks and the economy. In coal mining, the little coalmines were replaced by big shaft plants. Technical innovations like the Malakoff towers, that are typical for the image of the Ruhr area, the use of jack-hammers and dynamite, electrical bulbs and subsurface pumps, the development of the chemical industry that processes the by-products of mining, the extension of the transport routes via waterways, railroad tracks and streets, and the construction of the bridges over the Rhine made the Ruhr area Europe's biggest industrial hotspot after the German-French war.

The "Ruhrpott" was based on iron and steel, as well as on the newly developing chemical and electronics industries. Around the year 1800, today's big cities like Dortmund and Duisburg did not have more than 5,000 citizens; Gelsenkirchen and Herne not even one thousand each. As a result of the permanently growing need for industrial workers, population figures increased rapidly. If the required work force could still be found amongst the rural population of the Munsterland, Eastern Westphalia, and Hesse in the beginning, after 1870 one had to resort to the work force potential of the Eastern Prussian provinces. In 1852, approximately 375,000 people lived in the Ruhr area already, and the immigration of more than half a million workers from Eastern and Western Prussia, from Silesia and Posen, were an essential contribution to the population figures rapidly exceeding the limit of one million. Again, one had to recruit workers from rural areas. Former small farmers, farm workers and small craftsmen, who now frequently were of Polish nationality and did not speak German, had to be made fit for the new requirements of the industry. Besides the Polish workers, work forces from Croatia, Slovakia and Italy were also attracted to the Ruhr area. In the beginning, the in-streaming people could still be housed in the existing village structures of the area. The locals moved together a bit closer and rented part of their houses to the people who had moved in. Between 1840 and 1871, the number of inhabitants in a house had doubled in Essen. People had to resort to well-proven old means and rebuilt sheds and stables into flats and extended houses. Living together so closely brought back the old problems of rapidly growing medieval cities. Initially, the cities could not cope with the increasing hygienic problems, and were exposed to epidemics that spread quickly among the population that was working much too hard and too long, and could hardly buy the bread needed for sustenance, did not have enough sleep, and lived under increasing stress due to the housing conditions.[12]

---

[12] Thomas Parent, Das Ruhrgebiet (The Ruhr area). Vom goldenen Mittelalter zur Industriekultur (From the golden middle ages to industrial culture), DuMont Kunst-Reiseführer, Köln DuMont Verlag, P. 25ff.

But still there was an increasing shortage in living space. At this time, the first relatively comfortable workers' villages developed. But, they were mainly rented by foremen and master craftsmen. The juvenile workers—even nine-year old children labored as haulers in Germany's mines for up to ten hours—mostly had only "single homes" available that were built like barracks and thus served also as their social control.[13]

The situation of the industrial workers was aggravated with each immigration wave. The immigrants, separated from home countries, were housed in ghetto-like workers' villages. In most cases, families lived in one room only and frequently shared them with so-called "sleep tenants", i.e. workers who could not afford their own flat and could only rent a bed on which to sleep. The 19th century is characterized by the fact that industrial workers had to use both their working and their sleeping places, in shifts. In order to mitigate social conflicts and to tie the workers closer to them, some manufacturers built long rows of attached houses for "their" workers in immediate proximity to their industrial facilities.

But these flats also only allowed living in cramped confines. In addition, loss of a job, e.g. as a consequence of critical remarks or joining the trade unions that were starting to develop, also meant losing the flat. The settlements that were built by Alfred Krupp in proximity to his plants became famous. Approximately 30,000 people lived in the Krupp villages around the incessantly growing plant. In order to be allowed to rent a flat for oneself and his family, one had to be a staff member of the plant. On average, the cost for rent was approximately two and a half days wages. In 1855, at the Paris Industry Exhibition, a new type of house was presented. Subsequently, this housing estate with a cross-floor plan was built everywhere in the Ruhr area. Narrow streets developed, and their position plan was drawn on the drawing table with the ruler. Trees, parks and even squares were rare.

Of course, there are no such "workers' ghettos" in today's Silicon Valley in California. The essential parallel of the period of promoterism in Germany and the foundational boom in the Silicon Valley is migration. A major portion of the new digital workers of Silicon Valley, including its leading founders, were immigrants or at least workers from other areas of the US. Even if today's working and housing conditions differ considerably from those of the 19th century, there are numerous analogies in migration. Still today, they are most obvious in San

---

[13] Ibid.

Francisco's Chinatown, but also in the growing social differentiation of poor and rich in the USA, as well as in Germany. Another analogy can be found in the working conditions. Even if employees and workers in today's Silicon Valley do not live under such inhuman conditions, the strict demand for total commitment by the entrepreneur is a symptom of the entire dot-com era. Employees having a sofa in their offices in order to be able to spend most nights of the week there are not a rarity. There is an endless amount of reports of employees who sacrificed many years of their lives solely for the company in a way that did not permit any kind of private life. This shows clear parallels with the period of promoterism in Germany.

In a fourth point of comparison, there are analogies, too, in the enormous need for training and further education for the newly developed industries. In the 19 century, as it is the case again today, there was a lack of qualified engineers and technicians in Germany. The classical universities did not offer any courses in the areas of economy and technology. Only in 1821 did Peter Christian Wilhelm Beuth, as the head of the Prussian trade education, open the first "technical institute", which later became known as a trade school. The citizens had little interest in what they could learn there. Only the equipment with scholarships helped a bit to gain more people who were willing to learn for this new form of training. The provincial trade schools that were founded at the same time promised that each of them could send the four best graduates for higher education to Berlin. Although the so-called "polytechnic education" had become more and more necessary in the internationally tightening competition since 1848, the year of revolution, it still took more than one decade until the first polytechnic institutes were founded in Cologne and Aachen. The former Technical Academy, today's Technical University of Berlin, developed in 1879. Just before that, the polytechnic school in Munich, founded in 1866, was advanced to the first technical academy of Bavaria in 1866. The economic crisis in 1873 emphasized the need to deal with the technical and economic basics of the new international production and trade forms to an increased extend. Totally analogous, there was and still is a considerable need to catch up in the field of the new digital means of production. The well-known efforts for gaining IT specialists from abroad by means of a "Greencard" for the immigration to Germany and Europe from India, Eastern Europe, and Asia are only one example. In contrast, from the very beginning, Silicon Valley developed due to the numerous universities located there. The transfer of knowledge and know-how was made quickly and without problems, often even directly by early connection of the companies with science and long-term search for the best students and graduates in expert fields that are especially sought after. Without exaggeration, one can say that the new requirements of initial and ongoing training developed from the manifold incorporations of the academies. The aspired interconnection of education and training, scientific research and industrial practice, proved to be as difficult in the years of promoterism in the 19th century as it is in the digital era today. In Germany, in the second half of the last century, the entire academic system reacted much too late to the new challenges, totally analogous at the end of the 20th century, to those of digital production and the Internet economy. In the Silicon Valley, in contrast, the relationships with the academies were intensified. Frequently, graduates do a six-months or one-year trainee training after their academic education in Germany before they are employed in the industry or in the private service sector in order to be able to orientate themselves in practice and to cope with the requirements made here. This evidence of the incapacity of the university doctrine, except for some exemptions, applies to many fields of technology of the 21st century so that more and more companies train people from different expert areas with good math, information technology, natural science and technical knowledge themselves "on the job" to an increasing extent. It is obvious how many efficiency reserves there are just in need-oriented instead of discipline-centered education and training.

Finally, another analogy of Germany's period of promoterism shall be compared with the persisting foundation rush of Silicon Valley. It is the claim of leadership by innovation and technology that is aspired by all means.

Prussia and France already used the canons produced in the Krupp factories during the German-French war 1870-1 in order to shoot at each other. Nowadays, more elegant methods are used, but the core is the same intention. The importance of telegraphy for the advance in information that was so decisive for decisions in the 19th century is frequently compared with the importance of the Internet for the beginning of the 21st century. With regard to the enormous acceleration of the information and communication stream, this has become stronger in the recent years and will even increase further. Today, the dot-com companies do not only determine the action, but first and foremost also the speed. But the claim for technological leadership and advance in competition exists. Again and again this becomes most obvious with Microsoft's attempts to gain ground in the Internet industry, as in May 2008 during the "takeover battle" regarding Yahoo. It failed, but has not ended yet.

In an impressive way, the international disputes about the oil reserves also prove that the character of the aggressive leadership claims of the market and technology leaders has not changed. The oil price increasing almost daily and the dramatic increase in prices at the petrol pumps connected therewith highlights that the most. At the same time, it proves how high the backlog of green technology for the automotive industry is. But it also emphasizes the dimension of the shift to more climate and environmentally friendly drive systems and logistic solutions. That alone represents a huge multi-billion dollar business because the global automotive and supply industries have to reinvent themselves.

The Revolutionists of the Dot-Coms and their Effect on Startup Dreams

In order to understand what makes the dot-coms so unique and at the same time so interesting for the developing, even bigger, green-tech market, the backgrounds of Internet economics have to be inspected in more detail.

In the first place, there is the enormous diffusion speed of the new company type dot-com. Never before had it been possible to build up a company with such low effort as it was in the beginning of the mass diffusion of the Internet. In principle, it was sufficient to choose a suitable domain name and to create a homepage. If companies had to spend much money on advertising, CI (corporate identity) and image before, suddenly it was sufficient to have a good-looking Internet presence in order to make a one-man company pretend to be a successful global company. Access to the Internet, a provider to make the web page is available, and a catchy domain name were enough to start businesses actively or even just pretended.

Before the company Google revolutionized the search engine industry, everybody who was a bit skilled could provide for a good position in the search engines of Yahoo, Lycos and AltaVista. For this purpose, it was just necessary in most cases to use as many catchwords as possible in the so-called meta-file in order to increase the importance of the web site. These meta-tag files were nothing else but a little text file containing keywords concerning the Internet page. Since all search engines checked all domain pages at regular periods in order to read these files, this was the simplest way to work oneself up to the top of the result pages. The contents of the meta-tag files were used as keywords, i.e. search terms for the just-named big search engines, regardless of whether they really had something to do with the content.

Silicon Valley was and is said to be the capital of this "New Economy".[14]The daily newspaper USA Today even talked about the capital of the "digital era",[15] in which, of course, the technology-based companies of the chip, computer and software industry also had to build up the corresponding basic facilities.

The boom in Silicon Valley has been breathtaking from the very beginning. The companies did not have long planning periods, they did not care about norms or guidelines, they just simply started. In addition, every firm, even if it was very tiny, was respected there, as long as the products or ideas were innovative enough. Such a way of acting would have been unthinkable in Europe. When the Internet with its importance and the opportunities offered to the dot-coms turned the world upside-down, euphoria had no more limits, especially in the USA. Never before had technicians and amateurs been more motivated than in the late 80s and 90s. Everybody was dreaming of the millions that could be earned, and everybody already saw himself racing on the boulevards in a Ferrari.

The completely uncontrolled growth of pretended genius techniques and the very careless conduct with the provided financial means evolved from these high-flying dreams of young entrepreneurs. The speed of development did not leave any space for sophisticated and verified business plans. Being the first was the utmost priority.

The enormous speed of growth can be documented quite well with the example of web browsers. In order to watch the offers of the World Wide Web on the PC, every user needs a web browser. The name was derived from the abbreviation of World Wide Web, web in short, and the word "browse". From the beginning, special software has been needed for this purpose, and when the first version of the Netscape Navigator was presented at the end of 1994, this browser represented a little revolution. Even if there had already been web browsers before, they were all based on a standard that was predominantly suitable for displaying text. Originally developed by a team of students and employees from the

---

[14] Spiegel 11/2000, p.108
[15] USA Today dated November 16, 2000

University of Illinois under the name of Mosaic, this browser was posted on the Internet for free and won its followers in a short time. The student Marc Andreessen was responsible for the creative aspects of the browser and obviously he was the first who realized the importance of a good web browser in the growing Internet. In talks with Jim Clark, at that time founder and boss of Silicon Graphics, he discussed his visions. This led to the joint foundation of the company Mosaic Communications Corporation in Mountain View in California a bit later. Just a few months after that, the company had to be renamed due to licensing reasons, and was called Netscape Communications Corporation from then on. Mosaic turned into Netscape Navigator. Its first version was already able to run on almost all common computer systems and was delivered in all of the important languages. Netscape's business politics still have to be called genius. The web browser has always been free and was therefore always advertised as a "trial version". Netscape made their money by selling special server software that was also used for the Internet. Thus, in accordance with the speed of growth back then, the name Netscape became the top address for modern browser technology within one year. You can say that Netscape controlled the browser market for almost two years without being challenged.

The software giant Microsoft simply missed the entire development of the Internet. In Redmond, in the main office of the company, they started to think about the future of the Internet no earlier than at the end of 1995 and, more hastily than qualified, added Internet Explorer to the Microsoft "Plus Package", but not for free. When Microsoft finally realized that the Internet would become more than just a soap bubble, it was almost too late. In summer 1996, they launched Internet Explorer 3.0 and, for the first time, this was a really competitive product.[16]

In retrospect, the battle that broke out thereupon can only be watched with disbelief, because from then on, new versions of the competing browsers were released in three-month intervals. Even if the user benefited from the constantly new possibilities of the browsers, more and more often it occurred that a web site that was designed for the capacities of one browser could hardly be displayed or not be seen at all with the other one. In view of their market position, with one of the new

---

[16] Source: http://www.netplanet.org/www/browser.shtml Request of February 12th, 2008

versions Netscape started to claim money for their browser while Microsoft offered the browser for free, according to the original role model. This battle about the market shares of a web browser is a good example for the partly chaotic development of Silicon Valley, even if a "non-Californian" named Microsoft was involved.

No other former economic system made it possible to turn each computer connection into a company, fast and without complications. Whoever had an idea it could be tested on the Internet first. As soon as visitors clicked on the Internet address this was considered as breakthrough already, completely independent from the real business volume developing from that. In the early years, in particular, numerous new models of "Electronic Commerce"[17] developed from that, ranging from new worldwide sales opportunities to target groups for directed advertising.

Most of the forecasts regarding the development of the Internet-supported economy were, and still are today, highly exceeded by reality, even if disillusionment has already taken place. The speed of growth of the new Internet-based companies literally was accompanied by a fabulous possibility to earn money. This particularly went with a California that is mainly famous for the 1848 "gold rush" even to this day. The gold discovered back then attracted swarms of gold diggers from all countries and made sure that the state of California, like a wonderland, in the thinking of the people remained connected with the chance to gain a quick fortune. The digital era exceeded the profit that could be made by gold digging by far. Many people considered it a license to print money and within the shortest time it produced more millionaires than there had ever been in economic history. In many cases, employees of the firms got shares in the growth of the companies by "stock options" and were paid by means of shares in addition. Thus, the highest number of super-rich in history developed in one economic area in a completely legal way.[18] As simple as this sounds, this unique chance to make quick money by dot-com companies or general high tech companies, not only those from Silicon Valley, has to be understood as a very special characteristic. The

[17] cf. Blemel, F.; Fassot, G.; Theobald, A. (Hrsg.), Electronic Commerce, Herausforderungen – Anwendungen – Perspektiven, (Challenges Applications Perspectives) Wiesbaden, Gabler-Verlag 1999 18 cf. Business Week March 27, 2000, p. 112
[18] cf. Business Week March 27, 2000, p. 112

"share communism", for the first time practiced by and with the dot-coms, according to the "Economist" of October 7th, 2000, has lead to the biggest legal creation of wealth in the history of mankind. To a special extent, this also explains the fascination of many by the New Economy. Over night, personal richness by means of the Internet-supported economy seemed to be possible for everybody, even if the person had hardly been interested in the economy and the Internet up to then. Repeating that with green-tech attracts many creative spirits, not least because the economic pressure increases from day to day.

The ways in which money is really made on the Internet branch out more and more.[19] Normally, the 3-C model is used to categorize them. Here the 3 Cs stand for Commerce, Content, and Connection.

Here, commerce is understood as real trade with products or services, as with Amazon, possibly most famous online dealer in the world.

Content subsumes all providers of information and knowledge, and browsers also belong to them. For example, Google's core business is offering content permitting to find answers to any search terms within seconds. Connection enters the domain of telecommunication in the closer sense the Internet service providers like AOL, T-Online and similar have to be named here. But today these can hardly be separated from the providers of the connection hardware (e. g. DSL line).

Thus, only recently, T-Online, which had been marketed with a loud drum roll as a shareholder company a few years ago, re-merged with the mother concern Deutsche Telekom, a development that can be observed all over the world.

The 3-C model can be expanded by a few more Cs. Especially cooperation and communities should not be left out. One of the most popular cooperation networks is the worldwide and industry-crossing network Xing.

Networks of purely private character, bringing together people with the same interests, affections, attitudes, needs and other criteria, represent the growing area of communities. That these online

---

[19] cf. Volker Bätz, Internetbasierte Abwicklung von Consulting-Projekten und Analysen im Umfeld betriebswirtschaftlicher Softwarebibliotheken (Internet-based processing of Consulting projects and analyses in the environment of business economic software libraries) Inaugural-Dissertation, University of Würzburg 2001, p. 65

communities become more and more similar with real communities can be realized by the example of "Secondlife". The business model that is connected with the so-called Web 2.0 is said to be the carrier of hope for the digital future. Here, everybody can create his or her own virtual world. In Secondlife, you can be who you always wanted to be. Successful businessman, artist or bon vivant, everything is possible. There is even a Secondlife currency and, as in real life, you can become a millionaire with the right idea at the right time.

The above-quoted categories show the huge bandwidth with which fun and business can be interwoven on the Internet. But today, "pure format" providers can hardly be found. Content providers like YouTube provide a community component at the same time. Many connection providers maintain the community idea at the same time and offer loads of content as well. The list of examples can be endlessly continued.

In the broadest sense, the providers of hardware and infrastructure also belong to the dot-coms, because without laptops, PCs, network cards, DSL, W-LAN and all the other technologies, there would not be dotcoms and no customers for these companies. Not only digital startups used the Internet boom, but also classic enterprises directed their offers and communication ways more and more towards the Internet. Here again, communication and marketing theory were lagging behind practice.

The already mentioned special way of acting of the dot-com firms also has not been researched to a sufficient extent. There rarely was and is a regulated working day. Frequently, the individual, separated mini working area in front of the PC (called cubicle) is seen as the second home, and is of correspondingly individual appearance. Everybody brings with them what they love and treasure and relaxes with a quick glance at it. Work intensity is extraordinarily high and many duplicate an eight-hour day and even sleep in the office then, especially if project deadlines generate additional pressure. Quite often, work lust turns into real work mania and "workaholism" is considered a widespread virtue. A similar way of working will doubtlessly be necessary for solving the climate problems.

With the new high-tech goods, the Internet, originally just developed for connecting computer capacities of research and education institutions, started its triumphal procession. This mass-market motivated investors and the stock market to an up to then unknown extent and attracted investors with expectations of huge profits. In order to give young start-ups a chance on the stock market, too, the market segment "New Market" was founded in Germany in parallel to the NASDAQ. This way, almost every technical or net-based idea that sounded exciting found a venture capital provider. The fair new world of the Internet frequently enabled courageous entrepreneurs to make fabulous careers, many of them however without a happy end.

In Germany, there also was a dot-com boom mainly initiated by the former public enterprise Telekom going public. Again, in spring 1996, the company provided enough headlines with the hitherto biggest flood of claims by investors in the history of stock trading. Telekom's initial public offering was massively advertised in all possible forms, in particular by TV spots in order to make the share popular as "people's share", especially amongst the citizens who had had no experience in stock up to then. Subsequently, more and more people became interested in the stock market and also bought shares of other diverse new Internet foundations.

Already back then, numerous stock market experts considered the share prices of Internet companies as too high, but within this common euphoria such voices were simply ignored. The initial public offering by Infineon on March 13th, 2000, is said to be the highlight of the stock market party. It even made the trading systems of the securities market in Frankfurt collapse. Stock trading had become the new public sport of the Germans.

Overheating of the Market

Regarding the new type of business founders and "web workers," and the financing of their ideas, there are many questions to which scientific economic research has not had any answers up to now. When investments in the "New Economy" were globally increasing disproportionately from the middle of the 90s of the last century on, many people wanted to join in. As already remarked, until Deutsche Telekom went public in November 1996, most Germans had not been particularly interested in shares. This changed with the introduction of the T-share. The placement volume was even increased by 100 million to 600 million T-shares. The mega advertising campaign for the "people's share", initiated by the popular actor Manfred Krug, was efficient. In an analysis of "Börsengeschichte" (History of the stock market) it says: "With a subscription profit of more than 16%, the T-share fulfilled the expectations that were put on it by the investors to the fullest extent. In the run-up to the emission already, the increasing interest had caused an upswing in the Dax. On the first listing day of the T-share (November

18th, 1996) the Dax was listed at 2,763.84 points already. Encouraged by the success with the T-share, many investors now tried their luck with other shares, too. This led to the Dax exceeding 3,000 points a few weeks later, on January 17th, 1997, for the first time."[20]

But such euphoria in terms of environment investments cannot even be sensed yet. On the contrary, it is just fair to say that the green foundation wave, considering the irreversibility of many processes in our unstable climate balance, has been proceeding in a relaxed and rather calm way up to now. 15 years ago, the World Wide Web and the seemingly almost fantastic communication possibilities did not only motivate visionaries or junior entrepreneurs, but also experienced managers and, above all, investors. Especially the possibilities of handling business processes via the Internet offered space for new business concepts. They were connected with completely new terms and abbreviations like *B2B* ("Business-To-Business") and *B2C* ("Business-To-Customer").

Matching that, the newly developed economic sector received the name "New Economy". This immediately implied to the imagination the concept that the Old Economy had business models that were basically obsolete. New foundations, so-called start-ups, sprang out of the virtual world into reality. Americanisms that were widespread anyway, ruled the new economy and completely new kinds of dictionaries developed, like e.g. by Jürgen Frühschütz in Deutscher Fachverlag, the "ECommmerce-Lexikon"(Frühschütz 2001). It is typical that fundamental economic terms like expenditure and profit are missing. In turn, there are numerous abbreviated documents of the Internet language regulation in their long version. At the same time, cyber law developed, as described by Walter J. Jaburek, Norbert Wölfl in "CyberRecht" (Cyber law) with the matching subtitle "Marktplatz Internet schrankenlose Geschäfte" (Market place

---

[20] Börsengeschichte Teil 1(History of the stock market part 1), Internethausse und Megabaisse (1996-2002) Von der T-Aktie zur UMTS-Versteigerung 1996-2000 (Internethausse and megabaisse (1996-2002) from the T-share to the UMTS auctioning 1996-2000), in: http://zeitenwende.ch/finanzgeschichte; request of June 30th, 2008

Internet businesses without limits).[21] It seemed that on the Internet money could be made without limits.

The token ".com" became the brand mark of the new industry as dotcom, even if many people could not really understand that on the telephone, in the beginning at least. Even reputable US-companies from the EDP sector, like Hewlett-Packard, IBM, or even Microsoft, appeared like companies from the last centuries compared with the vitality and creativity of the New Economy. Dynamic junior entrepreneurs controlled the stock exchange transactions. The old-established companies were deeply shattered in their foundations and management structures. According to the American example of NASDAQ, the German Stock Exchange developed a new field of investment, Nemax (New Market Index), for the "New Market". Every start of a company at the stock exchange was called IPO (Initial Private Offer) only and produced high profits on the first trading day. The Nemax was started in April 1997 with 500 points, reached a peak of 8600 points around the turn of the millennium and dropped down to 353 points in the following years—a nightmare for German investors that left an image of the ratio between chances and risks of share trading amongst the German citizens that has not got anything to do with the normal stock market business. Once again, the time of "the economic weightlessness" ended with a crash after the revelation of "criminal activities" and strengthening of investors' protection by a court, the "out" for the New Market came in September 2002. Started in 2005, an attempt of an extra stock market for small venture companies completed the change between hausse and baisse even more rapidly than all its predecessors.[22]

Table 1: The development of the Dax performance since Dec. 30th, 1998:

Date	Dax	Performance Since 12/30/98
12/30/98	5006.57	
10/27/99	5363.86	+7.14%
12/03/99	6119.17	+22.22%

---

[21] Jaburek, Walter, J.; Wölfl, Norbert, Cyber-Recht (Cyber law). Marktplatz Internet – schrankenlose Geschäfte (Market place Internet businesses without limits), Vienna and Frankfurt, Ueberreuter-Verlag 1997.

[22] Holger Zschäpitz, Der Crash sitzt noch tief in den Knochen, (The crash still grips to the marrow) in: Die Welt, June 5, 2008

12/30/99	6958.14	+38.98%
01/14/00	7173.22	+43.27%
03/07/00	8064.97	+61.09%

Table 2: The development of the Nemax performance since Dec. 30th, 1998:

Date	Nemax-All-Share	Performance since 30/12/98
12/30/98	2744.45	
01/06/99	3197.82	+16.52%
10/27/99	2878.59	+4.89%
12/13/99	4150.08	+51.22%
12/30/99	4572.18	+66.60%
01/19/00	5030.33	+83.29%
02/04/00	6212.75	+126.38%
02/18/00	7224.74	+163.25%
03/02/00	8056.01	+193.54%
03/10/00	8559.32	+211.88%

Source[23][24]

"Due to the achieved success, the New Market experienced great inflow with companies and investors. At the end of 1997, besides Bertrand and Mobilcom, 15 further societies in the growth segment New Market were listed. Here, all new emissions could book profit on the first trading day, even amounting to more than 100% with some companies like BETA Systems, SCM Microsystems, or SER Systems. Other companies

---

[23] Source: Börsengeschichte Teil 1(History of the stock market part 1), Internethausse und Megabaisse (1996-2002) Von der T-Aktie zur UMTSVersteigerung 1996-2000 (Internethausse and megabaisse (1996-2002) from the T-share to the UMTS auctioning 1996-2000), in: http://zeitenwende.ch/finanzgeschichte; request of June 30th, 2008
[24] Börsengeschichte Teil 1(History of the stock market part 1), Internethausse und Megabaisse (1996-2002) Von der T-Aktie zur UMTS-Versteigerung 1996-2000 (Internethausse and megabaisse (1996-2002) from the T-share to the UMTS auctioning 1996-2000) , in: http://zeitenwende.ch/finanzgeschichte; request of June 30th, 2008

27

like BB Biotech, EM.TV, or Qiagen shone less by subscription profits then rather by rapid increases in share prices in the months after the emission."[25]

The examples for this stock market enthusiasm came from Silicon Valley or from the high tech industry in the broader sense. In 1994, the search engine provider "Yahoo" was considered as one of the first big companies in the New Economy. The enterprise was brought to life by Jerry Yang and David Filo, who were Stanford students when they began their idea. They collected interesting hyperlinks in the World Wide Web and stored them in hierarchical order on their web server. At the end of 1994, the project caught the attention of the risk capital provider Sequoia Capital. One million US dollars were invested in Yahoo so that Yahoo could be founded as a company in April 1995. One year later already, Yahoo was listed on the stock market.

The light-hearted faith in the New Economy partly lead to absurd developments in the stock market universe which, strange enough, were not seriously criticized by the financial scientists, not to mention the stock market operators. In the year 2000, for example, with 2,300 employees, Yahoo had a market value of more than 79 billion euros. In comparison, at the same time, the technology and automotive group DaimlerChrysler with 467,900 staff worldwide was only rated with a market value of 57 billion euros.

The merger between the online service AOL and the entertainment group Time Warner to form the new media giant AOL Time Warner in the year 2000 was almost tantamount to a coronation. The industry literally wallowed in self-content and everything that had just remotely to do with strategic redirecting also jumped on the bandwagon. What strengthened this faith in the New Economy in particular? In the remarkable "European Communication Council Report" at the end of the last century, the new objective facts of the Internet economy were comprehensively explained for the first time.[26] The strategic difference of all activities on the Internet is founded on a basically very simple fact: Digital bits feature completely

---

[25] Börsengeschichte Teil 1,(History of the stock market part 1) Internethausse und Megabaisse (1996-2002) – Von der T-Aktie zur UMTS-Versteigerung 1996-2000, from the T-share to the UMTS auctioning 1996-2000 in: http://zeitenwende.ch; request of June 30, 2008.
[26] ECCR, Berlin, Springer Verlag 1999, p. 15 ff.

different good characteristics than physical goods, their marginal costs tend to zero, and they are globally available at the speed of light. Copies cost almost nothing; they do not require storage houses and do not know borders. The electronic infrastructure determines the distribution possibilities and new business models. Indicators like customer logins led to fantasy values that can hardly be explained from today's point of view. These fabulous possibilities motivated many entrepreneurs to take risk capital that was suddenly available in abundance. In the years of the boom, nowadays well-known companies developed, like the book consignor Amazon.com in 1994, the online auction house eBay in 1995, the exclusive online department store Boo.com in 1999, and many others. Companies in Germany developed this way too, for example the multimedia agency Kabel New Media in 1993, or the online shop dealer Intershop in 1995. Since 1998, many new companies developed within a short period of time, which partly showed almost nothing but high starting capital.

On the Internet, the situation back then is reflected as follows today: "Scenarios developed that partly could not be outbid in terms of scurrility and ridiculousness: risk capital providers equipped start-up companies with fabulous amounts of capital although many of the underlying company concepts would not have withstood a founded analysis. New staff was employed without special basic knowledge, customer projects were calculated at the outer limit of profitability, free services were offered on the Internet without realistic plans for the generation of exemplary turnover with the service at one point. Instead, even more venture capital was pumped into many of those start-up companies because many believed in the loud-colored industry and heard the cash till ringing. Almost surrealistic credulousness and infallibility spread and became characteristic for the whole industry. Going public took place in weekly intervals and was celebrated as a triumphal milestone. The stock markets honored that with the establishment of their own technology indices, for example the *Nemax* at the German Stock Exchange."[27]

But in the history of economics this euphoric behavior was not new at all. The tulip mania at the beginning of the 17th century is the most famous example. Still today, it is not clear why the tulip became the most sought-after fashion flower, mainly in France and the Netherlands. In the

---

[27] cf. http://www.netplanet.org/geschichte/neunziger.shtml; Request from June 30, 2008 28 cf.

middle of the 16th century, traders and Habsburg's diplomats first replanted it from the Levante to gardens in Austria and Upper Germany, and then to those of the Netherlands. Initially, its cultivation became an aristocratic hobby and then the source of foolish speculations. Between 1633 and 1637, the coffee houses in Holland had turned into tulip markets, where very soon things were no longer about owning real tulips but about speculation and trade with imaginary value expectations. As long as everybody expected rising bulb prices, they bought with enthusiasm and prices increased. But on February 2nd and 3rd, 1637, trade in Harlem turned unsure, on February 4th there was panic whilst prices were dropping and within one week the plants that could not be measured by gold up to then had become worthless bulbs. Numerous investors were completely ruined by this "wind trade," which is the appropriate Dutch term for this kind of business.[28] This first major stock market disease that was internationally called "Tulipmania" generated the terms "monkey business" or "wind trade" that are still used today. And how did those behave who wanted to invest and thus increase their capital a few centuries ago? In a remarkable analysis, "What can we learn from financial disasters?" Howard Davies reports that even big names like Isaac Newton (1642-1727) have had failures. [29]

Even this genius was subject to then famous euphoria regarding the "South Sea Company". Davis writes: "The share price of the South Sea Company opened at around £120 per £100 par value in January 1720. It reached £950 in July, before collapsing to £290 in October. Most of the 'assets' of the company were found to be loans and installments due from subscribers to the stock. One of the big losers was Isaac Newton, who subsequently wrote, 'I can calculate the motions of the heavily bodies but not the madness of people.'"

Besides the known economic fact of the objective volatility of capital market development, uncertainties are always based on psychological influences that can be found again and again. They are as old as Julius Cesar's realization that "Men willingly believe what they wish." In the case

---

[28] Bonß, Wolfgang: Vom Risiko. Unsicherheit und Ungewissheit in der Moderne (About risk, uncertainty and insecurity in modernity), Hamburger Edition, June 1995

[29]

http://www.fsa.gov.uk/Pages/Library/Communication/Speeches/2003/ sp121.s html (request from April 15, 2008)

of the dot-com oversubscriptions, things were not much different. The investors did not want to see any risks but just the tempting profits from the first fabulous successes. Especially the small investors, inexperienced in capital investment, often did not suspect that they were running the risk of losing all their savings within no time if they put all their eggs in one basket. Sometimes, the mobilization of capital by the New Economy is just negatively judged one-sidedly. Here, one does not see that many positive effects are connected with it: in the first place the release of idle capital for new company foundations and for large-scale projects that could not be financed otherwise. In the period of promoterism, the newly developed banks already had this role. The interest of many small investors in the New Market and the Internet boom generated an abundance of companies going public like had not been the case for many decades. Due to the expected profits of the dot-coms, the internationally widespread interest in shares of big parts of the population experienced an enormous upswing. The "New Economy" experienced a real IPO boom. 46 companies went public in 1998 and in 1999 there were 140. Thus, the German Stock Exchange could introduce a blue chip segment on the New Market that should comprise the 50 biggest companies. At the same time, the New Economy was renamed to Nemax All-Share and the blue chip segment to Nemax 50. Just before that, in April 1999, the German Stock Exchange had brought into being the small cap segment SMAX that comprised small and medium-sized traditional companies."[30]

The following table lists the number of companies that went public on the regulated market from 1997 to 2008.

Table 3: Number of companies going public from 1997 – 2008

Year	Number of Companies Going Public
From 3/10/97	38
1998	79
1999	194
2000	173
2001	27
2002	7
2003	1

[30] History of the stock market, Ibid. 45

2004	10
2005	19
2006	47
2007	37
Until 7/7/2008	7

(Table established according to specifications by Deutsche Börse Group: Group: http://deutsche-boerse.com/dbag; Request of July 6th, 2008)

In the year 2000, 173 companies went public in Germany. This can definitely be rated positively because, especially in the build-up period, liquid means are essential for starting business development. Of course, the economically reasonable employment of the capital won by going public is likewise important. You can safely assume that a part of the money collected by going public was spent by unnecessary expenditure for luxurious cars or expensive and prestigious office equipment. In addition, there were the management mistakes of the dot-coms resulting from objective inexperience. On the other hand, the presumed rip-offs out of ethical-moral loss of values to conscious defrauding intentions surely played a marginal role.

In the period of promoterism, the objectively needed new control mechanisms were missing for the new Internet economics. If even auditors, as it was the case with "Enron" from the USA, do not manage to see through the real economic bubbles, how could that be possible for the controllers of the entirely new Internet? These new problems, connected with the nature of the net-supported business models, were even sharpened by the media.

To a great extent, media reported about the golden age of the Internet and, as generally known, they favored stories of success. Skeptical contributions did not find any readers or spectators and when the first problems that were also taken seriously by the media began to show. In most cases it was too late then, anyway. Here, a crucial change was initiated by the American financial magazine *Barrons*. On March 20th, 2000, it published a study under the title "Burning Up" in which 207 American companies from the Internet industry were inspected and ranked in a "list of death". The result of the study was that with most of the inspected Internet firms there was a terrifying gap between the market value and the economic evaluation of the company. Since the running costs of these companies were higher than the incoming means,

Barrons estimated that 51 of the inspected companies would be insolvent one year later at the latest.

In this connection, the fact that nobody really foresaw that is particularly remarkable. In fact, common sense should have told every investor that this would go wrong. How can a company be evaluated at 500 million dollars if the turnover amounts to only 5 million dollars? Even the most optimistic prognoses should have made it clear to everybody that such evaluations could only be pipe dreams. In addition, many dot-coms spent money as if it would run out of fashion. The most expensive offices, the grooviest company cars, free food for the staff, even free vending machines for sweets and drinks; everything was possible and it seemed to be like wonderland.

Even the Internet book dealer Amazon was predicted to go bankrupt in January 2001 if the burn rate (money burning speed) remained unchanged. One day later, Germany's biggest daily newspaper presented the results of this study as "The list of death of Internet firms" to the broad German public. But that was not all. In the following days, articles about burn rates, lists of death and negative cash flows, flooded the financial press. Consequently, many experts advised to sell Internet shares, at least in part."[31]

This initiated a development that lead to panic sales and also affected many newly founded companies that definitely would have had bigger chances under normal development. The crash of the dot-coms drove many to insolvency.

Bursting of the Dot-Com Bubble and Hangover

At the end of the 20th century it soon became obvious that many of the celebrated dot-com companies would not be able to fulfill their profit expectancies at all at present or in the foreseeable future. Frequently, the stock market value was just based on an idea and its birth was merely covered by material counter values. The "company history" achieved a higher value than the balance of the company. At that time, detailed business plans and other documents with which new founders sometimes planned themselves to death before the actual start-up were interesting

---

[31] cf. Börsengeschichte (History of the stockmarket). Internethausse and Megabaisse (1996-2002) Part 2: Nemax-Skandale und Guru-Schelte 20002001 (Nemax scandals and guru criticism), in: http://zeitenwende.ch/finanzgeschichte; Request of June 30th, 2008

for only a few investors. Correspondingly, in its anniversary article regarding the new economy, Spiegel Online sneeringly described the behavior of the shareholders: "The company makes losses and has no reasonable business model? Order the purchase!"[32]

The facts of the increments in quotations confirmed the completely exaggerated expectations. Subscription profits also crashed within a few weeks. Regarding the beginning of the megabaisse in March 2000, Börsengeschichte says: "If in February all IPOs still started with subscription profits that partly brought three-digit record subscription profits for the investors (e.g. Biodata 433%, Popnet 340%, Softline 322%, Pironet 232%, Varetis 213% or OnVista 195%), the first signs of fatigue emerged from March on. Thus, on March 22nd, with the mega emission of Lycos Europe AG, there was no subscription profit and with ProDV, going public on the same day, even a subscription loss of 4.35%. Jobs & Adverts, going public a bit later on April 6th, even had to cope with losses of more than 17%."[33] At the same time, it turned out that there seemed to be some truth in the "list of death" of the dot-coms from the USA.

"Amongst the first companies that had to stop their business activities were names that are almost forgotten today, like the British fashion and sports dealer Boo.com, the Internet furniture dealer Homeportfolio or the media dealer Pseudo.com. In addition, companies like Deja.com, iCast or the Internet portal Altavista reduced big parts of their staff in order to save costs. Although Germany had been spared more or less up to then, the growth segment lost more than 30% by the beginning of April, and quoted at only 5,731 on April 5th." This crash initiated further panic sales. The liquidity that had seemed to be always secured up to then was lost.

Very soon already, the first insolvencies disturbed the high spirits and a considerable decline in prices in the opinion of experienced speculators resulted in direct massive share sales. Also responsible for the extreme crash of the new economy were numerous cases of fraud in which sham orders, wrong investor information and other foulness

---

[32] http://www.spiegel.de/wirtschaft/0,1518,470879,00.html;Request of June 30th, 2008

[33] cf. Börsengeschichte (History of the stockmarket). Internethausse and Megabaisse (1996-2002) Part 2: Nemax-Skandale und Guru-Schelte 20002001 (Nemax scandals and guru criticism), in: http://zeitenwende.ch/finanzgeschichte; Request of June 30th, 2008

frequently hit the small investors first. Thus, for example, the Spiegel reports in the abovementioned article about the traffic technology company *Comroad*, whose fantasy orders represented 96% of the balance. Again and again, other companies imputed to their products new characteristics in order to rectify further share splitting this way. The company Phänomedia, famous for their cheeky game "Moorhuhn," made many small shareholders lose the money they had worked hard for after falsifications of the balance became public. Holger Zschäpitz commented "The crash still sends shivers down the spine"[34]

Numerous stock market experts considered the share prices of Internet companies overrated from the beginning, but in the general euphoria that lasted until the turn of the millennium such voices were ignored. But in the year 2000 the crash became reality and initiated a general downwards trend at the stock market. In retrospect, the dot-com boom has been called a bubble. Many of the founded Internet start-ups had to close down; especially business models that should be financed by advertising only or that even wanted to make the surfer pay for the reception of advertisements (Paid4-Szene) could not survive. In the course of the years 2000 to 2001, the economy experienced the rapid disappearance of a whole industry sector that had been frenetically celebrated only months before. Companies whose financial means were exhausted suddenly could not resort to the, up to then, always comfortably topped up risk capital any longer and got into acute financial trouble within a short time. Faulty business-political decisions added one more thing to such critical business situations to trigger a company's bankruptcy within a short time. In addition, there was an event that, nowadays, is almost forgotten that burdened many of the up to then always profit-promising telecommunication: the auctioning of the UMTS licenses. After 173 rounds they filled up the public purse with 98 billion euros, but burdened the bidding companies even stronger than foreseen as it was soon shown by the share performance.

---

[34] *Die Welt* dated June 5, 2008, p.19

Source: Die Welt, June 5th, 2008
Figure 1: Dotcom bubble at the Nemax

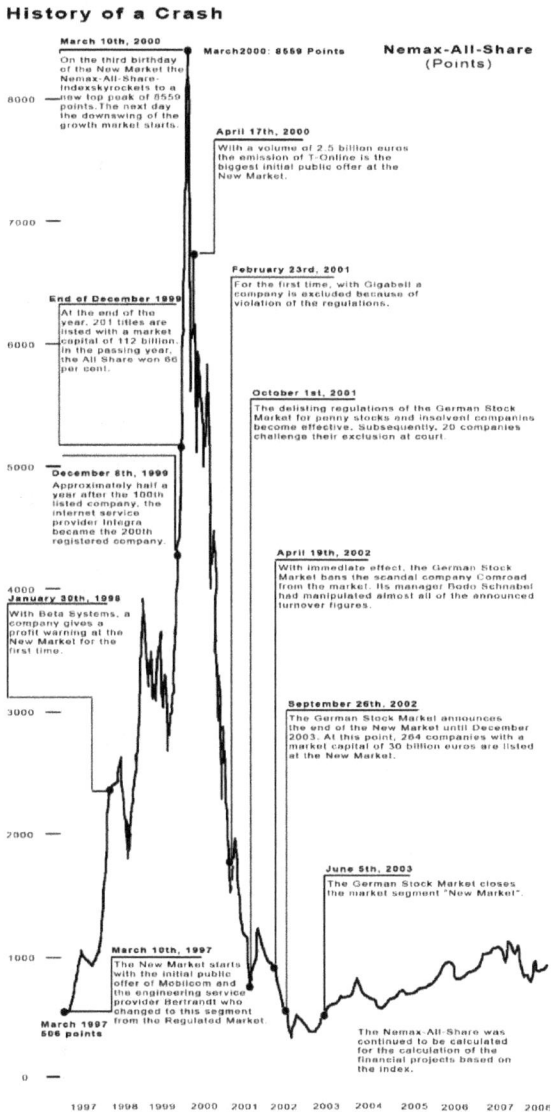

History of a Crash

Table 4: Slump in prices after the auctioning of German UMTS licenses

Bidders in	Share	Price	Price	Performance

36

Germany		8/11/2000	10/18/2000	
E-Plus Hutchison	Hutchison	16.25 EUR	13.30 EUR	-18.15%
Group 3G	Telefonica	24.06 EUR	19.66 EUR	-18.29%
	Sonera	33.45 EUR	17.70 EUR	-47.09%
Mannesmann Mobilfunk	Vodafone	252.00 EUR	126.00 EUR	-50.00%
MobilCom Multimedia	MobilCom	132.50 EUR	52.60 EUR	-60.30%
	France Telecom	135.60 EUR	98.00 EUR	-27.73%
T-Mobil	Dt. Telekom	48.30 EUR	37.22 EUR	-22.94%
Viag Interkom	British Telecom	12.54 EUR	10.32 EUR	-17.70%

Source: Börsengeschichte. Internethausse and Megabaisse (1996-2002) Part 2: Nemax-Skandale und Guru-Schelte 2000-2001 (Nemax scandals and guru criticism), in: http://zeitenwende.ch/finanzgeschichte; Request of June 30th, 2008

The Telekom share, in particular, was considered overrated after further purchases in the USA and lost considerable worth, a fact that fills many small investors of the people's share with bitterness yet today. In addition, those start-up companies that could already present sustainable returns partly got into very severe trouble thanks to the now emerging general caution of the investors and customers. The hangover got worse. All the positive effects of the New Economy, the 100,000s of newly created jobs, the courage to found globally acting companies and the citizens' interest in shares soon fell into oblivion.

In the centers of the New Economy movement, mainly in the Californian Silicon Valley, a real recession developed with the crash of the new market that nobody had expected. Many start-ups had to lay off a big portion of their staff in a short time, sometimes within a few days, in order to be able to rescue the company. Firms that had employed several hundreds of employees in their best periods reduced themselves to less than 50 employees. This development also took place in the German dotcom and New Economy centers like Hamburg, Berlin, the Ruhr Area, or Munich.

While the rapid growth of the dot-com companies had produced many clever spirits, amongst the employees that ended up on the streets then, there were also many boasters that only impressed by their brisk appearance and their ability to present great visions. All these colorful figures ended up in the card file of a "difficult to place" work force. It is obvious that the really qualified work force were the ones who were bereaved in the first place. The market that had been so massively pushed over ten years collapsed and demand for qualified technicians, computer scientists, and designers went through the floor. Here it should not be forgotten that many of these clever spirits had completely exploited themselves in the years before. Too much work, not enough leisure time, bad nutrition, not enough exercise, all of that took its toll. Many of them fell by the wayside and ended up in the bulk of unemployed people.

This way, much precious creative potential was lost and many of the job seekers in Germany and the whole of Europe felt like the losers of a development that ended in permanent mass unemployment and bitterness. Regarding that, Netplanet writes: "Retrospectively, after a certain time, the frustration of the 'losers' marks this dramatic period. Friendships broke apart, on web sites verbal wars were virtually held between ex-entrepreneurs and their former employees. But clever entrepreneurs even found their markets in the New Economy that had become unemployed to a great extent: So-called pink slip parties[35] were held in the centers of the New Economy where unemployed specialists could talk with new employers in an informal atmosphere. Only the incredible cynicism of the scene was reliably underpinned by such events because only a minority really found new professional contacts at this kind of events."[36]

The downward trend of the New Economy was even worsened by the events of September 11th, 2001 and the global economic recession. Even later on, in the years 2002 and 2003, companies collapsed that could not survive the hard times despite their strict course of consolidation.

At this time, men from the "Old Economy" were needed again in order to reorganize companies, even if many were worried about the capital they put into the new companies, and tried to avert total catastrophe. Some were lucky and succeeded in taking the values of the shares in the hands of the shareholders back to what they really are,

---

[35] In the USA, the dismissal paper is called "pink slip".
[36] ECCR, Berlin Springer Verlag 1999, p. 15 ff.

namely counter values to the material assets of the companies. If an entrepreneur manages to connect his financial needs with the value of the real material assets of the firm and not with fantasy values, as in case of many dot-coms, he can put his company on a salvageable basis. The old capital principles say that, in reality, share prices are bound to material assets, the real values of which cannot be changed by stock market speculations or crashes. This means that speculators drive the sales profit hopes to unreal heights. The example of the dot-coms made it particularly clear that greed permitted evaluations that did not have anything to do with reality. The growing turnovers in shares at the stock markets resulted from the increasingly accelerating trade in stock market papers. These purchases and sales do not have anything to do with the real economy and the available amounts of money. In the past, people purchased shares for the long run, as Ron Summer demanded for the Telekom shares. It was customary to hand over shares from generation to generation. It was completely different with the dot-coms. With the introduction of new media, and especially the Internet share, trading practices changed. Also, shares themselves were sold quicker and quicker. Profit expectations rose with every sale, even if it was just a marginal percentage. As with the tulip mania in the 17th century, a kind of roulette was initiated, and the stock markets turned into gambling halls where, as everybody knows, a great deal of money is lost in most cases. The roulette of the 90s was additionally fueled by the worldwide linkage of all share market locations by the Internet and, of course, bankers and brokers supported it with pleasure. They, in particular, always win this game because they are the bank holders.

Even if small investors turned back to stock market trade to an increasing extent in recent years in order to get a piece of the cake, too, they purchased less than one fifth of the shares of the German companies and are rather underrepresented in the trade turnover of the stock markets. In Germany, this is still a deficiency. The recurring fear of the small investors, fueled by the stock market crash of the dot-coms, that there is a shortage of money for the foundation of companies, even if the entire role in domestic economy has been minor until now.

In the "Süddeutsche" of January 24th, 2008 Franz-Josef Leven, Director at the German Institute for Share Promotion, said: "I simply assert that even if all private investors would sell their shares at the same time, this would not be of high impact to the market."[37]

On the one hand one can assume that the stock market spectacle around the dot-coms at the turn of the millennium was a mélange of greed of speculators, stock brokers and banks, the development of technical possibilities (Internet), and advertising and media that fueled the share purchases, as became very obvious with the Telekom shares. On the other hand, the dot-com bubble resulted in a basic cleanup of the Internet industry and a more objective inspection of conceptions also in this field. The industry got rid of tricksters and free-riders who had just been searching for quick money and laid off any kind of rationality in doing so. Even if the dot-com bubble burst, the Internet as such has survived and, with it, the big technology and Internet companies.

In the face of the horror stories of this crash one must not forget, of course, that there are always two participating parties. That became more than clear in this stock exchange game. Very quickly, companies delivering absolutely realistic turnover prognoses and aiming for fundamental, healthy growth had become completely uninteresting for the venture capital providers. It was the one who promised higher and higher profits that had good chances to get the needed starting capital. Most of the founders of new businesses of that time were brilliant technical spirits with an idea and were then supported in the search for capital by managers of the venture capital firms. Quite often, it came to strange duels between honest companies and managers who were eager for growth and profit and praised the definitely innovative product into spheres that did not have anything to do with reality. One or the other start-up entrepreneur found himself on the dock later on and had to vindicate himself. Of course, amongst the venturesome entrepreneurs, there were also spirits who practiced a new form of interpretation of applicable laws and, in their addiction to make much money, never thought that they could also lose the game.

Within a short time, through the employment of enormous financial means, on the back of innumerable innocent investors, a technology was promoted that could never have been developed within such a short period of time without this gold rush. An enormous leap in technology remains as the benefit for all. Even if the investors paid the price, in the

---

[37] http://www.sueddeutsche.de/finanzen/artikel/434/154037/; Request of June 30th, 2008

end everybody will profit because the computer and software development, as well as the Internet as it is today, would never have been developed in its current form otherwise.

The stock exchange roulette still continues in the year 2008 and a great number of big companies in the field of new media participate in it, as the latest multi-billion dollar takeovers in the IT sector show. "Microsoft is partying like it's 1999," could be read in the "Wall Street Journal," for example, meaning the takeover of YouTube and DoubleClick by Google, of Skype by Ebay and of Facebook by Microsoft. They were made in the hope for a growth potential that again should be mainly based on advertising. Of course, here one also thinks of the growing market in Asia and hopes for a high success quota and new profit chances by means of special offers. The frightening thing is this: Facebook, in particular, due to its abundance of available personal data that is provided by the users themselves, allows for very targeted advertising possibilities which, in turn, promise the advertisers a very high success quote. Facebook was founded by the then 20-year old Harvard student Mark Zuckerberg in 2005. In 2007, Yahoo offered him one billion dollars for this company, and that although the annual turnover amounted to "only" 150 million dollars. These "value assessments" by Internet companies suggest upcoming turbulences in the field of new media, especially as these billions of turnover show the open competition that has broken out between Google and Microsoft. "Microsoft has invested in keeping Google out," judges the analyst Rob Enderle according to the *Times.* Even if the final outcome of an interest in Yahoo by Microsoft is still open, the efforts prove how strategically important the dot-coms are still considered to be. At the same time, such recent spectacular attempts to get a share or sales also show that still much money is put in the Internet economy and new growth potentials are seen there. They attach to the successes of the meanwhile established Internet companies like Amazon, eBay or Google, which were not so heavily affected during the entire dot-com crises. This way, the Internet boom, even if at a more moderate pace, continues and gives hope to the new technology-driven dot-greens.

Future of the Dot-Coms and Conclusions

In Germany one gains the impression that just thinking about the positive aspects of the New Economy triggers incomprehension, precisely because it resulted in the well-known crisis. Here, in the USA it still applies today that more than 20 billion dollars were invested in Silicon Valley's high tech sector in the year 2000 and more than 5 billion[38] in the meager years after that. Even people in Germany are just talking about burnt money, in Silicon Valley they also offset the gained experiences against that and dream of the next boom.[39] Starting points for that were and are things like mobile Internet technologies, nano technologies and, foremost, the clean technologies that still have to be explained in more detail.

This upswing is pushed by higher investments by venture capital companies with new target directions of monetary investment. The main direction of impact for that is called climate and environment protection or simply "green technologies." The trend leads from "old" high tech industries like chip production to fields like mobile industries and intelligent software, bio-medical devices as well as products and services for a clean environment. At an unusual speed, Silicon Valley has been developing more and more into "Green" Valley. In the German media, a ZDF contribution in January 2008, and then the 10th issue of the magazine "Stern" in February 28th, 2008 called attention to that in a way that was appealing to the public. Here, it is about more than a campaign or a flash in the pan, as some readers of the "Stern" believe in the later discussion about the lead article "Das bessere Amerika" (The better America). Those who think that California was behind the times compared with Germany's environmental benchmarks will be disabused soon.[40] The author is of a completely different opinion here. The German environmental industry has experienced a similar challenge as the classical electronics industry experienced due to the development of micro-electronics or, formulated even sharper, the replacement of horse carriages by taxies.

At present, the venture capital providers are in the starting blocks in Silicon Valley. One of those companies that already helped to bring into being Google and Genetech is the venture capital firm Kleiner Perkins Caufield & Byers. Since last autumn, the former Vice President and Nobel Peace Prize Laureate Al Gore has been collaborating as an advisor. The subject is to filter out the best ideas and projects for

---

[38] Ibid.
[39] cf. *Building The Next Silicon Valley*, Roven 2003
[40] Stern 12/2008, p. 20

green and clean technologies" and make them work.[41] "The message is: You can transport the skills of Silicon Valley and must transport some of those skills outside of the valley," Al Gore recommends. "But in fact the capital and the later stage businesses are all over the world."

Creative spirits for better climate and environment protection are sought after like never before. Therefore, the start-ups in this field try to compose management teams with a mix of science and business know-how. Meanwhile, many IT specialists are entering this sector. The background is not just the trend towards "Green IT" that was clearly visible at the latest computer fair in Hannover in 2008, but the climate change itself. The globally installed computer technology already produces as much CO_2 output as air traffic. JeanBaptiste-Joseph Fourier (1768-1830) discovered the natural greenhouse effect in 1820. He still was of the opinion that water vapor was the most important greenhouse gas. Then, John Tyndall (1820-1893) discovered CO_2 as another greenhouse gas and Svante Arrhenius (1859-1927) from Sweden warned of the imminent global warming already in 1896. It is mainly caused by CO_2 emissions that develop when coal, oil and natural gas are burnt. Coal or gas power plants for the generation of electricity also have their share in that.

Mainframes like Google's for operating the worldwide data search engine need enormous amounts of power with all the consequences for the consumption of resources and environmental impact. IBM already altered the advertising slogan from Big Blue to Big Green for the establishment of climate-protecting computer technology and invests approximately one billion dollars per year in that field. "Heating with Data" was the headline of a disillusioned contribution about the economic compulsion to a more environmentally-friendly IT industry published by the news magazine *Der Spiegel* no. 13, 2008. Many IT engineers from Silicon Valley want to effect more for environmental protection and, at the same time, of course, also remain in the industries where there is the highest cash flow. To them this step means a complete change to new environmentally-friendly technologies and new customers, e.g. in the field of solar technology.

Founders and employees from the IT sector who had only to do with soft and hardware over years can help the green enterprises a lot. Initially

---

[41] *San Francisco Cronicle* http://www.sfgate.com request from Nov. 13, 2007

and foremost, they transfer the foundational spirit and their course of action to the environmental industry. Many representatives from the much more dynamic high tech companies are sure that a completely new spirit can be brought into the environmental industry just by the changed Silicon Valley company style. Some say directly that the Silicon Valley virus has to be spread within the environmental sector in a positive sense.[42] According to the same source, David Cope, head of the water and food processing company Novazone, thinks that it is absolutely crucial that the right mix of the team is the biggest challenge for newly developing environmental companies: "You have to find those people who are ready to re-invent themselves."

This also applies even if the environmental sector is not so new for the IT specialists. Paul Holland, responsible for the green technologies at Foundation Capital, reports in the same source: "We really find staff that have just been working in the fields of software or networking in the recent 20 years. And then it turns out that they have a university degree in environment technology."

According to Russel Hancock, CEO of Joint Venture, the green upswing is also particularly interesting from the point of view of safety for the future. The current economic situation of the USA would influence Silicon Valley, Hancock said to the Wall Street Journal. Thus, in the region there would be less and less jobs with a medium salary from $30,000 to $80,000 per year. But in Silicon Valley the costs of living were 47% higher than in the rest of the USA. The instable stock market and the sub-prime crisis would lead to the people in Silicon Valley "having more and more difficulties in feeling safe." From there, too, there is an increasing tendency to turn to future-oriented technologies with background knowledge from the IT sector.

From the recent years, the makers of this "green revolution" know that they have produced completely new industries out of their own power, paired with venture capital. Out of this self-confidence, the awareness accrues that they can achieve the same success in new environment technologies. One gains the impression that this special Silicon Valley virus has an almost stimulatory effect and produces very high self-confidence. In the past, this led to numerous other regions in the world trying to copy the idea of the foundation wave from California.

---

[42] cf. Martin LaMonica and Katharina Guderian, on May 30th, 2007, in: http://www.silicon.de/cio/strategie, Request of June 30th, 2008

From that, more than thirty "Valleys" developed alone, reaching from the USA to Europe to the Russian Taiga. Even if there are still massive differences between Taiga and tourism valleys in terms of the local and climatic conditions, one thing seems to be the same: the obsession and the incredible will of the people working in such foundation centers to push through something groundbreaking.

In October 2007, Todd Woody characterized the new rise in a comment regarding the publishing of the environmental report "Sustainable Silicon Valley-CO_2 Report 2007" as follows: "Silicon Valley these days is the epicenter of all things green, home to renewable energy entrepreneurs, ecologically minded venture capitalists and global warming-fighting CEOs."

In the *Los Angeles Times* of February 28th, 2008, in a lead article, Jessica Guynn described the new sense of departure as follows: "Even as the rest of the business world frets about the gloomy economy, Silicon Valley is living the Hightech high life. Nowhere is that more evident than at Founders Brunch, a private, invitation-only gathering where new-boom kids and industry veterans pick up whispers of the next big trends, invest in one another's ideas and push one another to think big."[43]

The description of the informal meetings says a lot about the spirit ruling there. Nobody drives up in an Armani suit or a Porsche, but rather in worn jeans trousers, t-shirts, and possibly on a pushbike. Visible status symbols do not count. The expressed ideas and their chances for the future are crucial: the faith in the feasibility of the new. The meetings are a colorful mix with no formal rules. One gets to talk and decides to meet again, or maybe not. Present are providers of ideas and money. Frequently, being invited to a "Founders Brunch" is based on an e-mail or the participation in a blogger forum about an exiting topic.

Just the way of meeting and the thereby ruling culture without paper can be compared with the invitations to founders' seminars or information events that are typical for us and shall particularly tempt new sponsorship possibilities. For example, the "Enterprise Europe Network" invited to a meeting about support contents and project applications just at the point of time when this work was under development, in this case

---

[43] cf. Jessica.guym@latines.com, Come for Brunch. Bring Billions, in: *Los Angeles Times*, Business; http://www.latimes.com/technology/lafifounders26feb26,1,6009894. story?ctrack=1&cset=true), Request of June 30th, 2008

for the program "eContentPlus." Although the network advertises with the hardly readable slogan "We are at the side of the companies," a detailed inspection of the invitation leaves the impression that one is rather asked for his money than being advised. A participation fee of 59.50 euros plus 9.50 euros (19% VAT) was charged for the four-hour information event about the EU program. Another 30 euros were due for an individual consultation for a project draft that had to be provided in writing beforehand. In this case, the inviting party was the Berlin Partner GmbH from the well-known LudwigErhard-House in Berlin Fasanenstraße. It goes without saying that the three-page written invitation was sent with detailed information about deadline and terms of payment. This alone probably characterizes the difference between the approach in Los Angeles and Berlin more clearly than any other explanation. That just a few young founders feel attracted by such meetings becomes obvious with the participation figures. Frequently enough, the young creative do not dare to give away their still half-baked ideas. Professionals know from experience that the way to the subsidy funds of the EU or other bodies is long and bureaucratic. They avoid it and know that the chances of getting financial support are bad anyway. The big concerns, on the other hand, can afford specialists just for combing through the jungle of subsidies and find additional support this way. This shows, too, that the foundation virus in our country is still merely infectious but hits very fertile soil in other regions of the world, like in the Taiga as it was reported under the title of "Silicon Taiga."[44]

Of course, the above-described backgrounds have to be included into all these observations. Be it the completely different mentality of the Silicon Valley pioneers yesterday and today, or the still deep-seated sting of mistrust that can be sensed especially here in Germany. Companies searching for venture capital today normally fail with the deputies of the venture capital firms who have to check the flood of business plans and, quite often, merely have the required knowledge of a single industry and rarely dispose of a sense for real visions. Today it is normal to send one's business plans to the capital provider via e-mail, it has become almost impossible to communicate with a really competent partner. It rather seems to be a big roulette game, so that many ideas get lost without leaving a trace.

---

[44] *Der Spiegel*, March 10th, 2008

Exactly at this point we should take the companies from Silicon Valley as an example again. Despite enormous losses, they did not lose their optimism and faith in innovative new technologies. Because just now we would do the right thing if we threw our acquired skepticism overboard and founded even more new companies as dot-greens with a mix of pioneering spirit and optimism.

2. The new Gold Rush: Green to Gold

Green Business Strategies as a new Challenge

Amongst the future technologies of the 21st century, environmentally-oriented ones have a front-row seat. In typical American advertising manner, "going green" has been catching the eye of many companies and public institutions since the spring of 2008 in a way that you almost feel like you are being shifted to an eco-advertising fairground. Here, California has been considered as "the better America" and an example for a long time now, as the "Stern" issue 10 formulates in a leading article. As an example region, Silicon Valley is in the fore. Even President George W. Bush, who always turned the crank backwards in the brakeman house of the international eco train, changes sides in the last remaining year in office. The *Newsweek* of May 5th, 2008 shows Bush on the front page under the amazing headline: "Turning Green." After a short clearing of his most popular activities against environment and climate protection, especially the collection of the Kyoto Protocol 2001 for the reduction of CO_2 emissions and the opening of Alaska's nature protection areas for oil drillings, the news magazine wonders: "Lately, however, Bush is turning... well if not green, then at least lime or chartreuse.... What is behind Bush's late-term epiphany about the environment?" [45] Pragmatically, *Newsweek* gives ten main proposals by which the tortured planet could be helped the most.[46] They range from suggestions for the radical reduction of packaging and waste, which is particularly urgent in the USA, to "Zero Waste", to energy-saving LED illumination and solar cells of plastic, to the abolishment of inefficient cooking methods and, of course, the petrol consumption of the old road cruisers. The persistence of shockingly high oil prices leads to painful price increases at the gas pump. At the end of July 2008, in California, a gallon of gas cost 4.10 dollars a pound. This corresponds to approximately 70 eurocents per liter, thus still low-priced compared with Europe. But the skyrocketing increase by almost 40% since the end of 2007 upsets many Americans. The annoyed car drivers try to establish car pools, form clubs of "Hypermilers" in order to drive as many kilometers as possible in a petrol-saving way, drive way under the recommended speed limit on

---

[45] Environment and Leadership. The New Green Leaders, News Week. 5. May 2008, p. 34
[46] Ibid., p.50

motorways, or use electric golf cars for shopping. This summer, as the first federal state, Utah introduced the four-day week for its employees in order to save petrol and energy.[47]

To the automobile giant General Motors, for example, the start-up company "Aptera Motors" from Carlsbad, California, is named as an example. From the next year on, this company will offer cars with hybrid or pure electric engines. The perspective is that one shall be able to charge them up by means of photovoltaic on the garage roof. *Newsweek* asks ironically: "Are you listening, GM?"[48] Obviously, more and more American enterprises hear the signal for the new international running competition in environment and technologies.

If you compare the approach in America with the approach in Germany, some important differences cannot be overlooked. Thus, when the environmental movement in Germany and Europe started at the end of the 70s, they initially changed local politics and from 1980 on, as the Federal Party "Die Grünen," also the federal politics. The center was ecological, social, violence-free and basic-democratic politics. In this respect, the 1980 program says: "The ecologic world crisis is aggravated from day to day: raw materials are running low, one poison scandal follows the other, animal species are being eliminated, plant species are dying out, rivers and oceans turn into cloacae, humans are threatened to atrophy intellectually and mentally within a late industry and consumer society, we burden the following generations with a sinister heritage."[49] The correctness of these statements has not changed up to now. Despite that, the economic redirecting in Germany, Europe and the whole world started under the utmost pressure, normally enforced by environment scandals or real catastrophes. Also by reason of their deliberately different outer appearance (trainers, jeans, turtleneck), over years, one did not take the concerns of the greens as seriously as needed. Only after success in elections on local and state level have the greens succeeded in entering federal politics. Here, ideological objectives dominated the program, too: "A complete change of our short-term-oriented economic

---

[47] Dowideit, Anette: Der Benzinpreis macht in den USA sogar Strafzettel teurer (In the USA, petrol prices even make traffic tickets dearer), Die Welt, July 2nd, 2008, P. 9

[48] Ibid., p. 52

[49] Archive "Grünes Gedächtnis" (Green memory), Preamble to the program 1980

purpose-oriented way of thinking is necessary. We think it is a mistake that the current waste economy promotes happiness and life satisfaction. On the contrary, people get more and more hustled and dependent. Only to the extent to which we free ourselves from the overestimation of the material standard of living, to which we enable self-realization again and bethink of the limits of our nature again, creative power will be released for redesigning a life on an ecological basis."

Up to now, from this economy and technology-distanced basic position, rather innovation-skeptical and technology-hostile, sometimes even destructive politics (e. g., against the production of gene plants in agriculture) are flourishing. In Germany, "green politics" are often put on the same level with deindustrialization (e.g. pull-out from nuclear plants), technology prevention (e.g. Transrapid technology) or innovation abdication (e g. for fashion products). In the German and European self-understanding, going green is still primarily connected with eco-ideological intentions, with a general educational right of nature, climate and environment protection and, above all, often enough with pronounced renunciation thinking.

In the USA, the new green politics and practices come from a completely different approach: the hard, immediate economic and the connected social-pecuniary constraints to save energy and redirect. At the petrol pump, climate change effects far more than the frequently far-flung climate objectives for 2020 or even 2050. When the petrol price climbed over the 4-dollar mark in San Francisco in spring 2008, news and panel discussions concentrated on this fact for days. In a "positive" global view, President Bush promised that he wanted to get Saudi Arabia to produce more oil and thus achieve stability in prices. The helplessness of the governments proves that entrepreneurial acts have to show a faster and, above all, more effective way out. "Entrepreneurs will turn us to green faster than government mandates" is the rational opinion of Ed Ring in the *AlwaysOn* magazine that is based in Silicon Valley.[50]

Simply and completely independently from ideologies, the swing in the USA initially and mainly results from economical constraints, the so-called "practical environmentalism" in contrast to the "emotional environmentalism" that is wide-spread in Europe. Hereinafter, the first approach is simplified and understood as "eco pragmatism" compared with the well-meaning "eco idealism". Having a clear conscience and a

---

[50] AlwaysOn, GoingOn, Issue 10, Fall 2007, p. 3

clean feeling supplement the pragmatic pressure, but does not effect it alone and especially not across the board as it can currently be sensed in Silicon Valley and the whole of California. Who has to pay $11 for parking a hybrid rental car at the hotel car park instead of R25 will rather take a hybrid vehicle next time without having a lecture about air pollution in San Francisco.

The already-mentioned almost extreme classification of any kinds of ecological efforts in the USA as "green business" justifies the question of what the difference between all the company strategies with the sticker Bio, Eco, Clean, Greentech, Emission free, or Sustainable really is.

Without doubt, the particularly inflationary used prefix "bio" has the longest tradition.[51] The Demeter organization as a forerunner of today's "hip" bio farming was prohibited by the Nazis in 1942 and not officially readmitted in the GDR after the war. In Western Germany it also lived in the shadows only and, in principle, it regained a new profile by bio cultivation in recent years only. The accentuation of the bio products as eco innovations is important in two respects. On the one hand, many green company foundations come from the nature and soil protection movement; on the other hand the prefix "bio" has a very reputable but also controversial meaning.

In practice, the clear differentiation between bio and gene technology is still difficult since there are no clear differentiation characteristics. They are also cross section technologies and used in many industries. Not least, they are subject to permanently new potential assessments.[52]

With the bio product labels that spread more and more, the situation is similar with in basic production methods. Normally, it is very difficult to find the difference between the rather market-oriented and the real product-technical special characteristics. The bio business has developed into a booming industry and is willingly used for bio cosmetic measures by some offerers. The news magazine *Der Spiegel* comments as follows:

---

[51] Hans Bentzien, Ein Lesebuch von früher und heute, von bekannten Leuten, von ihrem Werk und vom liebreizenden Ort (Hans Bentzien, A storybook about the past and today, about popular people, about their works and about a charming place), Berlin/Bonn, Westkreuz-Verlag 1999, P.13
[52] cf. Technologien des 21. Jahrhunderts (Technologies of the 21st century), OECD Paris 1998, P. 80

"Many pretendedly meaty testing labels sound important but are thickly applied company cosmetics in the first place."[53]

The situation of the "eco term" is not much better as proven in the standard works "Ökotricks und Bioschwindel" (Eco tricks and bio deception) by means of numerous examples as early as 1990.[54]

Internationally, the new generation of technology-based green companies faces big challenges if it is about real climate and environment protection. For that, so-called "maintenance men", creative makers of new products, materials, services and distribution markets, but also new organization structures and politically-administrative solutions in the sense of Schumpeter are needed. There are many indicators that the market on its own does not cope with the requirements of the climate problem and that operating a ruthless economy in the sense of "grasshopper capitalism" still requires different ways of intervention. For that, many more eco-founders are needed, also named "green entrepreneurs" in technical literature. Here, the already normal emphasizing of environment management is exceeded, needed are fundamentally sustainability-oriented foundations.

Robert Isaak characterizes these companies as follows: "In contrast, a green business is one that is designed to be green in its processes and products from scratch, as a start-up, and, furthermore, is intended to transform socially the industrial sector in which it is located towards a model of sustainable development."[55] Thus, extremely high requirements are made on the new green entrepreneurs. They are globally targeted towards the new cleantech world that is about to take the role of the hitherto existing high-tech industry. The "Cleantech Forum" conference that took place in Los Angeles at the end of February 2008 clearly accentuated that it is a completely new dimension.

In the *Chronicle* of February 28th, 2008 David R. Baker outlined: "Known both as green tech and clean tech, the industry develops alternative fuels, better ways to use existing resources and other

---

[53] Das große Moral-Monopoly (The big morale monopoly), in: *Der Spiegel* 19/2008, P. 102

[54] cf. Adler, Adam; Mackwitz, Hanswerner, Ökotricks und BioSchwindel,(Eco tricks and bio deception) Publishing house Orac, Vienna 1990

[55] Issak, Robert: The making of the Ecopreneur. In: Greener Management International, No. 38/2002, p. 82

ecofriendly products. Most of the companies are young, and many call Silicon Valley home. California cleantech companies won $1.79 billion in venture capital funding last year, 45 percent of the nationwide total $3.95 billion."

In an empirical study about green market leaders in his book "Ecopreneurship und Wettbewerbsstrategie" [56] (Ecopreneurship and competition strategy) Holger Petersen studied a number of companies regarding themselves as leaders. Out of these:

- 11 leading on global level
- 15 on continental level
- 43 on national and
- 4 on the regional level

The majority of the interviewed enterprises are medium-sized companies in the fields of nutrition (14), power and heat supply (13), living (11) and mobility (6). More than two thirds of the companies were founded after 1970 with the rise of the environmental movement in Germany.[57] Only relatively few successful green companies can look back to a company history of many years. This also proves that an "eco economy history" practically does not exist yet although some of today's particularly topical "green productions" have very old historic ancestors in reality. More recent new dissertations, like the one by Jens Clausen "Umsteuern oder Neugründen? Die Realisierung ökologischer Produktpolitik in Unternehmen" (Rerouting or new foundation? The realization of ecologic product politics in companies) (Hannover 2004), do not give clear delimitations between the different internationally comparable "green business strategies". Likewise, in Silicon Valley all the environmental sins have not been eliminated yet, there are enough attempts to jump on the bandwagon by means of a green coat. Going-green is "in".

Pseudo eco-entrepreneurs must be referred to because they risk damaging the reputation of entire industries again and again. This does not only apply to new founders but also to established companies and their environment respectively CO_2 reports. Sometimes, even prominent people are caught red-handed publicly uttering green tirades and subsequently boarding their private jets.

---

[56] Petersen, Holger, EcopreneurshipVerbreitung ökologischer InnovationenMarburg, Metropolis-Publishing house 2003, p. 102
[57] Ibid. p. 104

Here, in the sense of the opening question, the characteristics of the typical and simultaneously special features of eco companies are of interest. Their research still has not got much scientific background. International literature likewise talks about "environmental entrepreneur", "ecopreneur" or "green entrepreneur".[58]

Next to them there are the so-called "enviro-capitalists" that have already been correctly evaluated in their progressive role in the standard publications by Terry Anderson and Donald Leal in 1992.[59] Normally, their acts concentrate on local, nature-related effects. But the green change has become obvious on an international level too. For a long time already, formerly eco-abstinent regions like the Gulf States or growth tigers in Asia or India have been competing for green company foundations. Most of the requests address Silicon Valley and not Germany, as many here believe in a frequently imagined predominance in the field of environment technologies.

Even the rich oil producing countries have recognized the signs of the time and emulate the new company foundations from Silicon Valley with the new green standard.

"It's very clear let's extend our activities in the energy sector. It's what we do best," said Sultan al Jaber, Chief Executive Officer of Abu Dhabi Future Energy Company. "We're creating the Silicon Valley of alternative energy in Abu Dhabi". 15 billion dollars are already available for this purpose.[60]

India is more advanced already, and so are Singapore and China. Everywhere, they work with enormous effort to get basic innovations in the fields of clean-tech or green-business running soon. After the job losses in the fields of military technology, the personal computer industry and even in software development, all signs are green on the environment sector. Even big enterprises like Wal-Mart have switched to the green wave. At the end of 2007, new guidelines for green purchase conditions came out, mainly for small and medium-sized companies, as new suppliers were adopted. Following this trend, more and more products with a green seal can also be found in German supermarkets.

---

[58] cf. e.g. Michael Schaper, The Essence of Ecopreneurship. In: Greener Management International, No. 38/2002, p. 26 ff.

[59] cf. Anderson, Terry; Leal, Donald, Enviro Capitalists. Doing Good While Doing Well, Rowmann & Littlfield, Lanham, Oxford 1997

[60] Comp. http://www.masdaruae.com/Requestof June 15th, 2008

Without doubt, Silicon Valley, which also has been shattered by crises in recent years, has found a new "hot spot" in green technologies, too. Here, the focus is on new alternative energy production technologies. In San Francisco, insiders are already talking about the change from dot-com companies to watt-com firms with enormous growth perspectives in the next years due to the persisting global hunger for energy. Consciously, hinting at the dot-coms, this book talks about dot-greens.

The political uncertainties in the Near East regions fuel this trend. Thus, more and more money flows to California. "A study just out from Dow Jones Venture Source indicates that more than half of all clean-tech venture capital in the United States last year went to Californian companies."[61]

Changed Markets and Frame Conditions for Sustainability

In the recent years, the image of the "green consumer" has changed radically. If eco-consumers were considered a fringe or niche group for decades, nowadays the self-confident consumer is the center of strategic rerouting. Well-informed and climate-conscious Californians belonged and belong to the precursors today. With his environment program, Governor Arnold Schwarzenegger personally advocates more climate protection. The measures he planned and pushed through in extraordinarily climate-endangered California are radical and address the sense that still is the most developed in the USA: earn money. Without doubt, California is the head of the green renewal of America. At the same time, environment and climate-political decisions for California are made which, as is generally known, exceed the American average by far. Due to the practically realized measures, Schwarzenegger is specifically popular as a politician and with his new environmentally conscious lifestyle, like many other personalities, becomes an example for millions of people. New web sites like "ecorazzi.com" rigorously observe how seriously the new lifestyle that is better for the environment and the climate is lived by these prominent people.

Analyses of the "carbon footprints", i.e. the CO_2 footprints respectively extent of the carbon dioxide emissions of practically every

---

[61] Bob Keefe, Money for Clean-Tech Research Mainly Flowing toCaliforniain: Cox News Service, March 10th, 2008

action are far ahead. Although different greenhouse gases are held responsible for the greenhouse effect, it is CO_2 in particular that leads.

CO_2 is generated when carbon-containing substances are burnt. There are global efforts to reduce the emission of the gas although CO_2 is also generated in modern plants or emission-reduced cars with combustion engines. The global total emissions amount to about 36 billion tons per year.[62] But since there is no effective and at the same time economizing method for the separation of CO_2 at hand yet, this amount emits to the atmosphere and considerably contributes to global warming. The concentration is measured in ppm parts per million, i.e. the thousands part of one percent. Meanwhile, CO_2 constitutes 0.04% of our atmosphere. In the course of the history of the Earth, the portion of CO_2 in the atmosphere of the Earth has been subject to considerable fluctuations that have different biological, chemical and physical reasons. But over 650,000 years at least the share has always been lower than 280 ppm as numerous scientists confirm. During the last 10,000 years, this CO_2 concentration value has remained relatively constant. Thus, the balance of the carbon dioxide circuit has mostly been stable during this period. With the beginning of the industrialization in the 19th century, the CO_2 share in the atmosphere has increased to 381 ppm (in 2006) and its rise is currently increasing by 1.5 ppm per year on average.[63] Everybody contributes to that by driving a car, using energy, and going on planes. In England and the USA, many books for measuring one's personal CO_2 footprint have been published.[64]

In Germany, you can determine your personal CO_2 account online with different CO_2 calculators.[65] Here, the living conditions up to the nutrition habits play a crucial role and a kind of CO_2 selling of indulgences is already developing.

The Anglo-American efforts exceed separating and recycling of waste that has been particularly cultivated in Germany over several decades by

---

[62] cf. Wikipedia, Carbon dioxide, request from July 25, 2008
[63] cf. Ibid.
[64] cf. I Counttogether we can stop climate chaos. Your step-by-step guide to climate bliss, Penguin Book Ltd, London. 2006; de Rothschild, David: The Live Earth Global Warming Survival Handbook, Virgin Books Ltd., London 2007; McKibben, Bill: Fight Global Warming Now, Holt Paperbacks, New York 2007
[65] cf. http://www.spiegel.de/wissenschaft/natur/0,1518,470825,00.html

far. You can even feel a bit of irony in the fact that the Europeans are considered as the world champions in waste separation and recycling on the one hand, but obviously lost the innovative demands of the new clean-tech over all this passionate separating and collecting.

Internationally, one expects a new green economic wonder and a trend that is generally called LOHAS, derived from Lifestyle of Health and Sustainability. Here, health and sustainability hold key rolls and do not represent an eco fig leaf.

In February 2007, the Zukunftsinstitut in Hamburg (Future institute Hamburg) presented a study titled "Zielgruppe LOHAS. Wie der grüne Lifestyle die Märkte erobert." (Target group LOHAS. How the green lifestyle captures the markets)[66] This new mega-trend changes the entire work, consumption and life style, as well as the production methods and technology connected therewith faster and more radically than hitherto existing ecologically motivated political and strategic objectives. What is the key secret of this green economic wonder, the global going green movement or the apparent ecological revolution that has become subject to discussions more and more frequently? Without being taken in by new marketing slogans, the following can be stated: "If one of the most important venture capitalists says that the green business market has more market potential than the entire Internet market then this is definitely a statement."

The person in question is John Doerr, who brought Google on the stock market and was responsible for the financing of companies like Amazon.com, Symantec and Compaq. This statement was made by Doerr in a speech in front of the elite of American politics and economy at the TED Talk Conference in California. Sparked off by the confrontation with his 15-year old daughter, he started to look into the subject of climate protection. And in good old American entrepreneurial manner, apart from the problems, he also sees big chances for mankind.[67] Such statements fuel the fantasy of many market participants and, above all, of investors. The emerging green economic wonder addresses the mass market and meets geo- and national-political frame conditions that support the

---

[66] cf. Horx, Matthias: Zielgruppe LOHAS,
www.zukunftsinstitut.de/verlag/studien_detail.php
[67]
http://www.ted.com/index.php/talks/john_doerr_sees_salvation_and_pr ofit_i n _greentech.html

change and enforce it due to changed economical starting data. In his remarkable Zerstörung" (Balance or destruction), [68] Franz Josef Radermacher indicated that the frame conditions play a much bigger role than assumed with focus on the market alone. "The main difference between the developed societies is the kind of frame conditions of their markets."[69] Rademacher shows that competition alone is not important "But much more crucial is the second aspect and these are the frame conditions under which competition takes place. Here, in the first place, it is about the requirements of the citizens of the state, the social matters, the maintenance of the variety of cultures and the protection of the environment. In the frame conditions it is fixed what are unchangeable and preserveable assets with regard at the social conditions, the variety of cultures and the integrity of the environment. If necessary, they are also pushed-through against property interests and growth expectancies."[70] The frame conditions have changed in the whole world. The hitherto gratuitous atmosphere has to be billed in such a fundamentally new way that everybody understands that it is about survival in the literal sense.

Since the last UN World Climate Report of 2007, it has been an undisputed fact that a climate change has started that cannot be denied by any reputable researcher any longer. It will accelerate or can be stopped if we act resolutely.

But our atmosphere and the climate constitute the elementary basis of life for everybody, Jörn Altmann compares very clearly in his book of principles "Umweltpolitik" (Environment politics) in 1997.[71] Already 500 km above the Earth there is absolutely free interstellar space. In the first place, the stratosphere including the ozone layer embedded therein, as well as the troposphere, also known as weather zone up to about 10 km, are of special interest for our climate. Only this very thin and vulnerable

---

[68] Radermacher, Franz Josef, Balance oder Zerstörung – Ökosoziale Marktwirtschaft als Schlüssel zu einer weltweiten nachhaltigen Entwicklung (Balance or destruction Eco-social market economy as key to a globally sustainable developmet), Ökosoziales Forum, Vienna 2002
[69] Ibid., p. 17
[70] Ibid., p. 18
[71] Altmann, Jörn, Umweltpolitik. Daten, Fakten, Konzepte für die Praxis (Environment politics. Data, facts, concepts for practice), Stuttgart, Publisher Lucius & Lucius 1997

skin of the troposphere can be seen from space as the blue skin of the Earth because it contains particles that reflect the sunlight.

The atmosphere (derived from the Greek word "atmós – air, pressure, steam") that is so important for our lives consists of a mix of invisible gases, water drops and ice particles, as well as dust, soot, and other particles. 78% from that are (N_2), 21% oxygen (O). 0.9% the inert gas argon (Ar) and about 0.04% consist of carbon dioxide (CO_2).

But this little share of carbon dioxide crucially participates in the greenhouse effect. "The Earth has got fever, our planet is ill. And the humans are the virus that makes the fever rise." With this message, the Intergovernmental Panel on Climate Change (IPCC)[72] startled the global public in the first half of 2007.[73]

For the first time, the increase of greenhouse gases in the atmosphere caused by men and the destructive consequences were straight out named by the World Climate Council.

"The global atmospheric concentrations of carbon dioxide, methane and laughing gas as a consequence of human activities have been remarkably increasing since 1750 and surpass the pre-industrial values determined from ice drilling cores for several thousand years by far. The global rise of the carbon dioxide concentration...is primarily a result of the consumption of fossil combustibles and the changes in the usage of land while the increase in methane and laughing gas is mainly caused by agriculture."[74]

Furthermore, the most important climate killer is clearly worked out as being caused by men: "Carbon dioxide is the most important anthropogenic greenhouse gas".[75] And the health-endangering effect of carbon dioxide must not be underestimated in addition. Dizziness and headache are caused by about 5 percent of CO_2 in inhaled air. Higher concentrations accelerate the heartbeat, increase blood pressure and can lead to difficulties in breathing and unconsciousness. This phenomenon is known as carbon dioxide narcosis. CO_2 concentrations in the breathable air of 8% or more lead to death within 30 to 60 minutes.

None of the reputable climatologists in the world ignore the facts of the UN report any longer:

---

[72] required only in the German version.
[73] UN report, p. 29
[74] UN report, p. 147
[75] UN report, Ibid.

"The global atmospheric concentration of carbon dioxide has risen from a pre-industrial value of about 280 ppm (parts per million) to 379 ppm in the year 2005, the atmospheric concentration of carbon dioxide in the year 2005 exceeds the natural bandwidths determined from ice drilling cores of the last 650,000! years (180 to 300 ppm) by far. "All those who express their worries about the world climate and call for prompt rerouting are willingly denounced by the so-called "climate skeptics" or "climate critics" as "scare mongers". In the center of the attacks is, as a representative for many nameless climate protectors, Al Gore, who was honored for his devotion with the Nobel Peace Prize.

His book that was already published in 1992 "Earth in the Balance— Ecology and Human Spirit" has become a manifesto for new thinking and acting in terms of environment and climate protection. The documentary film initiated by him "An inconvenient Truth" shattered many of those who had been unconcerned up to then, and is a very descriptive proof that it is not about any kind of scare mongering but naked facts that are visible everywhere. For many, Al Gore was not only the Vice President and later candidate for president of the USA, a politician with visions and a developed sense for reality, but an inconvenient mobilizer against the climate skeptics. Al Gore understands "Ecology" as "the science of balance and some of the same principles controlling the healthy balance of the elements."[76]

Again and again that emphasizes the need for a realistic attitude regarding climate change:

"We can see but we are blind. We can hear but we are deaf."[77] Generally known observations of the climate change from the last 100 years confirm that we are within a much more serious process than was first recognized with regard to the consequences for life. First, this concerns the global rise of the average temperature, second the rise of the sea level and third the reduction of the snow layer on the northern hemisphere which can be recognized with the bare eye already. The German Chancellor and Environment Minister gazed at the latter in a camera-effective way at glaciers in Greenland. The increase in extreme

---

[76] Al Gore, Earth in the Balance-Ecology and Human Spirit, New York, Penguin books, 1992 – German first edition: Wege zum Gleichgewicht – Ein Marshallplan für die Erde (Ways to balance a Marshall plan for the Earth), Frankfurt/Main, S. Fischer Verlag, 1992 P. 23
[77] Ibid. p. 43

weather events provides another proof but is willingly explained in a different way.

If one just watches the obvious limits of inhabitability of the Earth, the global rapid growth of deserts catches the eye the first.[78] About 860 million people, thus almost 15% of the global population, are starving. On the other hand, the climate-caused rise of the seas does not only threaten far-flung regions, Bangladesh is targeted, but also our North Sea countries.[79]

The loss of many species from flora and fauna, bemoaned nowadays already, is also part of the eco system of our Earth like the growth of the population. World population amounts to 6.3 billion at present. In the last decades, growth has been decreasing but on a high level. Currently, the annual growth in population is estimated at 1.14% to 1.9%. If we remained at the bottom limit, the world population would increase by 72 million people per year (6 million per months or 200,000 per day).

Everybody needs drinking water, food, clothes, housing, heating, power, traffic routes, schools, hospitals, jobs, etc. So which number of population really marks the upper limit for a human livelihood? The pherologists, derived from the Latin word fero (to carry), occupyied with this special question of ecology, are often addressed with hostility and scientifically disputed. According to the actual assessments of the UNO, world population will settle down at a level between 7 to 11 billion until 2050, whereby big differences in the standard of living are still assumed. In his trend-setting book "Ein Planet wird geplündert" (A planet is being plundered), Herbert Gruhl indicated the necessity for radical ecological rerouting of our way of economizing towards the maintenance of the habitability of the Earth already in 1975. Optimistic assessments like those by Herman Kahn in "Vor uns die guten Jahre" (The upcoming good years) (1976) or in "Die Zukunft der Welt" (The future of the world) (1979), were based on higher population figures, but with an income and consumption that were considerably lower per head, namely 20,000 dollars. The "atmosphere consumption" was not taken into account here.

---

[78] http://www.dradio.de/dlf/sendungen/einewelt/387504/ Request of February 3rd, 2008

[79]   cf.
http://www.spiegel.de/wissenschaft/natur/0,1518,463967,00.htmlRequest of February 2nd, 2008

Nobody owns the atmosphere but we all pollute it every day without respect for those following. We cannot remain unconcerned about that any longer, neither from the frog's nor from the bird's eye view. Finally, there is no life without healthy air or if the entire natural system of our Earth fails. In their fundamental work "Natural Capitalism"[80], Paul Hawken, Amory and Hunter Lovins have shown the crucial starting points in 1999 already. They all start with a changed attitude and elementary understanding: we are not God. In the blurb of the book the authors warn:

"We are running the risk of losing the natural capital of the Earth. Not only the resources are endangered by exhaustion, life itself is retreating. The highly intelligent and complex system of the planet is of life-maintaining importance to us. Nonetheless, we behave in a way as if its services were worthless. In reality, the value of these services is almost endless and cannot be replaced by any kind of technology."

The new market and frame conditions that fuel the market have to be seen in front of this background. As the following overview shows:

- Health: 118 billion dollars. (includes natural/organic foods, supplements, personal care, alternative medicine, yoga, health/fitness, media)
- Eco-tourism: 24.2 billion dollars (includes eco-travel and adventures, new age/spiritual travel)
- Alternative energy: 400 billion dollars (includes green pricing programs, renewable energy certificates (RECs))
- Alternative mobility: 6.1 billion dollars (includes hybrid vehicles, biodiesel, car sharing)
- Construction biology: 49.7 billion dollars (includes ENERGY STAR products and homes, other green-certified homes, materials and solar panels)
- Lifestyles: 10.6 billion dollars (includes home furnishings/supplies, natural pet products, cleaners, apparel, philanthropy)
- Socially responsible investing 215 billion dollars (including privately managed accounts, SRI screened mutual funds, etc.) Natural Marketing Institute (http://karmakonsum.de/neue-marktstudielohas-aus-den-usa,48,2007-03.html

---

[80] German = "Eco capitalism. The industrial revolution of the 21st century wealth in accordance with nature"

The long Way to Green-Tech Base Innovations

Who is surprised when the representatives and scientists' associations' from the industry sectors that are particularly responsible for climate damages due to the consumption of fossil combustibles, resolutely argue against these causal interrelationships? For example, the representatives of the American Association of Petroleum Geologists allege that there are no verifiable connections between human acts and the petrol industry specifically, as well as climate change. In contrast, in numerous media reports they revealed that the highest government institutions in the USA, as well as important oil concerns, consciously play down the consequences of climate change and even provide financial support to those scientists who appear rather calming than upsetting. Even investigation committees of the Congress in Washington found themselves forced to criticize the political influence on objective climate reports. A report of December 2007 said:

"The 16-month investigation of the committee reveals systematic efforts of the White House to censor climate scientists by controlling their access to the press and by reworking their statements towards the Congress. The White House made special efforts to mute discussions about the connection between increasing hurricane intensity and global warming. The White House also tried to minimize the importance and the safety of climate change by thoroughly reworking the government reports about climate change. Other activities of the White House comprise editing legal expertise...about climate change."[81] Critics of the IPCC report belong to different nations and society groups from science, economy and politics. The political need for action because of climate change is discussed particularly controversially. Finally, here it is foremost about the future usage of fossil energy carriers and the carbon dioxide emissions that are proved to produce greenhouse gases. The criticism that starts at different aspects, points against the IPCC thesis that at least an important share of the observed warming process was made by men (anthropogenic). Instead, natural causes are assumed.

Ostensibly, sun activities are preferably consulted. Exemplary is the latest book by Henrik Svensmark and Nigel Calder "The Chilling Stars" from 2007. In the book, a new provocative climate theory is presented that was summarized in a report by the BBC as follows: "The book sets out to prove that a combination of clouds, the Sun and cosmic rays sub-

---

[81] cf. Committee Report December 12th, 2007

atomic particles from exploding stars have altered our climate far more than human carbon emissions."[82] As early as 1997, Nigel Calder's book "Die launische Sonne" (The volatile sun) with the subtitle "Widerlegt Klimatheorien" (Disprove climate theories) was published in German.[83] According to that, every climate change stands and falls with the sun's activity and thus they plead indirectly to carry on like before in all technological areas. Such publications and many others could be ignored in the sense of unproven scientific journalism if there was not a danger connected therewith that has to be taken seriously. The lobbyists and political representatives of the old environment polluting and climate destroying politics and the concerns behind them try to distract vehemently from the true, self-made causes at the expense of the entire human race, according to the principle: "After us, the flood".

It is known that one learns from mistakes, but what seems to be so easy in the literal sense turns out to be a difficult task in everyday life. Our children already show us that they would rather make their own mistakes than learn from the experience of their elders. No wonder that from the global point of view it has almost never been possible not to repeat mistakes that have already been made. This is a dangerous weakness, as the Austrian author Festl formulates: "In the face of the fact that humanity is not able to learn from the mistakes of the past, we cannot afford to make any mistakes in future."[84]

Despite all warnings, progress in the sense of clean technologies takes place much slower than necessary. This is not only because there are not enough success-promising and drastic innovations, but mostly because the old still wins over the new much too often and spreads faster than innovations can get a foothold on the market. The reason for that can be seen in three factors: for many big companies in the industrialized states it is still economically profitable to offer already outdated products on new markets that can be produced at low costs but with environmental impact. Thus, even old scrap can still generate profit over several decades. The European automotive industry is completely on this track.

---

[82] BBC, February 2, 2008
[83] Dr. Böttiger Verlags-GmbH, Wiesbaden 1997
[84] Ernst Ferstl, einfach kompliziert einfach (simply complicatedly simple), vabene Verlag, 1995, P. 20

With the economic development of developing and emerging industries the focus is much too often put on traditional products than on integral, benefit-based concepts and services. For example, instead of developing environmentally harmless concepts for mobilization, the status symbol automobile is globally marketed with combustion engines and with hybrid drive in the best case.

Very often, producers in the developing and emerging countries do not dispose of the financial power to buy the latest technologies. In particular, patent rights and the license fees and conditions connected therewith prevent the transfer of urgently needed, environmentally more harmless technologies or products.

Hitherto, there is no founded historic refurbishment of the "history of environment technology" and, above all, of the speed at which it is pushed through, although there are some books about the general history of environmental efforts.[85]

From our point of view, the following epochs and the theoretical as well as practical concepts for the spread of environment-oriented technologies and cultural changes connected therewith have to be differentiated:

First the environmental changes caused by sanitation technology, which we can simplify as sani-ecology. It already finds its pioneers with the growth of the cities in the Middle Ages and the new hygienic requirements caused by plague and other diseases at that time. The battle against environmental pollution, e.g. from tanneries and dye works, was an urgent problem already in the Middle Ages.[86] From this point of view, the inventors of the first water toilets deserve much more attention, starting with the Roman latrines to the first manorial "Temples of Convenience," as they were described by Lucinda Lambton.[87] Hygienic innovations are frequently underestimated, down to the invention and introduction of soap for washing and keeping the body clean. The first toilet with flush from a cistern created by Sir John Harrington in 1596 was 179 years ahead of its time because the first patent for this was registered

---

[85] cf. 1. Fischer, Helmut: 90 Jahre für Umwelt und Naturschutz ,Geschichte eines Programms (90 years for environment and nature protection, history of a program), (Bund Heimat u. Umwelt);

[86] cf. H. Kühnel (Publisher.), Alltag im Spätmittelalter (Everyday life in the Middle Ages), Weltbild Verlag 2006, P. 62ff.

[87] The Gordon Fraser Gallery Ltd., London and Bedford, 1978

in England no earlier than 1775. Subsequently, sani-technology started to spread.[88] Centuries after that this basic principle of water flushing systems for toilets has remained unchanged. Only now, due to the general shortage in water and the high degree of ground water pollution, new filtration and recycling considerations are to be made and researches for innovative solutions for an elementary human need are executed. This example already shows how slowly the change to innovative greentech takes place in the broadest sense. Martin V. Melosi wrote a first fundamental and comprehensive report about the history of urban environmental technique.[89]

The *second* mass debate in new environmental questions is closely connected with the movement that we will name limit-ecology. In 1972, the world bestseller "The Limits to Growth" was published in New York for the first time and in the same year in German under the title "Die Grenzen des Wachstums." The main authors, Donella H. Meadows, Dennis L. Meadows, and Jorgen Randers, wakened the world with hitherto never expressed thoughts. Essentially, they can be summarized by the following three main statements.

The absolute limits of growth on Earth will be reached within the next 100 years through growth of the global population, industrialization, environmental pollution, limits of food production and exhaustion of natural raw materials. Thus, population figures and the industrial capacities drop drastically.

Only by turning away from the growth trend and towards an ecologically-economic balanced state, the materialistic bases of life for every human being could be maintained with a certain margin for individual objectives and needs, even over a longer period of time.

The faster and the more consequent the human race decides to generate this state of balance, the better are the chances to reach this state.[90]

We know that the predicted limits, in the sense of the highest impact on the environment, have not yet been reached. Limit ecology contributed

---

[88] Ibid. p. 5

[89] cf. M.V. Melosi, The Sanitary City, Environmental Services in Urban America from Colonial Times to the Present, University of Pittsburgh Press, 2008

[90] Meadows, D.H., Meadow, Randers, J. et al. The Limits of Growth, DVA, Stuttgart1972, P.17

much to the almost fundamental connection of environment/technical solutions with renunciation ideology. This worked like a built-in brake when acceleration was crucial and often enough it made the discussions become heated.

The authors Meadows and Randers also had to admit that and twenty years later they formulated new limits of growth.[91] In 1992, the original American edition was titled "Beyond the Limits", the German title was a bit more friendly "Die neuen Grenzen des Wachstums; die Lage der Menschheit: Bedrohung und Zukunftschancen." (The new limits of growth; the situation of mankind: threat and future chances).

In this book, the limits were outlined a bit more precisely in the following three main directions:

The decline in food production, in availability of energy and in industrial production is determined by a more sensible usage of the natural resources and the degradability of irreversible input of contaminants into the environment.

The rise in consumption and the growth of the population have to be revised by means of political practices of acting in a way that energy efficiency and the use of material resources are considerably increased.

Sustainable fitness for the future as constant expansion can only be achieved by compensating long- and short-term objectives and more livable perspectives, e.g. by maturity, sharing in partnership and wisdom.[92]

This book did not remotely have the success of the one published in 1972. Many people questioned the newly formulated limits and most of the environmental activists concentrated on the minimization or prevention of polluting emissions into our environment. Therefore, this *third* direction of reorientation of the environmental movement is called chemo-ecology. With many spectacular, media-effective activities, Greenpeace effected that often enough the environmental sinners stood in the pillory of "Contaminant of the Month". Only very few believed in the limits of the inhabitability of the Earth.

In their book of 1992, Meadows and Randers specified the ozone layer as the only border that can be geographically defined, and defined

---

[91] Meadows, D.H., Meadow, Randers, J. et al. The new Limits of Growth, DVA, Stuttgart 1992
[92] Meadows 1992, P. 13

hydrofluorocarbons (HFC)[93] as the main destructors. This had the effect that many people considered themselves as environment protectors if they renounced products containing HFC, which was used as blowing, solvent or cooling agent. In 1978, the first prohibitions for HFC gases in aerosol cans became effective and relatively quickly, industry globally shifted to mostly HFC-free production. This provides one more proof that market competition alone does not meet the requirements of the environment without changing the frame alternations described above. The discovery of the hole in the ozone layer and the dangers for the foundations of life connected with that led to the first global counter-reaction that created hope for the future. At the same time, it is surprising today that climate change has practically remained unmentioned in "Beyond the Limits of Growth". Of course, there is no mention of a climate catastrophe.

The *fourth* reorientation and movement in environment technology that spread in parallel with this is called meno-ecology (saving ecology). It focused on saving resources in general and on lower surface usage with each product, the minimum energy consumption of all products and services.[94] The mips-concept, the material intensity per service unit, was considered the new dimension of ecologic economizing. Thus, the intensity of material and energy of our wealth moved into focus. The new goal was dematerialization, the search for tons and kilograms of environment consumption took over the search for nanograms of poisonous substances in the environment. The reduction objectives concentrated on a factor and efficiency economy to the four- to ten-fold, in some areas to even bigger saving effects. Lately, audit and eco controlling connected therewith aggravated the lifecycle analysis of the products and services up to the carbon footprints, i.e. the CO_2 emission to the ecorazzia.

The *fifth* new wave of the ecology movement is called green business ecology. It unifies high-tech, clean-tech, eco-intelligence, eco-entrepreneurship and innovative passion with the new LOHAS lifestyle and mass markets. The new innovation-focused movement effects the green economic wonder of the 21st century.

---

[93] Medows, p.178 ff

[94] cf. e.g. F. Schmidt-Bleck, Wie viel Umwelt braucht der Mensch? (How much environment does man need?), Birkhäuser Verlag, Berlin, Basel, Boston, 1993

What would the climate-friendly, resource-protecting, contaminant-free car look like today if all the power and engineering arts had entered into the development and market introduction of truly ecological greentech vehicles? Here, the emphasis is put on the implementation on the market, not the conception or studying period.

Tests have found that even many car freaks have problems differentiating the very latest model from the latest or before-latest model of any car makes.

The innovative researcher Gerhard O. Mensch called this phenomenon of high similarity and technical exchangeability of new products and techniques of the most different producers "stalemate," which he gets from chess. His book "Das technologische Patt" (The technological stalemate) that was published in 1975 is considered a classic of the innovation theory today and describes how confusable many mass products with common technology basically are. In the history of the economy, the consequences of the technological stalemate regularly end up in deep recessions and economic crises.

The small, so-called "incremental" innovations do not create any jobs and not enough demand for replacement needs. Fundamental innovations or so-called basic innovations, especially from the point of view of the environment, look different. Verifiably, growth and prosperity of entire national economies depend on the way they succeed in mastering such fundamental breakthroughs from the technological point of view. Well-known examples from the history of technique and economy are the original introduction of the steam and tool machines, the development of the electricity economy, the triumphal procession of the automotive industry more than 100 years ago or the introduction of telephony and TV as well as lately the market launch of PCs, mobile phones or the World Wide Web, the tourism industry and the airline operation.

Figure 2: Innovation ebbs and innovation flows

Source: Forum Wissenschaft, Bd. 40, Marburg 1998 (the line with the squares corresponds with analogue results by J.V. Duijn in "The long wave in Economic Life", London et. al. 1983). The results of these parallel studies were discussed with Gerhard Mensch in Spring 2008 and included here with his approval.

In these industries, in particular, many new jobs were generated with their market implementation, new products and services. In this analysis of fundamental breakthrough innovations, Gerhard Mensch finds out that they do not occur regularly in the history of the economy, but rather in waves at the end of depressive phases. The technological stalemate is interrupted by such fundamental innovations.

The cyclic innovation depressions correspond with the long waves of business activities, for the first time discovered in the USA in the year

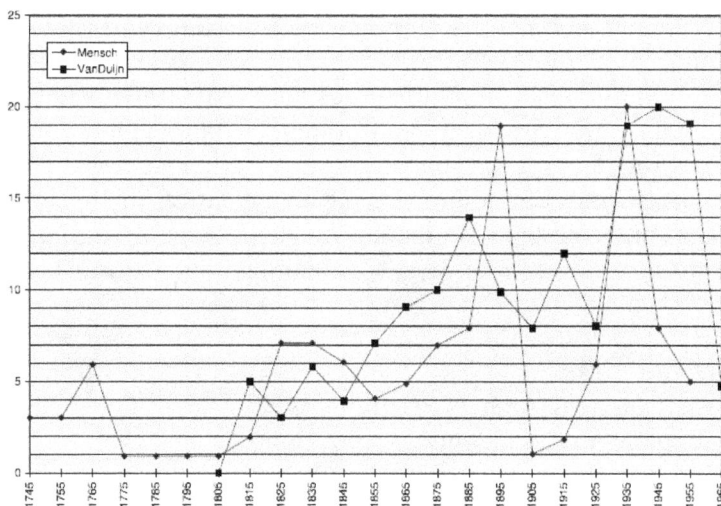

1926 by the Russian economist Nikolai Kondratieff (1892-1938). All the basic innovations supporting them are based on technologies that are obsolete at least from the ecological point of view and are stagnating today, but frequently should also have been long surmounted from the point of view of the enormous irreversible usage of resources and waste production. From the historical point of view, in the sense of the five run

70

out Kondratieff cycles, [95] amongst them count in keywords: the industrialization period with steam and tool machines as well as the cotton-based textile industry until 1850, the steel and railway development from 1850 to 1900, the upswing of electronic engineering and chemical industry from 1900-1950, the automotive industry and the closely connected petrochemical, as well as the upswing of information technology from about 1990 on.

But did they bring about something fundamental for environment and climate protection or did they rather make the situation worse? The answer is on the tip of the tongue. Most of the innovations were made with view at environment and climate protection ranking in the second or third respect only, often enough even disregarding the new dangers caused by them. But even if they talk about "eco-innovations" or "bio-products", not all new products contain nature and sustainability.

Recently, the term "innovation" itself has frequently become subject to inflation. Originally, it did not name anything else but an innovation that one would really get running. Consequently, even the cleverest idea, like the hydrogen engine, is not an innovation without practical market implantation.

Innovation in the sense of green business characterizes not only the idea, but mainly the practical realization, the implementation of eco-novelties in the market for business and market success. Therefore, innovation is always the connection of an invention in the interest of climate and environment protection with usage, i.e. exploration or implementation. Consequently, the innovation formula of the environment age is:

> Inventiveness
> + Environment/Climate Friendliness
> + Implementation/Commercialization
> = Innovation

If you closely inspect really fundamental environment and climate protecting products and technologies from the point of view of the real environmental consequences, often enough you will not find any groundbreaking innovations. The practical implementation of climate

---

[95] cf. Leo N. Nefiodow, Der sechste Kondratieff, (The sixth Kondratieff) Rhein-Sieg-Verlag, Sankt Augustin, P. 3 ff

innovations falls far short of the possibilities of our high technologies even if more pressure goes in the right direction. Staying with the example of the automotive industry, the wheel really had to be reinvented but in the sense of a completely new mobility concept. The paradigm shift to be connected with that should focus less on the "car" as a prestige product instead of the basic, much less prestige-oriented service "mobility" or "transport".

Stopping the Diffusion of Old Technologies

The spread of the automobile with an out-of-date drive system is a particularly good example for the consequences of sticking to obsolete concepts. Suddenly, many automotive groups cannot explain to themselves why only the latest oil price increases accelerate the search for alternatives. Instead of searching for innovative key technologies with which 17 million square meters of Russian earth could be bridged or 1.3 billion Chinese could be mobilized, the emphasis is still placed too much on the traditional solution that proved to be an ecological and, increasingly, economic dead end in industrialized countries already. Although numerous experts have long recognized that not only the threshold countries have to strike a new path here, except for hybrid cars from Japan, real alternatives that are fit for the market are missing.

"There are nine million bicycles in Beijing" Katie Melua sang in her famous hit "Nine million bicycles." Millions of bicycles waiting to stay at home and being replaced by a motorcar? About 20 years ago, cars still were a rarity in China's capital. Highly visible, bicycles dominated street life. Thinking about mobility concepts of the future, it seemed to go without saying that new, environmentally friendly solutions had to be searched and found.

How high the missed chances in China have become already becomes obvious with the fact that the highest growth rates of the automotive market reached more than 70% per year. However, besides Russia and India, China counts amongst the most strongly growing automotive markets. As "Der Spiegel online" reported on November 16, 2006 in its report "Maos Erben geben Vollgas" (Mao's heirs drive at full throttle), Chinese banks assume that in 2010, every other Chinese household will own a motorcar. That would mean 180 million more private cars that need oil and that blow their exhaust gases into the atmosphere. Although the Chinese government supports alternative drive systems like hybrid engines and fuel cells, these are already coming too late for the first wave

72

of mobilization. The few taxis and busses that are operated with gas, for example, do not make a big difference on Chinese streets. One would think that the sale of the latest motorcar models with consumption and contaminant-reduced engines would take place here. But instead, the market leader VW, for example, took the chance to sell their out-of-date models that they had not been able to sell in Germany and other traditional markets any longer. Fortunately, the market already reigned in the People's Republic of China. The car-thirsty Chinese did not want to sit in sturdy, square-cut boxes that did not correspond with their needs. Thanks to feeble figures in the recent years, the people from Wolfsburg have been forced to offer something more modern from the year 2005 on. Now, the ecological conscience of the car manufacturer awoke, too. According to the Tagesspiegel of October 11th, 2007, they want to become the most environmentally friendly car manufacturer in China.

There are even more reasons for hope. Already now, China is struggling with energy shortage and there are numerous initiatives for the construction of more environmentally friendly mass transit systems. The big trump of the Chinese is their high system-caused command economy. If the leadership makes a resolution, there is no stopping for party activists and private entrepreneurs. The Chinese are makers. Whereas here in Germany at least two years go by for planning, permissions and environment compatibility checks for the construction of a new traffic project, within this time the underground train is already running on the new track in China. Travelers going to Shanghai two times within one year are hardly able to orient themselves with all the new buildings. What may Chinese managers think when they sneak along the signs at German motorway construction and hold up places that indicate construction periods of several years? Yet today, Shanghai would be without motorways and without the Transrapid to the airport, whose equivalent still only runs on one single test route in Germany. In China, economic activity comes first, even if environment protection projects become more and more important just by reason of the instinct of self-preservation.

With climate and environment innovations China could become the precursor for new mobility concepts. It is high time because already today many of the big Chinese cities belong to the metropolises with the worst emission impact. If traffic on the basis of common fossil combustibles continues to increase, from the point of view of health the remaining cyclists will also be forced to switch to alternatives soon. In parallel,

73

something similar is happening in the bordering Russian Federation. There, the automobile market has gained even more momentum. According to a report in Spiegel online on February 21st, 2008 in Russia there are 250 passenger cars per 1000 inhabitants at present. In Germany, this quota amounts to more than 500. Besides the upcoming doubling of the passenger car stock, Russia also has great chances for ecological progress because the average age of the passenger cars in Lenin's country is 10 years, in Germany, on the contrary, about 16 years.

Here, at least, the motorcar manufacturers could take their responsibility and turn the former Russian fuel-guzzling cars into the most modern and environmentally friendly car pool in the world. But possibly the real market and the assumption of the West European consumption patterns contradict such dreams. Because whereas with the former Cossacks with less means costs play an important role, the "Nowi Ritsch" (nouveau riche) want, beyond the upper class cars, status cars and off-road vehicles. Up to now, climate friendliness does not play a role in purchase behavior.

If intervention on the part of politics does not take place here, the perspectives for environmentally friendly vehicles are as overcast as the air over Russia will be with the corresponding growth of individual traffic. Because if there is no demand on the market there will hardly be offers and where economic interest is endangered, in the past environmental protection had to take a backseat.

"Pro environment" thinking and acting have been poorly developed up to now, although, of course, there are also environmental activists and much ecological progress. But one must not forget that, for example, a big portion of the savings in CO_2 are a result of the breakdown of the old industry that was controlled by the command economy.

But still today, the position of environment technologies becomes visible with the spread of latest technologies for ecologically sustainable production that is particularly urgently needed by the developing countries. Most of the developments come from the USA, Japan or Western Europe where the latest technologies are protected by patents. This protection of the intellectual property, and thus also of the expected profits, strengthens the trend that out-of-date and less environmentally friendly technologies continue to be employed in those countries that hold the biggest chances for an ecological new beginning. This is because the manufacturers in the developing countries either cannot afford the needed license fees, cannot fulfill the imposed conditions, or the costs of the end products are so high due to these sums that they are ultimately not successful on the global market. Although technology transfer is on the very top of the action list in the Kyoto follow-up protocol, the governments of the industrialized countries insist that the protection of intellectual property has to be maintained. If this opinion is not loosened, the transfer of clean technologies will remain a word sleeve with dirty contents, our out-of-date but affordable inventions whose patent protection has long run out all that these countries can afford. Threshold countries like China can, in part, afford to buy modern technologies in order to ensure efficiency and quality. But just then, at the crucial point, the environment technology savings are made. Thus, for example, very modern steel works are erected where the de-dusting installations are missing and environmentally friendly cooling systems are omitted. As a result there are smoke clouds that can be seen from a far distance in an air you can hardly inhale.

Who is responsible for the present technologies not being employed here? It is both a global and local challenge for investors, suppliers and politicians. The latter finds many connecting links here to intervene, be it by means of laws, taxes or subsidies for more environmentally friendly technologies.

But the consumers also have to take their obligations. Because it cannot be emphasized often enough that in the end they decide, with their demand and readiness to pay, whether environment protection is also economically profitable.

Therefore, we do not only need to spread new technologies but also have to spread a new consumption culture with a focus on a considerable increase in efficiency. In the industrialized countries, more and more people notice the emptiness behind full stores, refrigerators and furnishing. But just a few seriously live energy reduction at the favor of the environment and immaterial values. Pushed by the media and advertising industry, everything is done so that the hunger for consumption does not decrease. The consequences of the Americanization could already be felt in the states of the former Eastern Block where Coca Cola became the symbol for a full life. But appealing to the poorest population classes of our world to take new ways of consumption would be rude and ironical, because in order to become happy by money and consumption, a certain base of income has to be achieved. This simple fact can be understood especially well with one of the most popular motivation and explanation theories of human behavior.

According to the pyramid of needs of one of the co-founders of humanistic psychology, A. Maslow, at first our basic needs like hunger and thirst, safety and social needs have to be fulfilled to a certain degree before a human being starts to care for "higher" desires like acknowledgement, self-realization and a healthy environment.[96]

While millions of people hope to advance from a life beyond the poverty level, there is almost no space left for a developing environmental protection culture. Where hardship reigns, the environment will fall by the wayside. In addition, in many countries the cultures of the original inhabitants who frequently lived in close connection with nature were destroyed. As an alternative there is frequently no more real, authentic culture of these peoples but just a poor copy of a free market economy to which a big part of the population has almost no access. Can one really expect that people actively address the problems of our environment in this situation? Possibly not, as little as the western world can hope that in terms of consumption and economic development these countries follow a completely different path than our nations did. Because to them an environmental culture was also not handed down on an industrial silver platter. Also in Europe, a real culture of environmental protection emerged in the 60s and 70s of the last century only after a certain level of consumption saturation had been reached. Consequently, in order to achieve fair environmental protection, it is indispensable that a new consumption culture develops mainly in the industrialized countries. But just preaching restraint in consumption here or looking back at old times when people lived in more harmony with nature cannot lead to the goal. This kind of environment culture has long survived itself. Instead, we need new concepts that make our cultural and material achievements compatible with ecological requirements as it is impressively demonstrated by new environmental movements like "bright green".

We cannot turn back the clock of civilization but we can use the potential of mankind in order to act and finally start to employ our scientific-technical findings for the sake of the environment and humanity. This way we can set benchmarks for the acting intelligence of our generations.

---

[96] Maslow, Abraham H. (1943). A theory of human motivation. Psychological Review, 50, p. 370-396

Search for the Golden Path out of the Climate Collapse

At the World Climate Meeting in Bali at the end of 2007, everybody was very busy to agree on accountable targets, especially for the reduction of CO_2. Finally, a sailing list was produced according to which concrete and continuative agreements should be concluded after the end of 2009. Every responsible statesman knows that climate change has already gained scary momentum. But the interest conflicts for really consequent redirecting are still in the fore. Many critical contemporaries have healthy doubts that the governments will even be able to alter course. They rather rely on entrepreneurs and refer to the tradition of Silicon Valley again and again. The Internet boom initiated here had not been foreseen or steered by any government even if there were state subsidies within the scope of military aid programs as already shown. Therefore, the advocates of market-economic processing promote the development of super products rather than the imposition of super taxes, like those on CO_2 emissions. This is vividly discussed as a main topic in Great Britain as well as in California. In Germany, many people still consider the required rerouting as a "good man discussion". The State Secretary for the Environment, Sigmar Gabriel, rightly assessed in the Spiegel interview in the fall of 2006 that Germany was "not level with the ball".[97]

Basically, on the one hand, it is about the reduction of harmful greenhouse gases wherever possible and, on the other hand, about the implementation of completely new, more climate-friendly technological solutions. In the field of tension between both strategies, initially the reduction of emissions is always the faster and often easier way. Amongst that counts, in the first place, the increase in energy efficiency in all areas, including private households. At present, Europe has just managed to achieve an improvement in energy efficiency of 1%, highly insufficient in order to reach results on a global level. "Until the year 2050, at least we must halve the global emission of greenhouse gases compared to 1990. For us as industrialized countries this means a reduction by 60 to 80%."[98] At the same time, it is indispensable that every individual puts their actions to the test.

With the climate adaptation we are facing difficult questions in Germany as well as the rest of the world.

---

[97] Spiegel 45/2006
[98] S. Gabriel, in: Spiegel 45/2006, p. 92

What do these adaptation measures have to look like? Who has to put them into practice and until when? Which roles do state and administration, enterprises and the civil population play? And, what are the costs of concrete adaptation measures? A competence center "Climate implications and adaptation" (KomPass) is just being developed at the Federal Ministry for the Environment.

How difficult it is to solve the upcoming task on an international level is shown by a few figures. Just until 2030, globally about $550 billion will be invested in the energy market every year, approximately 60% of that in power supply and 20% in gas supply.[99] Here, investments for the reduction of CO_2 emissions have not even been considered. The consumption of power and natural gas will double in this period. The regulation pressure on the energy industry is getting much higher in order to concretely imply the focused and already agreed savings in carbon dioxide until 2020 and later 2050. If the pressure put on the producers is not high enough, without doubt all the consumers will also be involved. All the consumers will understand soon what it means to have the sun deliver the global annual energy consumption within just one hour for free. But even in Germany, the pioneer country of the solar industry, merely 0.32% of the electricity stems from photovoltaic.[100] Why such a "gift from heaven" has not yet been better accepted, also in innovation politics, shows again how enormously important the above mentioned comprehension of unavoidable adaptation strategies at the favor of the climate is.

Like never before in the history of the economy, a race towards green will have to start that will bring about both many new winners as well as losers. Who jumps on the bandwagon on time and participates with new conceptions will doubtlessly belong to the winners of the new millennium. The history of industry and infrastructure knows examples that prove how fast new things can implement themselves. The motorways, especially stressed by environment protectors, are part of that. In the USA, the first motorways evolved only 100 years ago, enforced by law with the up to now globally biggest infrastructure measure.[101] Such legal initiatives become necessary by joint international efforts for saving the climate and explain what Al Gore means when he is talking

---

[99] Wintjen, p.18
[100] mobil 08/2007, p. 68
[101] Federal Aid Road Act, 1906 102

about virtually mobilizing all powers at the favor of our climate. At the same time, the consumers will continue rethinking and include the contribution to climate protection by the companies from both the economical as well as the emotional, moral and cultural point of view, much more into their buying decisions.

One thing has become apparent in recent years: The flood of reports, studies, documents and films regarding the seriousness of the climate situation is not a warranty that the international community will really join for concerted practical actions against the more and more threatening dangers of climate change. Sometimes you get the impression that the media expenditure stands in opposite ratio to the real practical measures that actually could stop the frequently summoned climate catastrophe.

This became very clear at the diverse international climate conferences under the roof of the UN, often with ten thousands of participants, where they have been struggling for an internationally effective climate regime during the last years.

The last of these conferences in Bali in December 2007 was no exception, although the World Climate Council (IPCC) with its 4th report about the current stage of proceedings did not hesitate to articulate clear words. They struggled with agreeing on a new negotiation circle in 2009 in order to find a follow-up regulation for the Kyoto protocol that is rather tame from the climate-political point of view from 2012 on.

But also off the global stage, the partly heavy political strife between the EU member states about the climate-political program of the community left the impression that the farewell of "business-as-usual" conduct in Sunday speeches is still easier than in practical politics.

On the other hand, this contradiction between word and action is not amazing. Stabilizing the greenhouse gases in the atmosphere on a level that, according to today's assumptions, can limit the average global rise in temperature within a historically relatively short period of time to +2°C compared with the pre-industrial period, is not available for free. Whether it can be mastered just by the enterprises and the market mechanisms is still doubtful.

The incurred costs of the consequences of climate change in a great number of countries that are unavoidable anyway are not even mentioned. It is not reassuring if the costs of such a climate regime are always indicated in such low percentage values or they even talk about a "zero sum game" without economical losses.

Some masterminds suspect that here very elemental growth and development conditions of national economies, their performance and competition fitness in the ranking of the world economy, the rerouting of gigantic investment flows, the redistribution of income, fortune, extent and structure of occupation and jobs and, thus finally, also the capability of political and social stability of societies are for disposition. The same way the Internet turned the economy inside out and generated completely new global players, green business will change the world to an even greater extent.

The global change of the climate regime cannot only be tackled as a solely entrepreneurial venture. The rise of greenhouse gases cannot be locally or regionally limited and "fought". A climate-friendly regime at one end of the world can be limited in its effect by a "business-as-usual" behavior at the other end, or even be destroyed. Here, finally, is the crux of the search for the golden middle: the distribution of the burdens supporting one consent and collaboration of all is anything but a simple calculation example. In order to get everybody onboard for a sustainable low-carbon development of the economy, a differentiated approach of countries and groups of countries finally is the only practicable way: an eye has to be kept on aspects like the polluter-pays principle, the capability and possibility to reduce emissions, functionality, inexpensive proceeding etc.[102]

From this angle, the pioneering role of the developed industrial countries in restraining, stabilizing and possibly reducing greenhouse gases is a matter of course and not a task just for the Californians alone. De facto, it is naturally also accepted in politics and practice. A post-Kyoto regulation will reflect that again. The mitigation of such a claim with the repeatedly voiced reference to fast growing threshold countries like China and India where the greenhouse gas emissions increase rapidly is not effective, is a climate-political retreat battle. Important reasons for that are obvious:

First the historic-moral responsibility of the industrialized states for the present situation cannot be denied. It is the carbon-intensive growth and development path of the western industrialized states since the industrial revolution that led us into the climate trap. Denying and

---

[102] cf. Regarding this and herein after compare Walter Stock: Auf dem Weg in den Co2 Überwachungsstaat (On the way to the Co2 surveillance state), unpublished copy

refusing the threshold and developing countries the growth and development possibilities referring to the required climate-caused modesty would be highly dishonest and finally unenforceable, too.

CO_2 Emissions	CO_2 Total 2005 (m t)	Changes compared to 2001 (in %)	CO_2/Head 2005 (in t)	Changes compared to 2001 (in %)
USA	5,817	2.5	19.61	1.2
China	5,060	62.6	3.88	44.2
Russia	1,544	1.6	10.79	2.8
Japan	1,214	7.2	9.50	6.7
Germany	813	-4.3	9.87	-4.4
Great Britain	530	-2.0	8.80	-4.3
France	388	0.9	6.19	2.1
Australia	377	1.9	18.41	-3.1
Brazil	329	5.6	1.77	-2.2
India				
Indonesia	1,147	13.2	1.05	7.1
Hungary	341	20.3	1.90	39.7
Bangladesh	36	17.2	26	13.0

Source: Internationale Energieagentur (IEA), 2007

Second, a climate-politically justified strangulation of growth and development in developing and threshold countries because of the elementary interest of the industrialized states in a steadily functioning and dynamically developing global economy would be disastrous. A climate-political shock therapy towards these countries would be extremely counterproductive under the aspect of keeping up the stability of the world economy. Such "climate-political" solutions that finally are at the expense of an aggravation of the poverty problem are out of the question.

Third, the differences in competence and feasibility regarding the following of a less carbon-intensive growth and development strategy between developed industrial states and developing and threshold countries cannot be excluded. If the first-mentioned are able to realize a

CO₂ reduction strategy and to cope with it, then they are obliged to employ the available superior resources for that, namely for themselves as well as for the developing and threshold countries.

In other respects, severe shifting and slumps in the world economy would also be pre-determined if the industrialized states try to "sit out" the consequences of climate change, assuming that the "North" would still get away the best in such a scenario.

Consequently, there is no choice between climate-political pioneering role and doing nothing. For a foreseeable period of time, the developed industrialized states will have to take the bigger part in all measures for restraining and stabilizing the global greenhouse gas emissions. This does not have anything to do with good will or concessions.

Inseparably connected with this part is the task of creating conditions and incentives so that developing and threshold countries can reroute to a climate-friendly growth and development course, too. If this is not achieved, the contribution by the industrialized states would have to be even higher.

Actually, the open question is simply which stabilization level of global CO₂ emissions should we be headed for. A stabilization level (of the CO₂ concentration in the atmosphere) could be achieved even later and later in case of too slow and insufficiently coordinated proceeding with the reduction of emissions. The concentration would thus be pushed upwards even more and above the critical level of 450 ppm (and a rise in temperature connected therewith of more than +2°C).

On the other hand, it does not make sense to state an unrealistically low stabilization level (probably with a lower rise in temperature) that would have to be enforced relatively early by means of comprehensive and drastic measures. There is no consensus and no set of preconditions for this.

So there is a time window for CO₂ reduction in which a way has to be found between the two options that can establish the balance between the economical costs of a fast reduction strategy and the possible risks and the costs of a postponed CO₂ stabilization. If this "window of opportunity" is missed, at a later point of time drastic reduction measures at enormously high costs will remain the only option, but without having prevented a possibly already perilous temperature level.

From this transfer process that can only take place gradually towards a less carbon-intensive growth and development course, it has to be realistically concluded that the rise in greenhouse gases in the atmosphere will persist until 2030 and possibly even longer.[103] This has also got much to do with the fact that fossil energy sources will continue to take a prominent place in the global energy mix. At the same time, this means that the anthropogenically caused global warming trend and the rise of the sea level will continue in the next two decades. Just as a reminder: a certain degree of global warming could not even be avoided if the greenhouse gas emissions could be frozen at the level of the year 2000.

The urgency, speed, effectiveness and range of emission-reducing measures grow. They could take the political systems to the limits of their capacity. This becomes even more obvious in the face of the slow and non-uniform fulfillment of the obligations from the 2005 Kyoto protocol by the industrialized countries. The worries regarding the readiness and competence of industrialized countries to play a pioneering role are justified.

The wry look at America no longer helps in the face of the starting change and the pioneering role of California. To the EU and their member states it also means that the gap between "exemplary" climate-political rhetoric and the results from the reduction of greenhouse gas emissions has not been closed yet. For example, EU countries like Spain, Portugal, Italy, Greece and Austria do not fulfill their objectives. The observation of the EU reduction target of 8% compared with 1990 by all EU states has rather got the character of a nail-biting event.

Therefore, if the change in the development of greenhouse gas emissions is to be achieved and a stabilization at a level of about 450 ppm is to take place by the middle of the 21st century, considerable disproportionately high contributions by the industrialized states for the reduction in a relatively short time frame of about 40 years are compulsory (60-80% compared to 1990).

If one accepts a limit regarding the acceptable concentration of greenhouse gases in the atmosphere, unavoidably the question arises according to which principles and regulations the shares in the possible pollution of the limited asset atmosphere are to be distributed.

You can twist and wriggle as much as you like, finally possibilities and rights of the usage of the atmosphere can only be regulated according to the principle of equality. This will result in a principally identical CO_2 emission quantity per head on the global level. This opinion might seem

---

[103] IPTS-Study, 2007

to be utopian at present if you watch the huge differences between the countries in the CO_2 emissions per capita.

Despite all that the climate political discussion has long become unimaginable without this approach.[104]

But also in politics they seem to suspect that the process will go in this direction if you want to involve all the actors into a necessary global climate regime and tie them into adequate reduction obligations.[105]

Finally, one also cannot see why an American should have more rights to use the atmosphere (in the sense of higher CO_2 emissions) than a Chinese if the global CO_2 impact on the atmosphere has to be limited in any case and cannot be endlessly expanded.

Table 6: Distribution of CO_2 emissions to "rich" and "poor" countries

OECD	Share in%
North America (with Mexico)	28
European OECD States	16
Japan, South Korea, New Zealand	8
Remaining World	
South and South-East Asia	10
Africa	4
China, Mongolia, North Korea, Vietnam	15
Middle and East European Countries (non OECD)	10
Middle East	5
Middle and South America	4

Source: Calculations in: The UN World Climate Report (2007, p. 37)

In other respects, the introduction of an equality principle would still permit differentiations and deviations under consideration of further criteria (e. g. consideration of a development bonus, of peculiarities in economic structure, of demographic developments etc.).

Consequently, this principle cannot and will not mean that a leveling of the wealth between the inhabitants of a country will be the consequence, because different degrees of productivity and CO_2 efficiency of the GDP development will not be annulled by this. In principle, equally

---

[104] WBGU, Berlin 2003, Rahmstorf/Schellnhuber, 2007, p. 118ff
[105] Rahmstorf/Schellnhuber

high CO_2 emission per capita will therefore normally by accompanied by different baskets of goods for this. But these differences are then based on a "climate-neutral" foundation and will be determined by the level of energy and CO_2 efficiency in the economies.

But with the enforcement of the principle of equality with the distribution of the globally available "pollution cake" the fairness gap in a future consensus-competent climate regime is not yet closed. The establishment of an adaptation regime for the control of the consequences of the already prevailing climate change is just the second aspect of such a climate regime. Here it is essential: without a sustainable avoidance strategy the adaptation will turn out to be completely insufficient and partially effective at best.

A financially well-equipped climate adaptation regime will challenge the pioneering role and thus the paymaster role of the developed industrial states, namely out of the same reasons that supported such a role with the reduction regime for greenhouse gases already. Because without acknowledgement and realization of the polluter-pays principle there will not be any sustainable adaptation measures regarding the already occurred negative consequences of the climate change. A possible gradually levied charge on greenhouse gas emissions could be a way of application of the principle and produce a sustainable financial basis for adaptation measures.[106]

Thus, such a regime would not only go far beyond international relief operations in the case of the increasing number of climate catastrophes in developing countries but also beyond half-hearted attempts to install funds for the development of climate protection as proven by the Marrakech fund. The aggravation of water shortage, expansion of arid regions, undermining of fundamentals of agriculture, etc. are not to be fought foremost within the scope of humanitarian relief operations.

What will the world of our children and grandchildren look like in the year 2050? The extremely carbon-based development and growth strategy for the generation of the modern industrial society for about 250 years is doubtlessly facing a paradigm shift. It would be amazing if the social and political status quo that bore this kind of industrial society were not exposed to a change, too.

In other words, it will be difficult to harmonize the social and political status quo with the challenges of climate change within the

---

[106] k Blok et al., 2005, p. P6

current national and international framework. The all clear signal that could still be given by the Club of Rome after the first shock about "The Limits of Growth" will not be possible again. This time, things are different. The finiteness of the atmosphere and the claim of a great number of international actors for this asset block quite a lot of technocratic emergency exits. An economical, political and social system that has provoked this condition cannot effect its disintegration and surmount in unchanged form. In fact, the reinvention of the industrial society and its regulation mechanisms is at issue. Exactly this challenge determines the expectations of the green revolution. Although there are doubts whether this challenge can be mastered just by entrepreneurship following the American example.

If one realizes the extent of the task, having to revolutionize an industrial society that is based on high carbon intensity worldwide in a historically very short period of time, one cannot avoid to focus on a new symbiosis of market and governmental regulation for the enforcement of this paradigm shift.

There is simply no time left for time consuming try and error procedures in order to explore and put into practice the most effective and efficient ways of acting because the required massive investment shifts in low-carbon respectively carbon-free economic activities cannot wait any longer. Getting stuck in carbon-intensive infrastructures in the long run due to wrong or half-hearted decisions now would have devastating consequences. Clearly spoken, this means that the market (price) mechanism of coping with this paradigm shift in economy will and has to take a back seat. Governmental regulation will take control of the action. The pressure of dealing with climate change is unavoidably the time of police law.

Because in the near future, no market mechanism in the world will be able to stabilize the CO_2 concentration in the atmosphere at a certain level, with the required safety and probability, in order to limit the global rise in temperature to a life-friendly level. Above all, in the face of the extremely unequal distribution of greenhouse gas emissions, the market mechanism is blind and not suitable to prevent the unavoidable reduction and stabilization from turning into another aggravation of the poverty problem in the world.

In principle, the world community has passed into developing a political mechanism in order to fix quantitative requirements in the form of upper limits for the global development of greenhouse gases and to break them down to single states in the scope of "multiple-year-planning" with milestones (2020, 2030, 2050). Then, in a political process, the single countries distribute their national greenhouse gas contingent that will be lower and lower from period to period, to economic domains, sectors and single economy actors. Here, climate-induced world-economical overall planning takes place giving development corridors to the countries, economies and sectors that have to be observed. The question remains open, what happens if the single states do not fulfill their planned targets.

Of course, planning can and must not be made in an economically arbitrary way but still there are strong limitations in the principle of voluntariness and the recourse to purely market-economical incentives and mechanisms. Only in the context of setting a quantitative framework, can price mechanisms be reemployed. For example, this could be done by the emission trade that offers a possibility of finding inexpensive solutions for the reduction of emissions.

The development of the segment of renewable energies in the energy mix will probably be possible as a politically "prescribed" solution. Binding parameters by regulations for CO_2 emissions/km that have to be observed are the consequence, because the effectiveness of the price mechanism is much too sluggish.

The development of building efficiency has been out of the range of discretion of the individual for a long time already, meanwhile even including compulsory standards with the choice of the energy to be employed because it seems that the market is no longer considered as being qualified to select the "right" type of energy. Thus it is consequently right that the usage efficiency of long-lasting household items will be more and more regulated by provisions. This first climate induced regulation wave could be followed by others if the present generation of instruments should prove to be insufficiently effective with the reduction of greenhouse gases, for example special driving prohibitions for above average CO_2 producing vehicles or mileage restrictions. Then, it would just be a short step from CO_2-regulated production to CO_2-regulated consumption by the individual, which can be legitimized by the serious necessities of the climate change.

In the face of these facts many of us sorrowfully look into the future. But one must not forget that people almost always only start acting when it really hurts. Exactly that is the present situation. Up to now, all the careful attempts by the industry and politics have not been accepted by the consumer, or they have been forced on them half-heartedly only. The USA, branded as climate sinners for a long time, are waking up. With great efforts, the USA will now alter course. In doing so, that is my own prognosis, the same innovation wave and gold rush mood will prevail as it did in Silicon Valley in the time of the dot-coms. This is, on the one hand, because there are high profits attracting, on the other hand because there is an unavoidable economic and ecologic necessity. The market potential of the dot-greens exceeds the potential of the Internet market by far.

Green Tech as Profitable Investment Targets

Still, one of the most important indicators for the sustainability of new technologies is the investment volume. Here it becomes most obvious what the money providers bet on last year. The London consultancy firm New Energy Finance estimated according to indications by the Süddeutsche Zeitung "Venture capital firms and private money providers in the whole world invested 8.6 billion dollars in alternative technologies, 68% more than in 2005. Here, the main portion of the money for eco-startups comes from the USA, from the most successful industrial park in the world, Silicone Valley."[107]

For greentech, all the signs are set to investment. The "tipping point" when "green and clean" turn into a mass market is said to have been reached. "Clean technologies are the hottest investment class on the venture capital sector", Ira Ehrenpreis, General Partner at Technology Partners affirms. In the USA, in the recent year, more than 3 billionn US dollars flew into cleantech companies, more than 14% of all venture capital investments, compared with 4.2% the year before. "Thus, the cleantech segment even has overtaken the semi-conductor industry", said Ehrenpreis in the Venture Capital Magazine.[108] At the same point it continues: "The 450 participants of the IBF Forum consider cleantech the biggest chance for investors in the 21st century. The reason: "The perfect storm" as it is expressed in Hollywood manner; a mix of innovation and trends that make an explosive growth of the market unavoidable.

---

[107] cf. H. Breuer, Ökowelle in Silicon Valley,(Eco wav in Silicon Valley) in: Süddeutsche Zeitung,
http://www.sueddeutsche.de/wissen/artikel/881/114767/ Request from March 24, 2008
[108] http://www.vc-magazin.de/news/titelstory Request from June 12, 2008

Differing from the Internet bubble at the end of the 90s, cleantech euphoria is not generated by investors and a handful of companies. In this case, the end customers the population are willing to pull together."[109]

Six areas are awarded special attractiveness: renewable energy sources, power network infrastructure, bio fuels, water, transport and ecological construction. These are all mass markets and, above all, problems that concern everybody. The €uro-greentec-journal ranks the topics of ecology and environment technology as THE macroeconomic mega trend of the 21st century. But there are different opinions about the technologies that are essential for that. For example, the magazine AlwaysOn.GoingOn.com, located in Silicon Valley, assigned the 100 most important top green-tech companies to the following economic sectors:

- Automobile and Transport
- Bio Fuels and Agriculture
- Energy Management and Efficiency
- Nano Technology and Materials
- Other Energy Technologies
- Solar Technology
- Waste Management
- Water

A panel evaluated 100 top companies worldwide for these fields of technology that should be observed because of their technological innovation power.[110] This list is the first that has ever been made for startups and established companies in the USA. Concerning the peripatetic acting of governments P. Kelly states in the report: "While presidents and prime ministers around the world are focused on choosing among different responses to the ecological crisis, it is the entrepreneurs and companies profiled on this list that are most likely to give them and us the tools and options needed to be truly greener."[111] This already shows healthy self-confidence towards politicians because many of the companies listed here are not even known in Europe and Germany yet. For further information the respective URLs can be found on the *AlwaysOn* website. The vast majority of the firms are not even 10 years old.

---

[109] Ibid
[110] . cf AlwaysOn, The Blogozine On Innovation//Fall 2007, p. 24
[111] Ibid, p.24

Table 7: Top Green-Tech Startups

Automotive and Transportation	Biofuel & Agriculture	Energy Management & Efficiency
AC Propulsion	Altra Biofuels	Blade Network
CleanAir Logix	Amyris	Technologies
Myers Motors	Biotechnologies	H2Gen Innovations
Mygistics	Chemrec	Silver Spring
Phoenix Motorcars	Cilion	Networks
PML	ClearFuels Technology	SmartSynch
Tesla Motors	E3 Biofuels	Verdiem
Think Global	Gevo	
ZENN Motor	Greenfuel	
Company	Technologies	
	Imperium Renewables	
	LS9	
	Mascoma	
	Mendel Biotechnology	
	RangeFuels	
	Solazyme	
	Targeted Growth	

Energy Storage	Nanotech & Materials	Clean Energy (not solar or biofuel)
A123 Systems	Artificial Muscle d.light	Airtricitiy
Bloom Energy	design	CoalTek
Cobasys	EoPlex Technologies	General Compression
Deeya Energy EEStor	FiberTech Polymers	Great Point Energy
GridPoint	Hycrete	Nordic Windpower
Jadoo Power	Nanoexa	Orion Energy
Lilliputian Systems	Nanostellar	Powerspan
ZPower	Serious Materials	Verdant Power
	Space-X	

Solar	Waste Management	Water
Ausra	Earthanol	AbTech Industries
Better Energy Systems	EnerTech Environmental	Aqua Sciences Aquarius
BrightSource Energy	Intechra	Technologies

Daystar Technologies	iReuse	Atlantium Technologies
Energy Innovations	LanzaTech	Bio-Pure Technology
HelioVolt	MBA Polymers	Derceto
Innovalight	TechTurn	EnviroTower
Konarka Technologies	Ze-Gen	GeoPure Water
Miasolé		Technologies
Nanosolar		IDE Technologies
Silicon Valley Solar		Industrial Plug and Play
Solaicx		Microvi Biotech
SolarCity		MIOX Corporation
Solaria		NanoH2O Novazone
Solexant		P2W Pollution To
SolFocus		Water
Stion		PAX Water
Stirling Energy Systems		Technologies
Zytech Solar		Poseidon Resources
		Seven Seas Water
		Superall Products

Of the top-green companies listed here, 45 are from California, none from Germany. Of course, this may have to do with the proximity of the rating persons to Silicon Valley, but it also shows that there is no reason for Germany to rely on the achievements of the past or even an imaginary leadership in technology. Even if in the motherland of daringness the activities of the venture capital provision have decreased due to the aftereffects of the Subprime Crisis at the end of 2007, according to experience there are good reasons to pay much attention to these companies in the future. According to information by the US American National Venture Capital Association, in the first three months of the year 2008 only 5 venture capital financed startups dared to enter the parquet of the Wall Street stock market. Opposed to that, in the fourth quarter of 2007, there were still 31 startups financed by venture capital. The figures of the first quarter 2008 correspond with the low of the dot-com crises, they said. Other than Microsoft's plan to take over Yahoo, the buying activities in Silicon Valley have also decreased. While in the fourth quarter of 2007 big businesses still took over 83 venture capital financed startups, they only bought 56 venture capital financed firms. This year especially the shares of high-tech companies are not much sought after. Since the beginning of this year, the high-tech index Nasdaq Composite has dropped by about 11%. Apple securities went down by 21%, Google shares lost 31%. In addition, a decrease in job growth is predicted.

91

According to information by the Center for the Continuing Study of the California Economy 10,000 new jobs will be generated in Silicon Valley this year. However, in the year 2007 they still produced 17,000 new jobs, in the year 2006 there were 25,000.

In spite of that there are best chances, mainly for financings on the clean- or green-business sector. Analogous to the worldwide popular climate protection film "An inconvenient Truth" by Al Gore, the climate protection share index "GreenTec Climate 30" comprises 30 companies from the six most important climate-related topics like renewable energies, more energy-efficient transport, CO_2-reduction, more energy-efficient end devices, water and recycling. The business of the future will take place here, whereas in Germany it is still difficult to acquire venture capital.

Connoisseurs of the industry find themselves confirmed: In the "Innovationsindikator 2007" the German Institute for Economic Research stated that often enough there is not enough venture capital in this country. With the question for availability of capital for establishment funding, Germany ranked at place 13 out of 17 researched countries.[112]

Even if financing would require 40,000 euros maximum, the majority had no access to loans, venture capital or public subsidies or credits. With its annual statistics 2007 the German Private Equity and Venture Capital Association e.V. (BVK) provided another proof for the difficult stand of venture capital in Germany: even if the number of financed companies increased by about 10% to 978 compared with the average of the last three years, the invested means dropped by more than 25% to 839.7 million euros.

According to information by the greentech-journal the market for climate-protecting technique will continue growing disproportionately until the year 2050. Economists estimate that the market for solar and wind energy and other climate-protecting techniques could reach a volume of 500 billion dollars in the year 2050. The market grows rapidly. If clean energies merely put 55 billion dollars on the scales, at the end of 2007 it was 77.3 billion dollars already. In 2007, the market for wind energy increased by 28%, the one for solar energy by 52%. The global capacity for the production of electric power from renewable energy sources has grown by 50% since 2004. In 2006, the "new renewables"

---

[112] cf. http://www.vc-magazin.de/news/titelstory/index.hbs Request from April 14, 2008

(small hydraulic energy, modern biomass plants, wind, solar energy, geothermal energy and bio fuels) produced the same amount of power as a quarter of the nuclear plants did worldwide. The dimension hydraulic energy alone covered about 15 percent of the global power consumption. This offers unequalled chances to investors.

The perspectives for solar industry are still rosy: In the past years many countries have improved the frame conditions for the sector by means of support programs. Therefore, the international photovoltaic markets develop very dynamically. According to a study worked out by the European Photovoltaic Industry Association (EPIA), photovoltaic will be able to cover almost 10% of the global power demand until 2030. The turnover of the solar sector shall rise from currently 9 to 300 billion dollars per year.

But despite this good prognosis there will not only be winners in the future development in this sector but also losers. In front of Japan and clearly in front of the USA, Germany is the biggest market worldwide. Here, the solar market grows more dynamically than in the other states. The German production of solar power has grown by the tenfold since 2003, above all thanks to the remuneration fixed in the Renewable Energies Act (EEG). The German Solar Industry Association (BSW) assumes that in the future market growth abroad will be even higher than in Germany. Particularly promising were the European markets Spain, Italy, France and Greece where feed-in remunerations according to the example of the German EEG were established. Beyond Europe, the highest market dynamics were in the USA where many federal states established support programs for photovoltaic appliances. Meanwhile, China has established an independent photovoltaic industry but produces for export foremost. Corresponding support as starting ignition for the inland market growth is still missing.[113]

Whichever way the future chances are bundled, the still young green clean-tech market will extend its top position to multi-billion dollar businesses.

---

[113]

http://www.greentecjournal.de/download/greentecjournal/GTJ_0810.pd f Request of May 23rd, 2008

Venture Capital and other Financing Forms for Startups

Silicon Valley is famous for startups being able to collect money for the establishment of a company and the proof of the sustainability of the concept with extraordinary success. Of course, hard work is behind all that. It also applies to Silicon Valley that everybody has to question his chances of success critically beforehand. In the first place, a kind of industry filter is helpful here. Per se, money is available for very few industries anyway and from these industries only a few companies are qualified for venture capital (VC) investments. In the opinion of the FTD of January 17th, 2008 there are two main reasons for that:

"First, the funds normally concentrate on certain segments of the high-tech industries: biotech and pharmacy, medical technology, information technologies (e. g. Internet service, software, hardware, media and telecommunication) and the relatively young field of "clean-tech" around innovations in energy technology.

Second, they regularly employ a similar business model with the companies in which they invest: successful companies have to be able to make profit that justifies the risk of failure. And since this risk is extremely high, only such business models are interesting for VC investors that can successfully bring in a manifold of the investment in case of success within the investment period."

Depending on industry, the risk-profit profile looks differently. In the opinion of the FTD, investors in the biotech and pharmaceutical industry assume that they have to invest an average international amount of 40 to 50 million dollars per company. In case of success, the 20- to 30-fold of the investment can be made in return. It is these sums that attract VC providers again and again to invest in innovative developments. All the other classical VC industries from software to medical technology follow the classic technology model: On average, 10 to 20 million dollars are sufficient but the probability of success is higher than with biotech investments. But here the investors calculate with a lever of about the 10-fold of their investment within three to five years. For the needed investments on the clean greentech sector such experience values from the VC scene frequently do not exist yet. Therefore, the FTD advises: "Who wants to get hold of VC has to check first whether he belongs to the target industries of possible investors. And second, whether his business idea is suitable to multiply the value of the company by ten with the help of a low 2-digit million amount of capital and within a few years, in the field of biotech correspondingly more.[114] But the experience from Silicon Valley shows that the VC providers approach the market less according to definitions but pragmatically. Since they normally invest one to two-digit million sums per portfolio company with their funds, initially a need for capital amounting to that sum has to be recognizable from the business plan. For young entrepreneurs this means that from the very beginning they shall reflect whether their business idea can be sensibly expanded with the corresponding amount of capital e.g. by the expansion of distribution channels and whether they are interested in doing that themselves. Who rather wants to remain "small but nice" than conquering the global market should better look out for different investors.

Not all incorporators even have the chance to show up on the radar of venture financers: The money providers concentrate on a few industries from which they think that they have particularly high potential. In most cases, these target industries can already be identified by the names of the funds or the VC societies, which often contain terms like "Life Science" or "Technology". The VC societies compose their teams correspondingly: As a rule, these teams contain industry experts from the investment fields.

Of course, it is difficult to forecast which companies actually belong to the hip sectors—the range of favorites is definitely subject to permanent changes. A few years ago, for example, software companies were still hip, today almost nobody invests in this sector any longer. In turn, an increasing amount of capital flows into the sectors of biotech, pharmacy and medical technologies as well as into information technology. According to FTD of January 10th, 2008 "in addition, the VC-scene has discovered the "clean-tech" market, e.g. companies from the environment of regenerative energies. At present, the chances to get hold of venture capital are particularly good here."

With generalizations of the experience from Silicon Valley, the country-specific conditions have to be particularly considered, of course. In Germany, in the national economy, the smaller businesses play a crucial role, as researches by the Institute for Family Businesses at the private University Witten/Herdecke and many other economy research institutes confirm again and again.

---

[114] FTD http://enable.ftd.de/was-ist-eigentlich-venture-capital/?pager=2 Request from June 12, 2008

95

The smaller businesses are the economic but also the social, financial and, above all, the ecological backbone of our country. Without medium-sized companies, Germany would not function and there would be no internationally competitive environment industry.

Furthermore, smaller industry also plays an unbeatably important role for the safety of supply but also for the variety of products, as the engine of innovation and even as taxpayer.

But apart from these generally known statements about the smaller businesses, there are further characteristics for a business culture of medium-sized firms that are of crucial importance for their success.

- The person or family orientation of the company management
- Independence of the company in legal and economic respects
- The competition orientation of the company by a focused market share and the absence of monopoles and oligopolies.
- The high personalization of responsibility for the success of the company amongst employees and owners.
- Orientation towards the highest self-financing quota possible
- The development of an independent company philosophy with special responsibility for environment and climate protection.

Especially from the last-mentioned point of view, the small and medium-sized companies own the pioneering and key role today which, without doubt, was inherent to the generation of entrepreneurs from the IT sector who created the "new market" a few years ago. And despite all the euphoria and painful awaking from too venturesome dreams, they nonetheless essentially contributed to the breakthrough of the high-tech-based modern information and communication technology. In the economy of today, nothing works without this technique, without the World Wide Web, without e-mail and the Internet, neither with big, small or medium-sized businesses. Something very analogous emerges on the environment market with the new green revolution. There is not one single basis innovation in the field of environment or climate that stems from large-scale industry. On the contrary, often enough, the concerns initially defended themselves intensively against novelties from the ecological point of view. Their actions mostly took place under high pressure by the public and often enough at 5 to 12. The entire industrial and environment-technological power of Germany results from its variety in the smaller businesses. After the word tinkling the Federal Government runs "resolute politics for the smaller businesses". With the reduction of bureaucracy they were "on a good path" in order to relieve medium-sized companies. With the inheritance tax it should be made sure for private companies and family businesses that "that assets that are kept within the company also profit from tax advantages when the firm is transferred to a next generation." Unfortunately, reality is completely different and often enough the smaller businesses do not only fight against the growing market power of the big companies but also internally for qualified successors. As proof: less than ten percent of all family businesses in Germany have been family-owned for three generations and are managed by relatives. But the medium-sized companies have an excellent reputation and, in many respects, the entrepreneurs act completely different than the paid managers of big company groups. Therefore, to a special extent, the financing instruments for innovations also have to be adapted to the interests of the medium-sized companies. In the following, the importance of the smaller businesses becomes obvious:

Importance of small and medium-sized Companies in Germany

Qualitative Characteristics

- Unity of property, risk, control
- Unity of leadership, decision, responsibility
- Flat hierarchy, consensus between management and staff
- Local relatedness, market and customer proximity
- Personal relationships between company and environment

Company size	Employees	Turnover	Balance Sum
Micro enterprises	0 - 9	up to 1 Mio. €	up to 1.4 Mio. €
Small enterprises	10 – 49	up to 9 Mio. €	up to 10 Mio. €
Medium enterprises	50 - 249	up to 50 Mio. €	up to 50 Mio. €
SME total	under 250	up to 50 Mio. €	up to 50 Mio. €

99.7 % of the Companies in Germany belong to the SMEs and provide...

...41 % of the turnover subject to VAT,
...52 % of the gross investments,
...49 % of the gross added value,
...82 % of the apprenticeship places and
...71 % of all employees.

Figure 3: Importance of small and medium-sized Companies in Germany

Here, financing of innovative projects also has to allow for the conditions that are custom in our bank environment as the following illustration shows:

Risk-adjusted design of conditions

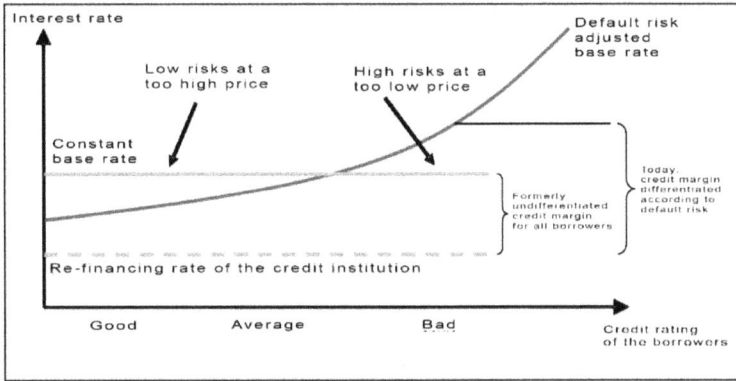

Figure 4: Risk-adjusted design of conditions

Of course, this makes the German and the European financing system completely different from the procedural methods that are custom in the USA and especially in Silicon Valley. The risk-adjusted design of conditions is the model for all companies that are looking for a loan under the conditions of Basel II. This cannot apply to startups. That is why they need different financing sources. Otherwise, they do not even need to start.

The past has shown which system really promotes innovations stronger, whereby venture capital is not the only financing source as the following overview shows.

Overview over alternative Financing Instruments

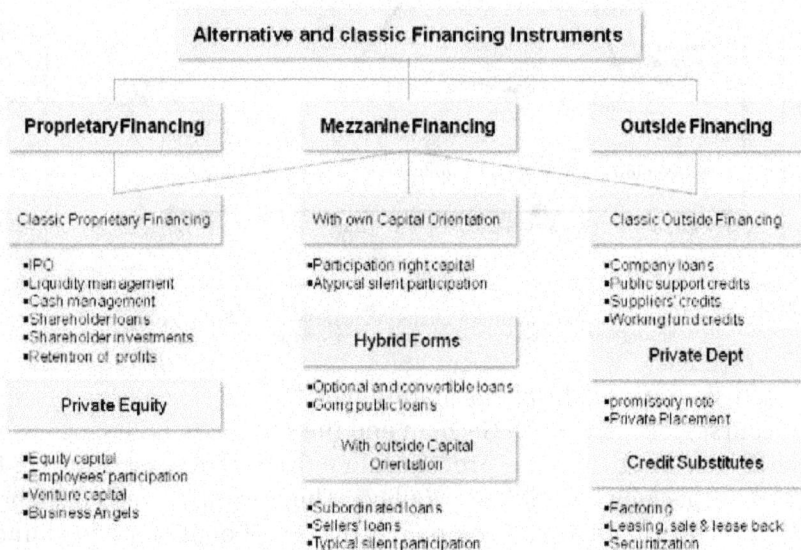

Figure 5: Alternative financing instruments

However, VC financing from the USA is considered the most successful model worldwide and one can assume that today's Internet economy would not exist without this instrument. Surely, the same applies to the upcoming greentech upswing.

3. Ways from Silicon Valley to Green Valley

Buck's Restaurant as Innovation Club

The Silicon Valley myth assigns to the area almost magical innovation power. Since many novelties were connected with the worldwide breakthrough of the Internet, due to the self-created network, the region became internationally popular much faster than ideas from Nowo Sibirsk Many people do not really believe at which places the new ideas really come into existence in Silicon Valley. Frequently, it happens in an unspectacular way, almost incredibly simple and without long-term prepared meetings with fixed agenda. In Silicon Valley, most of the ideas were really born in pubs or garages. Of course, there are no statistics about that, but in all informal meetings seem to play a central role. Again and again, one also reads or hears there that the first sketches of ideas were made on the paper place mats that are common in many restaurants and are simply taken away, no matter how much ketchup traces were left on it. The open atmosphere of Silicon Valley makes the difference. The content of ideas of workshops is higher evaluated than the office or the facade of the company. This even applies to respectable idea conferences like the annual TED conference. TED stands for Technology Entertainment and Design. How often do you find such events in Germany? With charismatic personalities and top contributions by speakers like Al Gore or Craig Venter which the audience will remember for a long time, even beyond their field of expertise! Is there any place where technology is connected with entertainment, fun and pleasure? For example, some even see the "Genome Guy" with his last lecture at the TED as the savior of mankind because he is concerned with the development of microbes that split up CO_2 or invent new bio fuels respectively new medicaments. You can get such information about novelties via the Buck's homepage.[115] Can you find a similar reference on just one web page of a restaurant in Berlin or Munich that likes to name itself "Munich Valley" because of the strong high-tech industry? Not even the restaurant chain "Einstein" gets such an idea and in the Munich Hofbräuhaus there are not even specifications regarding beer innovations, upward price innovations excluded. Does anybody in Germany enjoy listening to a politician and who feels so addressed by the message that he becomes thoughtfully himself and, above all, active? A gastronome, chef, farmer and multi talent

---

[115] cf. http://www.buckswoodside.com/ Request from April 15, 2008

like Jamis MacNiven honors Al Gore's talent for that in his restaurant in Woodside, Silicon Valley.

It is among the particularly popular meeting points and insider tips for visitors.[116] The boss belongs to the most well-known personalities of the Valley and, due to his body height already, he overlooks his exotically equipped restaurant like a commander. From breakfast time on, the meeting point is very well attended and you really find many guests with laptops and work documents. The atmosphere of the restaurant resembles a colorful collection of travel souvenirs, weapons, antiques and oddities up to spacesuits and telescopes. No wonder that by guests like the Harvard Astronomer Roy Gould and Microsoft's Curtis Wong a World Wide Telescope for the observation of stars was developed in the neighbor's garden analogue with the Google Earth perspective.

Obviously, the numerous eye catchers in Buck's restaurant stimulate the fantasy of the guests. The owner, simply called Jamis by everybody, writes weekly columns and counts amongst the most frequently interviewed personalities of Silicon Valley. Full of pride, he reports on his Internet homepage: "Since 1995 we have had over 600 TV, radio, glossy-print and fish wrapper press come to Buck's to speak with me and my customers".

At his rustic tables the information era was forged and here the next revolution takes place, the transition to the Green Valley or the birth of the cleantech revolution. Even if that is not yet visible in the restaurant and with the numerous big cars in front of the restaurant, the insider is sure that in ecological respect a new era has begun after the long deep sleep of the Americans. Everybody is not just talking about going green, they are doing something. That is exactly why Jamis supports the new eco innovation wave and its protagonists. The "Buck's" has a mediator role in this, helps to find and fix contacts as well as to provide new ideas with money. For that, the people in the restaurant shall feel like in paradise, find new contacts and incentives and remember the stay in any case. Although Jamis contributes in making new connections he does not cash in royalties for that but is happy to see prominent customers as well as curious or random guests. Who is looking for contacts can ask him or, mediated by him, have him placed at a table where the new idea might be heard. Where could you picture that in a German restaurant? Which

---

[116] cf. http://www.buckswoodside.com/history/index.html Request from April, 15th, 2008

restaurant owner would dare to guide a fundless inventor to the table of the bankers? This fact tells much more about the differences between the special cultures of Silicon Valley compared to Germany's country guesthouses than anything else. That this informal negotiation culture is not a single case proves a little story that was published by the Handelsblatt on May 5th, 2007. A policeman watched "suspects", a young Asian guy and a black man in jeans, at three o'clock in the night in a car park in front of a restaurant near Mountain View. He took them for a crossexamination because the sensed drug dealers. In reality, it was about a much bigger deal here the takeover of YouTube by Google. The people who were still negotiating at the car park at night were David Drummond, Google's chief jurisprudent and Gideon Yu, YouTube's financial head as the scene magazine "Valleywag" revealed. David Drummond is said to be media-shy and thus it is absolutely credible that he negotiates unconventionally in the dark or at a car park sometimes. After one of his launched statements regarding the planned participation of Microsoft in Yahoo, Microsoft promptly withdrew its offer. The clever jurist had loudly reflected whether the market-ruling methods of Microsoft were adequate to the character of the World Wide Web. On the other hand, the Handelsblatt speculated which impression a merger of Google and Yahoo would leave on the Internet advertising market.[117]

It sounds amazing but the restaurant chats from Silicon Valley could even concern world politics. After all, Yahoo holds e.g. 39% of the biggest Chinese Internet house Alibaba that combines ISP, web space and search engine. So if a shift in shares results from the negotiations during lunch or dinner, for example by a merger of Google and Yahoo, a new situation arises also for far-flung China due to the new ownership status.[118] In turn, every strategic change towards stronger environmental awareness has also global effect, especially due to the Internet presence. That is exactly why this book is called "From the Dot-Coms to the Dot-Greens". It is essential to spread the ideas of clean technologies at Internet speed. In this respect, the quality of the makers and the courage of the founders from Silicon Valley are like a fountain of youth for others, especially because absolutely not every new idea at the favor of the environment is

---

[117] cf. http://www.handelsblatt.com/News/printpage.aspx?_p=200811&_t=ftpr int&_b=1425529 Request of March 14th, 2008

[118] cf. http://www.silicommdada.com/ Request from March 14th, 2008

just based on a high grant by venture capital. Many things also happen growing upwards from the ground without high start-up capital. The Handelsblatt of March 13th, 2008 titles these founders: Startups "Von echtem Blut, Schweiß und Tränen"(About real blood, sweat and tears).[119] It addresses all those who want to start and take to success their companies without the typical VC injections. "Bootstrapping" pulling oneself out of the mud by the own hairs this is called by Americans, and there are more than just a few who try to make it this way. In the area of new environment technologies, for example, it is about becoming aware of new green business by means of intelligent software. Gabe Rivera, founder and CEO of Techmene, works on such problems without VC capital. Techmene is a very intelligent blog search engine that searches for new technical topics in the blogosphere (the German "pendant" is Rivva.de). Such examples show that one can also make it without loan capital. "A good idea, a handful of dollars, very much willpower, a thick skin in case of setbacks and very, very much work that takes a start-up absolutely further than just to a good VC."[120] Consequently, meetings at the most unusual places are absolutely not just about contacts between mind and money but also amongst the founders and combatants. This is why many founders also swear by other recipes, for example mutual support and complementing one another. Does one have to pay a programmer if one cannot program oneself? One does not have to, one only has to believe in the idea and, for example, gain interested combatants by giving share certificates for the collaboration. If the idea flops, at least one does not have debts but precious experience in turn. So in Silicon Valley one is also inventive in networking without direct and immediate cash flow and uses virtual collaboration in particular. Thus, the classic workshops are supported by the modern communication forms, whether in a restaurant or any other place. And everybody is of the opinion that personal meetings often work wonders and that the real world outdoes the virtual contacts by far. In order to stay in gastronomy: virtual working dinners are not tasty or to put it a bit more carefully not really yet.

What pushes forward the development of Silicon Valley gets attention. If it is just a pure "business deal", everybody who is watching gets rather bored. This becomes clear with the takeover plans of

---

[119] cf. Handelsblatt. com from March 14, 2008
[120] cf. Ibid.

Microsoft towards Yahoo that were sneeringly accompanied as "Microhoo". "With Microsoft and Yahoo a software company from the day before yesterday meet (That does not fit in the Valley anyway and is suspect to many people here. In addition, they overslept the Internet and then won the browser battle not by innovations but by hitting below the belt) with a descending champion from yesterday (even if they are still table leaders in many business ratios). This does not fuel imagination, in best case it lets some evil forebodings arise.[121] "Similarly harsh judgments also hit the Googleplex or the Googlenomics as soon as negative figures are looming. In the present situation they have a particularly paralyzing effect because the entire US economy is in a recession period or at least the fear of that has a negative influence on the economic processes. This attitude that is absolutely untypical for Silicon Valley concerns many analysts more than bad quarterly figures and the more eagerly they pick up even the smallest signs of new orientations. Here, "going green" is at the very top.

Practical Tips

- *The cultivation and maintenance of the personal relationships in a broad network are a factor of success and have to be designed actively but must never be delegated!*
- *Dot-green founders should learn to listen and be faster in drawing personal conclusions from the everywhere increasing environment and climate protection discussion.*
- *Everybody can practically tackle the shift to green business or dot-green founder without qualms about possible former ragging on "tree huggers"!*
- *Dot-green founders should have the courage to simply go to California and look around there. Even if one knows nobody, one will get into contact soon!*

Walmart's Green Ways of Purchasing

Can you imagine that Aldi or Lidl ask professors, doctoral candidates and students to check their supply sources? Not at all. Most of the big groups do not like others having a look into their purchasing books, even if they like to have a controlling look even in the bags of their staff or spy them out with a video camera, even as far as to the changing rooms as

---

[121] cf. Ibid.

recently with Lidl. Over decades, the retail giant Walmart also counted amongst the large businesses that were caught in their own "Bentonville Bubble". In German, the place of the headquarters in Arkansas, USA, already sounds a bit like "Betonvilla" and likewise cemented appeared the business principles of the discount retail group that was founded by Sam Walton (1918-1992) in 1961. In the center of the enormous expansion that started with going public in the year 1972 only, were operative effectiveness, growth and profit. With a turnover of meanwhile 378.80 billion US dollars in 2007, it is the worldwide biggest group with about 2.1 million staff in the year 2008. By building the first hypermarkets in the USA, the company strengthened its position and expanded globally, even if less successfully in Germany due to the market controlling position of the wellknown big German retailers Edeka, Aldi and Lidl. In 2006, the German Walmart subsidies were sold to the Metro group and today they trade under the name of real. The already traditionally low German margins in food trade of about 2% compared with the 5% expected in the USA forced Walmart to sell and caused an estimated loss of about 1 bn US dollars.[122]

All the more surprising is the fact that the biggest retail group in the world has changed their attitude beyond the binoculars of profit. They create networks with NGOs (suppliers) and staff, work together with governmental agencies and comb through their supply chain "green" in special, as the Stanford SOCIAL INNOVATION review reported in its spring edition 2008.[123] The beginning of Walmart's green activities go back to the year 1989. Back then, the activities of the group concentrated on environmentally friendly packages that had to be biodegradable or could be recycled. Single attempts to emphasize the ecological product quality with a green label partly even lead to negative press reports. The public noticed that e.g. with paper towels only the packaging was made of recycled material but the towels themselves were strongly polluting due to chlorine bleaching. After that, in the 90s, the environment activities disappeared from the agenda of priorities of the retail giant, at least at the surface. After a study had found out that 2 to 8% of all customers boycotted Walmart by reason of their general practices, the Head of the Board, H. Lee Scott, reacted in October 2005.[124] In a speech that was

---

[122] cf. wikipedia, wal-mart
[123] cf. Stanford SOCIAL INNOVATION *review,* vol.6, No.2, p.53 ff
[124] cf. BusinessWeek, Nov. 29, 2006

transmitted to 1.6 million staff in all stores and 60,000 suppliers worldwide, Walmart announced their new "Business-Sustainability Strategy". It embraced three ambitious objectives in order to reduce the environmental impact of the group: "To be supplied 100 percent by renewable energy; to create zero waste; and to sell products that sustain our resources and the environment."[125] The entire supply chain was confronted with this new ecological standard at the same time and the requirement to reduce the costs was also connected with that. The planned new network thinking and acting expanded the environment protection standard to the entire global supply chain. 14 networks were established that should help to realize at least one of the main objectives.

1. Target: Supply with 100% renewable energies by the following networks:
- Global Greenhouse Gas Strategy
- Alternative Fuels
- Global Logistics
- Energy, Design, Construction & Maintenance

2. Objective: waste reduction to zero
- Operations and Internal Procurement
- Packaging

3. Target: Sale of products that sustainably protect resources and the environment
- Chemical Intensive Products
- Seafood
- Electronics
- Food & Agriculture
- Forest & Paper
- Jewelry
- China
- Textiles

These 14 "Walmart's Sustainable Value Networks" brought about numerous new findings with high economic benefit due to improved awareness of environment and climate protection interests as well as new

---

[125] L. Scott, Twentieth Century Leadership, Wal-Mart, Oct. 24, 2005

social responsibility. The Stanford scientists Erica L. Plambeck and Lyn Denend interviewed 40 representatives of Walmart and their network partners and filtered out 7 rules of success of this networking.

Under the keyword "Networking the Walmart Way" they consider the following maxims as particularly important:[126]

1. Walmart expands its own management capacities by partnerships with NGOs in order to

- Determine design objectives and measurable criteria of the environment performance
- Push-through the certification of products as environmentally friendly
- Receive supplier support, especially on the lowest levels that had been too intransparent for Walmart as supplier up to then in order to improve their processes with groundbreaking technologies.
- Develop new income sources by environment protection.

2. The suppliers are motivated to become and remain Walmart partners by means of

- Agreements to buy or promote environmentally friendly products
- Consolidation of the business relationships with a smaller, better selected group of suppliers
- Preference given to more long-term, closer relationships with suppliers that include environment-oriented innovations in their focus.

For Silicon Valley and its high-tech companies, the approach of the biggest retail group worldwide confirms the need to address more environment-friendly solutions to an increasing extent also in the field of electronics. In the year 2004, the Stanford researchers Plambeck and Denend write the USA exported 80% of their electronic waste to developing countries. The pollution caused by that exceeded the level allowed in the industrial countries by more than the 100-fold. Disposing of "E-waste" and electronic waste in a safer and more environmentally friendly way is one of the objectives of Walmart's Electronics Network. Here, the subject is not only recycling of materials but also the avoidance

---

[126] cf. E.L. Plambeck, L. Denend, Case Study: The Greening of Wal-Mart, Leland Stanford Jr. University, Stanford 2007

of environment endangering substances from the design on. Another target is the enhancement of the energy efficiency of the electronics in total. The work of the electronic network achieved better results in the field of enhancement of energy efficiency than with the avoidance of dangerous substances. One reason for that is that energy savings can be measured in a better and faster way than recycling results or the avoidance of hazardous substances. Due to the complexity and the long electronics supply chain, the certification of all product components is difficult and cost-intensive. Apart from that, logically Walmart does not have the competence to assess single parts and components respectively assembly parts of complex electronic devices in a qualified way. But when the company is not able to provide the guarantee that the products that are labeled as particularly environment and climate-friendly really keep what they promise, they must not be marketed that way. For example, Walmart made efforts to be the first retail chain in the USA that corresponded with the RoHSregulation by the EU for PC deliveries. (RoHS = Restriction on Hazardous Substances). The retail chain guaranteed the Japanese company Toshiba a 12-week instead of the otherwise common 4-week supplier contract if they observed the RoHs-regulation of the EU. But they did not dare to market the environmental advantage explicitly.[127] Walmart has problems with recycling of electronics because the consumer does not benefit from taking back the old devices but rather faces effort and even costs, e.g. by transport to the dealer. In order to get better control of the problems, the group decided to cooperate with the Green Electronic Council (GEC), a nonprofit organization. They work together with electronics companies and their suppliers in order to improve the environmental and social performances in production. In the original they say regarding the targets of the cooperation with the GEC organization: "With the GEC, Walmart designed an Internet-based scorecard on which suppliers indicate how environmentally sustainable their products are. This scorecard includes measures of energy efficiency, durability, and end-of-life solutions".[128] In the future, collaboration is to be expanded by Walmart helping to market newer versions of improved electronic devices and thus getting the customer to replace more energy-intensive devices at an earlier stage.

---

[127] cf. SSI *review*, p. 58
[128] Ibid.

In this novel networking the retail giant sees the key for sustainable success that has both, an economic and a social environmentally friendly effect. Due to the high market power, such a change of direction naturally means more than a single offhanded action; this strategy initiated numerous further changes with the suppliers. But the principle still is: "More than anything else, Walmart's network approach must remain profitable if it is to be sustainable in the long run and if it is to be achieve CEO Lee Scots environmental goals."[129]

The involvement of the supply chains in climate and environment-related redirections has gained more and more importance in more and more large-scale businesses in the recent years. The Stanford Graduate School of Business, for example, regularly organizes "Global Supply Chain Management Forums" for that. [130] Here, the social and ecological responsibilities are of increasing importance. SER conferences stand for "Socially and Environmentally Responsible Supply Chains" and serve as a source of innovative solutions.[131]

In Germany, Supply-Chain-Management (SCM) has been used as industry-wide business optimization for the improvement of the entire logistics chain for about 10 years. "The concept SCM describes a system of suppliers of goods and services on several levels that agreed continuous collaboration. The customers within the chain tie up with one (Single Sourcing) or two suppliers (Dual Sourcing). This clear structure facilitates the analysis of the processes beyond the limits of the single companies. Objective is an optimization of the internal and external business processes."[132]

The improvements expected from that concern in the first place:
- Product and process quality
- Supply quality regarding reliability and time
- Reduction of the negative environmental impacts
- Enforcement of cost advantages as well as
- of the organization (cf. Ibid.)

---

[129] cf. SSI *review* Spring 2008, p. 57
[130] cf. gsb.stanford.edu/scforum/
[131] cf. gsb.stanford.edu/ser/
[132] Sustainability management in companies. (Concepts and instruments for sustainable business development), Berlin 2002, p. 107

109

"Green-Supply-Chain-Management" particularly concentrates on the ecological and social improvements as well as lately on minimizations of carbon footprints, consequently mainly on the CO_2-impacts of all activities and products. The latter increasingly developed to an innovation engine and instrument of comparative analysis that will receive much more attention in the future.

Practical Tips
- *Rigorously build up an own leadership program in energy saving and environmental design!*
- *Enforce "green standards" and rating programs for environment and climate protection through the whole supply chain!*
- *Consequently utilize all cost advantages of going green!*
- *Enforce the integration of green economic principles into all design and process activities!*
- *Choose the best values of leading manufacturers as the stan dard of your own acting!*
- *Arouse understanding everywhere for the fact that the green future begins today!*
- *Do not miss out one single field of the new need to think envi ronmentally, ranging from facility management to business trip regulations!*

From the Garage Company to the Green Giant

The most famous garage in the world is located in Palo Alto, set back next to an unimpressive wooden house in Addison Avenue No. 367. Just a brass board with the landmark number 976 of May, 19th, 1989 gives a hint that one is standing in front of the place of birth of the biggest technology center worldwide. The garage appears to be rather small. On the board it says: "Birthplace of Silicon Valley" and further in the original text:

"This Garage is the Birthplace of the world's first High-tech Region "Silicon Valley." The idea for such a region originated with Dr. Frederick Terman, a Stanford University Professor who encouraged his students to start up their own electronics company in the area instead of joining established firms in the east. The first two students to follow his advice were William R. Hewlett & David Packard, who in 1938 began developing their first product, an audio oscillator in this garage."

One is standing a bit helpless in front of the closed door and the far set back, apparently reconstructed garage. Who expects a company museum or a high-tech information pylon will be disappointed. The house seems to be rented out. The residents or company operators do not want to be disturbed by possible visitors. On a simple board at the house there is the company name "Palo Altan Green" and explaining "Another Palo Altan for Renewable Energy". What this has got to do with the famous company Hewlett Packard (HP) is not instantly comprehensible. The specified web site www.cpau.com belongs to Palo Alto, with about 62,000 citizens a rather medium-sized city in today's Silicon Valley. The streets were generously designed; there is almost no real center in the European sense. The single lots of land are built up with typical flat American single-family houses and abundantly covered with vegetation. That leads to the conclusion that water consumption is very high in summer. Near the garage with the indication to the new Palo Alto and renewable energies the observant visitor finds just one house with solar installation although the sun shines permanently here and California more and more suffers from water shortage and drought to aridity.

Again and again this garage incorporation is given as an example for the pioneer spirit and often transferred to other firms, starting with Apple to today's founders. Still today the starting capital of the two students and now globally largest computer company is declared with exactly 538 dollars. As the first customer the Walt-Disney studios bought eight sound frequency generators for the cartoon "Fantasia", Wikipedia reveals. According to Forbes, approximately seventy years later turnover amounted to almost 92 billion US dollars in 2007 (according to Wikipedia specifications even over 104 billionn US dollars). [133] Of course, this skyrocketing career had also got to do with the enormous demand for new electronic war equipment. W.K. MüllerScholz points out rightly what some authors forget: "For Silicon Valley the Second World War proved to be the basis of everything: not only for Hewlett-Packard. Because San Francisco was the central war harbor for the Pacific fleet in World War II as well as in the following Korea and Vietnam wars many soldiers stayed at the Californian West Coast at the end of the big battles, especially technicians and engineers."[134]

---

[133] Frequently, 1939 is specified as HP's real foundation year.
[134] cf. W.K. Müller-Scholz, Inside Silicon Valley, Ideen zu Geld machen (Turning ideas into money), Wiesbaden, Gabler Verlag 2000, p. 85

Hewlett Packard became globally popular with the first scientific calculator, the HP 35, which was launched in the year 1972 as well as the first personal computer that was brought on the market in 1980. With the first ink jet printer developed for private customers that was offered in 1984, HP occupied the market from which most people know the company today latest print technologies for private and business customers. Due to the purchase of Compaq in 2002, the influence in the field of computers became even higher, whereby the printer sector is especially essential for success today, even if disputed because the real business is made with ink and toner that have to be permanently replaced. For that HP developed technologies that are disputed in the EU from the point of view of competition law because they wanted to prevent the change to other manufacturers. These technologies are disputed because of data protection and competition law reasons and have partly been forbidden in the EU from the year 2007 on. Less public is the area software technology. With OpenView, software was developed that, amongst other things, is employed for the supervision of commercially used computers, but also for the processing of data backups. The annual investments in research and development have to be pointed out for which 3.5 bn US dollars are spent alone. Today, they do not focus on technological progress any longer, but to an increasing extent they include new ecological questions and challenges. According to Forbes' specifications, the foundation company of the Silicon Valley upswing counts amongst the "10 green giants" worldwide. This is surprising for many analysts because over several decades it did not seem all that the long-time industrial leader of Silicon Valley would lead the way in terms of eco sensitivity.

"The fact is, as more of modern life goes digital, the environmental impact of those computers and gadgets has gone from negligible to considerable. Hewlett-Packard has done the most to mitigate that. HP owns massive e-waste recycling plants, where enormous shredders and granulators reduce four million pounds of computer detritus each month to bite-sized chunks the first step in reclaiming not just steel and plastic but also toxic chemicals like mercury and even some precious metals. HP will take back any brand of equipment; its own machines are 100 percent recyclable. It has promised to cut energy consumption by 20 percent by 2010. HP also audits its top suppliers for eco-friendliness, and its omnibus

Global Citizenship Report sets the standard for detailed environmental accountability."[135]

Beyond the known economical growth objectives, HP's overall strategy follows new green targets that can be assigned to three big areas.[136]

1. Energy savings with the usage of computers and all kinds of computer technology
2. Taking back and recycling technologies for used computer technology
3. Eco auditing and control as well as reduction of the CO_2

In the first category, the increase of energy efficiency, HP is not the first company but meanwhile predominant also towards IBM and Dell. It becomes more and more obvious that computer technology in all has a high share in the increase of CO_2 in the atmosphere of the Earth. According to estimations they already reach the values of the entire aviation sector, thus about 3% worldwide. But an exact overview of the worldwide shares of the industries does not yet exist. Therefore, the big computer companies are particularly occupied with this topic. Central emphasis is put on the high-energy consumption of the data and server centers. Jointly, the companies AMD, HP, IBM, Intel, Microsoft and Sun have created a "Green Grid Consortium" in order to drastically reduce the energy costs. The following illustration shows how they have changed and will probably increase.[137]

---

[135] *Oliver Ryan,* http:/money.cnn.com/galleries/2007/fortune/0703/ Request of March 23rd, 2008

[136] cf. Source: OpinionWire by Butler Group www.butlergroup.com Request from April 12, 2008

[137] cf. http://www.economist.com/business/displaystory.cfm?story_id=878143 5 Request from April 4th, 2008

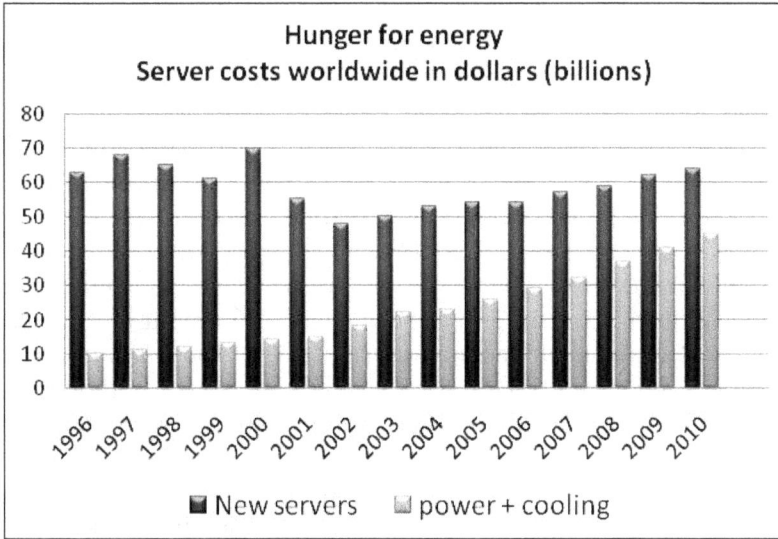

Hunger for energy
Server costs worldwide in dollars (billions)

New servers   power + cooling

Figure 6: Server costs worldwide Source: IDC

Such a joint initiative of principally competing companies of Silicon Valley is a typical way of proceeding because one often expects more from joint developments than from individual and secret processing. The new global challenges of climate protection have promoted this community spirit because the atmosphere can neither be divided nor privatized. For example, Hewlett-Packard follows the path of essentially improving the cooling systems of the computers. The system developed for that is called "Dynamic Smart Cooling". It connects temperature sensors with the fans in a way that the cold air is temporarily targeted directly at those server parts that need cooling. For that the corresponding standards still have to be developed and safety guarantees as well as intelligent networks for communication for the need for cooling have to be built in, but the direction is principally right. As a result, one expects energy savings of 25 to 40% from such dynamic cooling systems.[138]

The chip manufacturers have started to increase the performance per watt and practically include energy saving modules into the performance configuration. The new "Multi-Core Chips" range from dual to quadro core chips and increase the performance per watt by the factor 4.5. At the same time, they are looking for solutions to minimize the transfer from AC

---

[138] cf. Ibid.

to DC or to switch it off completely in order to avoid unnecessary energy consumption. Everybody knows that from the private sector if he just attentively watched the warming up of the mini transformers that are connected with every laptop. The power consumption of many data processing centers has doubled in the last five years and computer fairs have got good reasons why they display their new devices under the motto "Green IT". More and more companies complain that 10% of the technology costs are already determined by the power costs, tendency increasing. Furthermore, the need of "going green" in the sense of further reduction of power consumption becomes a requirement by the fact that the increasing number of "second life" residents in the computer network has not a real body but of course leaves ecological footprints with every log in into the virtual world. In fact, the own computer animations need a considerable amount of power.[139] Only recently it became obvious that every search request in the computer is connected with energy consumption, as it will be shown even more detailed in the section about Google.

Beyond the improvement of the energy efficiency, Hewlett-Packard steer their efforts for the reduction of the energy consumptions towards the improvement of energy efficiency. For this purpose, initially, they deal with the employment of more energy-efficient and thus economizing devices of all kinds. This step is simple and is normally made the first. In the second step, the entire organization of the processes and the possible savings from that are dealt with. If the most energy-intensive technique operates at just 10% instead of 70%, the company inevitably loses much money. In the third place there is efficiency, for example of business trips. According to HP's opinion, if they succeeded in changing the behavior of people, the most effective savings could be achieved this way. For example, HP equipped 13 worldwide HVCS (Halo Virtual Collaboration Studios). HVCS are highly effective virtual meeting facilities allowing for telephone conferences without time delays and high reality effect. By this alone, the travel costs were reduced by 8% and the CO_2 impact on the atmosphere was lowered by 32 tons.

Amongst HP's already mentioned special eco performances count reusage of products respectively assembly parts or recycling. They have been following this strategy since 1987 that focuses all products and their entire service life. Standard assembly parts for all HP products have

---

[139] cf. The Economist, March 1, 2007

increased service life already and also the effectiveness of production. More than that, in more than 40 states they erected recycling centers and recycling of precious raw materials of the computers or printers is the central point here.

Finally, like principally many other companies, HP makes efforts to ecologically improve supply chain management. Since 2002, responsibility for the entire supply chain has been stronger oriented towards social and ecological consequences. This does also include ethical aspects as well as health care for the staff, in all oriented at the own HP standards. In addition, the group announced in November 2007 that they collaborate stronger with the World Wildlife Fund of the USA in order to help with the mitigation of global warming by greenhouse gases from their own premises. The concrete targets were fixed and at the same time agreements for the employment of the respective best-suitable technologies for the reduction of the energy consumption of the own respectively leased facilities were met.

Even if in Greenpeace's opinion HP are not at the first place amongst the computer companies with ecological commitment, it is remarkable that the foundation company of the Silicon Valley, in the last years, has been making more and more efforts regarding this topic and supports new efforts.[140] This leadership towards other Silicon Valley companies shall be extended. Even if you assume that part of the activities mainly takes place out of marketing reasons, they still remain exemplary new going green initiatives.

Practical Tips

- *Learn from the start in the garage again and again that under any circumstances something big can develop from smallest beginnings!*
- *Raise garage thinking for flexible and faster reacting again and again and help enforcing it rigorously!*
- *Build up fast methods and quick structures for the change of the business principles from the point of view of sustainability!*
- *Meditate less how complex new questions like the reduction of the CO_2 output could be tackled but simply start at one point, as with power consumption.*

---

140 cf. http://www.greenpeace.org/international/campaigns/toxics/electronics /howthe-companies-line-up-6 Request of May 15th, 2008

A Ripe Apple Turns Green

Like many others, Apple's history is one of the rags-to-riches stories in the USA an empire developed out of nil and with not much more than an idea. As in all cases, a genius mind was behind that who never let himself be argued out of his idea and the belief in success.

The birth of Apple is the story of Stephan Wozniak and Steve Jobs two incorporators who could not be more different: one of them the quiet tinkerer, the other one the great sales talent with visions. The then third co-founder Ron Wayne left Apple before the development of the company became really interesting and can therefore be neglected here. Apple's 32-year history has always been marked by ups and downs, by genius ideas and fatal errors.

Back then, the name Apple developed rather from a threat uttered by Steve Jobs because nobody had an idea for a suitable name for their computer firm.[141] They stuck with this name.

As with most of the garage companies, Apple's beginning was a big struggle. The Apple I was a computer for tinkerers. At that time, it cost the sensational amount of 666 dollars and was mainly offered per shipment and, of course, at the electronic fairs in California. It was the Apple II, the development of which was financed by the Apple I that brought about the breakthrough for the little company. Still today it is considered the first successful personal computer. More than two million items were sold until 1985.[142] Already back then, Steve Jobs unrestingly pushed his numerous employees and very quickly Apple became the shining star in young Silicon Valley.

But they performed the real stroke of genius with the realization of an idea they had discovered at Rank Xerox: A graphical user interface, the so-called GUI. Apart from the graphic operating elements, the "mouse" as "indicator" was the really big innovation. Derived from the appearance of a desk, these two elements became the outstanding operating element for computers. That still is the basic principle of every PC today. Steve Jobs was more than fascinated by the then completely new form of operating a computer. Fanatically, he pushed the development of an own new computer with such an operating surface and with a "mouse". The first computer that was fit for sale, LISA, named after Steve's big disappointing love at that time, entered the market in 1983 and became a big flop. Too

---

[141] cf. Inside Steve's brain 2008
[142] cf. The Apple Story J. Gartz 2005

expensive, was the unanimous judgment and it seemed to set in motion the end of Apple then. When the failure became apparent after a few months, Steve Jobs instantly had developed a slim version of LISA in order to realize a price that was in line with the market. That was the real hour of birth of the Macintosh. The Apple Macintosh entered the history books of computers as the first computer that was really easy to operate, the computer for everybody. If Rank Xerox had not seen their user interface PARC as a pure research project, history had surely taken a different direction. But now Steve Jobs reserved the rights at this form of user interface and Apple became the wunderkind of Silicon Valley. Almost all developments that flow into today's user interfaces of the operating systems are based on the patents and developments of the early Apple systems. An essential component of Apple's success was based on the rigid human interface guidelines that Steve Jobs established for all software developers who wanted to write software for the Macintosh. Thus, he ensured over decades that everybody observed the basic principles and guidelines of the Apple operating system. In the first place, the users profited from this guidelines. They could thus be sure that every Apple program can be operated in the same manner.[143]

Despite its success, Apple has always been renowned as a company that is not very reluctant in the conduct with staff and competition. Driven by his visions, Steve Jobs demanded highest performance from his staff and was not very prude in conduct with his competitors.

In the mid-80s, this lead to hard internal power struggles at Apple. The loser was Steve Jobs who subsequently left Apple in 1985. But Steve Jobs successors could not prevent Apple from tumbling into their biggest crisis.

Apple's concept had long received competition and Microsoft's Windows 3.11 became, together with the PC, the biggest competitor. Apple's system was closed while Microsoft under Bill Gates professionally kept all doors open and thus made their own graphical operating system run on all computers that corresponded with a certain basic configuration. From this freedom of hardware selection, a merciless competition battle between the hardware companies accrued and consequently the price of the PC hit rock bottom compared with the Apple. Apple had slept through the most important development, namely opening themselves for the mass market.

---

[143] cf. Steve Jobs: Think different 2001

118

Thus, Apple faced the difficult task of finding a new way that would bring back the old glamour that the Macintosh had radiated back then. Steve Jobs went down a new path and founded the company NeXT with which he wanted to realize his dream of a computer with groundbreaking new graphical surface. He wanted to beat the already then out-of-date appearing Apple user interface and, above all, also Windows 3.11 by a mile and concentrated on the development of a Unix-based, completely new form of operating surface. At the same time, he had a computer developed that was definitely able to enter the history books as a milestone. But market success never came because the predominance of the windows-based computers could not even be outperformed with this technological innovation. Apple also remained unsuccessful and until the middle of the 90s it seemed as if the former star of the computer market would cease to exist forever. In 1995, Apple bought the company NeXT in a surprising deal and in 1997 Steve Jobs returned to the company Apple as CEO. The ups and downs of this blessed think tank started to change and Apple concentrated on their core competencies building innovative lifestyle computers that are easy to operate.[144]

In the year 2001, the presentation of the iPod, a MP3 player for the mass market, took place. Precious styling, simplest operation and own software to feed the MP3 player with music were the basis of the success that took Apple to a second hour of birth.[145]

With all this success, Apple had not been too interested in ecological activities in all these years. Apple's overall development outlines one of the big problems with which many IT companies had to fight in the recent decades. Surviving and concentrating on innovative products did not leave much space for ecological experiments. Thus, the market forced Apple over all these years to produce as low-priced as possible. Not so easy considering Apple's high quality objectives. Since then, Apple products have mainly been produced in Asia. Near Hong Kong, the Taiwanese Foxconn AG took the complete contract manufacturing for Apple. In the year 2006, specifically this company was denounced because of their inhuman working conditions. Thus, for the first time, Apple was forced to comment in public and to act correspondingly in order to prevent higher loss of image. Apple admitted deficits and promised change for the better. But that did not keep Greenpeace from putting

---

[144] cf. www.Brockhaus.de
[145] cf. The iPod Story Discovery chanel 2007

Apple on the last place of environmentally conscious companies on their internal ranking scale. But in the meantime it had turned out that Greenpeace had not accused just Apple but much rather the computer industry in general the whole production process of which is heavily confronted with environmentally harmful materials in its entire production process.[146] Today, in the face of continuously dropping hardware prices, it is definitely a feat to make high profits. And it is even a stunt to change production to not environmentally harmful assembly parts because the higher prices resulting from that had to be paid by the end customer in the first place. Of course, such a way of acting would only work if all manufacturers would commit themselves to it. In the face of this price battle the advance of a single company would press it out of the market very quickly. Despite these concerns, Apple dared to make the step in the right direction. Since Apple never belonged to the cheap providers but definitely orientates at lifestyle and exclusiveness, Apple's going green also is the right way from the point of view of market strategy.

Today, on the Apple website, everybody who is searching for it will find a detailed description of the ecological consciousness that Apple made their motto. The predominant usage of harmful substances like asbestos, plumb, cadmium, chlorinated and brominated substances is one of the biggest problems of the entire computer industry. Apple is absolutely aware of this fact and either reduced or completely abolished the employment of these materials from the production. A step that, on the one hand, swallowed a lot of money but on the other hand sustainably contributes to a highly improved image.[147] Thus, Apple gradually turns into the green Apple and the statements concerning the strategy are clear.

Since 2006 Apple have not produced any more CRT displays and even before the European Battery Guidelines came into force they renounced at the usage of plumb. Bromine-containing flame retardants, currently customarily used in production, shall become a thing of the past until the end of 2008. This is mainly achieved by the increased usage of aluminum with casings that make an additional flame protection unnecessary. Apple also renounced at the employment of other substances like polybrominated biphenyls (PBB) and polybrominated

---

[146] cf. www.greenpeace.org 2005
[147] cf. http://www.apple.com/de/environment 2006-2008

diphenyl ether (PBDE) long before the corresponding regulations became valid.[148]

With such measures, another problem surfaces that many computer manufacturers are confronted with today. Since the usage of poisonous substances also has not been economical for several years they renounced at them without blowing the trumpet. Thus, of course, they did not use a great marketing opportunity that would have given them the "green paint" years before already. Substances like decabromodiphenyl ether (Deca-BDE) are still permitted but have not been employed in the Apple products for a long time already. In the medium term Apple also want to renounce at the usage of beryllium. Currently, it still is indispensable in order to ensure the reliability of internal components but Apple will also be measured by this promise. The PVC portion of all plastic parts was drastically reduced and can be found, if even existent, in parts with a weight of more than 25 grams only and, unfortunately, still in cable coatings. But here Apple makes efforts to influence the total abolishment of PVC from production. Up to now, this simply failed because of the industrial standards.[149]

It is probably almost unknown that modern LCD screens contain arsenic, but so far arsenic has been an important component in order to prevent glass defects. In 2007 already, Apple put the first monitors on the market that completely renounced at the usage of arsenic and they promise to stop the usage until the end of 2008 completely.

The public commitment to the reduction of all these substances clearly shows the balancing act that modern computer firms have to perform today. Up to now, most of the consumers did not even know which really poisonous substances are contained in the little electronic helpers. Only the general climate discussion permits now to talk about that without losing image. Thus, announcing to renounce at certain substances more and more becomes a marketing argument and promises the consumers that they can have a clear conscience when they buy the corresponding products. Modern LCD screens have long replaced the old CRT displays but this was an extremely long and stony road. For a long time, LCD displays simply were too expensive and the technical efforts for more attractiveness were enormous. Thus, with the new displays, they

---

[148] cf. http://www.apple.com/de/environment
[149] cf. http://www.apple.com/de/environment Request of June 24th, 2008

always pointed out the low radiation but never that they also contain materials like arsenic or mercury. Mercury is mainly used for the background light of LCD displays and researches for the replacement by other environment-protecting materials are still ongoing. Here, Apple promises to stop the usage "in the foreseeable future" completely. A relatively empty promise that, however, in the face of the elaborate production methods of LCD displays, is not a burden solely for Apple. In this respect, the fact that mercury is no longer used with the production of iPods, is a small but important step already. Mercury shall be replaced by a complete shift to LED background illumination. Today, in more and more products, this is considered the most environmentally friendly illuminant of the future.

A big obstacle for companies like Apple in terms of usage of environmentally friendly materials is their dependency on suppliers. Because only if all purchasers agree to buy "green" products exclusively, the supplier is able to change his production without financial effort and push forward corresponding developments. But as long as many purchasers, above all the low-cost operators, do not care about the contained materials, a massive reduction of the harmful substances is not possible. One more time, legislation is in charge here because only if the corresponding regulations are present there will not be any more excuses. From this point of view, the enormous number of regulations absolutely makes sense and finally also supports those IT companies that want to take going green seriously and support it actively.

Another step in the right direction is the establishment of corresponding guidelines of conduct a business with which Apple is very familiar. From the beginning, all sectors of the company have been strictly regulated and there were severe rules not only for software development but also for the conduct of employees and suppliers. For example, there is a clear conduct regulation for suppliers, and all those who want to work together with Apple have to observe it. Here, the most important aspect is not only environmentally friendly production but also human work standards in the supplier firms. For Apple, because of the production in Asia, working conditions have always been a topic and since the initially mentioned revealment of the Taiwanese manufacturing company, these guidelines have even been tightened. No manufacturer can be blamed for doing this out of own economical aspects, too. Because nothing would be more damaging for the image of a company like Apple as if violations of the human rights like child labor or exploitation would be mentioned in the same breath.

Not only the renouncement at toxic chemicals or massive waste of energy means a big contribution to environment friendliness but the observation of the human rights also supports the image of the industry.

With the presentation of the Apple MacBook Air at the beginning of 2008, Apple proved the seriousness of their "green" efforts. This completely new notebook cannot only praise itself of being the flattest notebook in the world but also of having consequently reduced the usage of poisonous materials. From both, the technical and the environmental point of view, it is considered a real innovation and represents the success-promising beginning of committing themselves to the topic "ecologically acceptable" completely.[150]

Most manufacturers of the computer industry already occupy with another important field. Because apart from the used assembly parts, the elaborate, cost-intensive and mostly contaminant-loaded packaging of the devices has been an equally big deficit up to now. If the former packages of all Apples represented a cost-intensive mirror of the luxurious content, in this respect Apple have consequently headed towards expediency, too. Despite that, Apple's packaging today is still beautiful, precious, and promising, but the share of harmful substances has dropped to zero. Fully recyclable, Apple seems to have managed to cover the span between packaging the customer's expensive lifestyle product adequately and to renounce at everything unnecessary at the same time. The consumers themselves, those expecting a beautiful packaging for their expensive product on the one hand, but on the other hand complain about the ecological failures of this manufacturers, also determine the degree of renunciation.

Meanwhile, the capacity of computers of being recycled has also become another important aspect. In the face of the vast amounts of computer scrap, this also belongs to the important components of the eco balance and contributions of climate protection. According to their own statements, Apple started an own recycling program already in 1994. Meanwhile, this has become effective in 93% of all the countries where Apple products are sold. If in 2006 approximately 9.5% of recycled work materials were used, this year (2008) the share shall amount to 20% already. This would correspond with the double amount compared with

---

[150] vgl. http://www.apple.com/de/environment

123

manufacturers like Dell or HP. Own return programs help Apple with this ambitious plan. Thus, today every iPod user can take his old or defect iPod back to Apples' sales points. For that, every customer even gets a discount of 10% with the purchase of a new iPod.[151]

But in the face of all these activities it might appear to be quite alien if environment protection organizations or press permanently criticize single computer manufacturers because the problems behind the demanded ecological awareness are much more complicated to dissolve than you would assume at the first glance.

Practical Tips

- *Successful brand manufacturers, specifically, have no reasons to apologize for lacking environmental activities but have to become an example!*
- *With risk preview, new regulation guidelines should be preventively realized and adopted. There are no excuses for inactivity for anybody!*
- *The climate of the public opinion can turn to the opposite if environment protection is neglected and can have existencethreatening impact!*
- *From the point of view of the users (= customers) increasingly include the question in how far investments in the environment pay for the user.*
- *Adapt the old business models and design new, more ecofriendly solutions straight through from birth to re-usage.*

Google's New Green Strategy

Garages seem to exert magical attraction to American incorporators because the Google story also starts in a Garage. Namely in Susan Wojcicki's garage who, after the purchase of her $600,000 house, decided to rent her garage for $1,700 per month to the two (then students) Larry Page and Sergey Brin in 1998. A step that she certainly has not regretted up to now because short time later both Susan and her husband were already working for the rapidly growing Google company. In spring 2007, Susan's sister Anne married Sergey Brin.[152]

---

[151] cf. http://www.apple.com/de/environment/recycling 2008
[152] cf. http://www.validome.org/blog/news/Item-173 aus 2007

124

Initially, with the incorporators, the wish for a personal, easy-to-use research system for the completely confusing Internet, was in the foreground. It pushed them both forward. That this developed into a search engine that within months trumped everything available on the market was mainly because the Google page was completely free of advertising. Especially for students who always had a rather militant attitude towards all materialistic constraints anyway, this was an important argument. From the beginning, another argument for Google was the search speed. Yahoo and Lycos as well as Altavista and AOL did not only deliver much worse search results, but needed much too long to display them. In order to understand the success and thus also the gigantic seeming company value, one has to comprehend how a search engine and a web site work.

In the beginning, all former search engine operators like the abovementioned worked with manually established databases in which die web sites were stored. In order to be able to add a web site to a search engine, a program on a computer worked through loads of possible IP addresses of the Internet back then. The IP address, comparable with a telephone number, was automatically addressed and when there was an answer in the form of an Internet page, this page was analyzed. The program read through the program code and the entire text of the page and fragmented this text into single words that were compared with a big dictionary then. A special program code part with the title "meta-tags" that had been defined from the beginning on served as a guideline in order to transfer a web site into the search engine index. The operators of the web site entered into these "metatags" all those keywords that they connected with the content of their page. The search engine programs compared these metatags with the text content found on the page and the concordant terms and were then entered into the data base of the search engine. However, this simple and initially very efficient definition reached its limits very quickly. Because if after entering one search term 100,000 answers are found, the question of every web site operator comes very quickly: How to enter the front page? The formula was simple: the more metatags were found in the content of the page, too, the higher the page rose in the listings of the search engines. If the domain name was also meaningful in addition, there was nothing left in the way of a "first page" position.[153]

---

[153] cf. Search machine optimization by 2007

But more and more Internet users were annoyed with especially this proceeding because the first pages ware increasingly packed with completely irrelevant contents, mostly launched arbitrarily with many tricks launched by predominantly sex-oriented web page providers.

The wish for a more simple research system that quickly delivers really relevant hits in addition became a fix idea for our two students. It turned out very quickly that once again the really important things were very simple. You only had to differentiate between important and unimportant pages. The patented PageRanking principle, that made an evaluation of the found web sites, was based exactly on this principle. In order to integrate this system fully automatically, one assumed that a page belonged to the important and useful sites only if particularly high number of other sites refer to this one site in the form of links (references). This simple solution suddenly increased the efficiency of the search by a multiple because all the randomly placed metatags lost their importance as long as a site was not also addressed by corresponding links to the respective topic.[154]

Especially in times where Internet access mainly took place via modems, time was really money. As said, it took just a few months and the little Google idea turned into a global insider tip. The rest of the Google story is history already and Google themselves did not only manage to enter the history books but the word "to google" was also officially included into the Duden in 2004, as recognized term for the search on the Internet via the Google search engine.

Of course, Google's success is based on many more factors than just the page ranking method.[155] On the one hand, this has permanently been further developed and, above that, there are many other factors contributing to the success of the search results of the growing company Google, of course. But the lack of advertising of Google's web site and the quality of their search results still are their best references.

Especially in the times of the big dot-com bubble, Google very quickly became the unchallenged market leader. Of course, Google also earned money. In the beginning, they "just" licensed the Google search technology to other search engine operators. But nowadays the Google empire is based on an abundance of income sources. In the year 2004,

---

[154] Search machine optimization by the example of Google by Philipp Wiedmaier 2007

[155] cf. Company data www.google.com 2008

Google announced a turnover of 3.2 billion dollars and put 2.5 billion dollars of costs against that. This sum alone shows that the effort the group has to run now is enormous. Not only have the 16,608 employees (as of February 2008) justified such high expenses. In the fore there is the gigantic technical effort.[156]

It is exactly this problem that pushes forward all the IT companies today. In order to understand that, the technology and the problems arising thereof have to be inspected a bit closer.

In their search engine, Google have stored more than 8 billion Internet pages today. Each of these Internet pages needs about 10 kilobytes in the Google database, corresponding with an amount of data of 10,000 characters according to the universally valid definition. Every web site is completely indexed. This means that the search terms of each web site physically exist twice at least. In order to master this gigantic flood of data, Google use about 36 data processing centers today, with a total equipment of approximately 60,000 computers and a total storage capacity of about 50 petabytes. One petabyte corresponds to 100,000 gigabytes![157]

Furthermore, there is an uncountable amount of PCs in the subsidiaries so that one can assume that meanwhile Google are operating the biggest connected data processing center in the world. Bearing in mind that each of the employed computers consumes power, the tip of the iceberg becomes obvious already. But these enormous data processing centers also have another, completely different problem. Every computer consumes power, at Google many computers on a small area consume approximately 1,600 W power per square meter and, of course, they produce an enormous amount of waste heat. This means that they have to be cooled. So the biggest cost unit in Google's balance of success clearly is power consumption. Therefore, it is no wonder that the topic environment and ecology becomes more and more interesting for Google, also from the ecological point of view.

In September 2007, the daily newspaper "Die Welt" already reported in detail that the CO_2 output of the data network exceeds the entire global air traffic already today. The Internet with all its facets, information and games as a climate killer? Without a doubt, because everybody today who loves to behave in an ecological and environmentally conscious way but

---

[156] cf. Company data www.google.com 2008
[157] cf. Archive Heise Verlag 2006 160

plays on the Internet at night in order to indulge in his second identity in "Second Life", for example, directly had to be accused as an environment killer. For example, clever researchers have found out that every virtual identity in "Second Life" annually produces 1.17 tons of CO_2. Even if from the currently about 11 million members 50% played actively only, the result is an enormous additional amount. The accruing need to act for all manufacturers of the IT industry finally leads to all producers in the world thinking about the hunger of energy and the materials that are used in the IT systems today.

Before the companies are accused in public, more and more often they intervene themselves and present, not without pride, their predominant objectives, namely the reduction of power consumption and the attentiveness in terms of wasting our global resources. In the year 2005, the total power consumption of the Internet still corresponded with a production output of 20 big one thousand megawatt power plants, at least that is what the Freiburg Eco Institute claims. For Google a problem that they are already willingly facing. They openly admit acting massively against climate warming and they also demonstrate how that works. Research funds of approximately 100 million dollars only marked the beginning. They research and invest in clean energy. A clever tactic because the enormous power consumption can only be reduced with new, energy-saving hardware and they cannot be actively influenced. Like all the others, in this area they depend on the chip producers and the manufacturers of computers. In the beginning, they specialized in the use of solar energy and geothermal energy but meanwhile their targets have become more and more ambitious. Which, of course, also has the reason that Google realized very quickly: We can make money with that. "We want to produce power at lower cost than carbon power." Google founder Larry Page said in an interview. If Google succeeds in doing that, these investments are not longer borne by conviction but by purely economical factors.

A first step in this direction was made in the year 2006 already. Because, at the same time, the answer to the question of energy saving is the answer to the question "How do we reduce our costs?" Thus, the considerations on power saving rather quickly became an ambitious project that they wanted to test in peace at the company's headquarters. For a company like Google, the main interest is the investment of money in the most reasonable way. Therefore, numerous plans were checked for their feasibility in order to give the starting signal for an enormous solar project then.

Already today, Google produce 1.6 megawatts of solar power on their campus in Mountainview in California. The entire campus, every roof and even the car parks are peppered with solar cells. This way, they do not only produce low-priced power but also prevent the cars from heating up due to the solar-roofed car parks.[158]

But this solar project is only the beginning. As soon as safe information on costs and benefits is available, the locations of the other Google dependencies will probably follow soon. Especially the data processing centers are predestinated for alternative energy sources another reason why Google, apart from solar energy, also let research geothermal energy. Because the ideal case was achieved if they succeeded in catching the waste heat from the computers and use it again. Every user who ever spent a longer period of time with his laptop on the knees knows how much heat even such a small computer can produce. 1,600 watts energy consumption on one square meter is sufficient to provide a living room with comfortable temperature. At present, these data processing centers still have to be cooled with much effort and the energy used just for that is unquestionably gigantic. If they would succeed in catching this heat and put it back into the network as energy, the cost balance could be relieved by 2-digit percentage points.

But the company with the high sympathy bonus goes even further and shows everybody that it starts with little things.

All of the company cars are based on Toyota Prius models that are principally equipped with a hybrid system. In the USA, hybrid vehicles are the big hit, here in Europe they are denounced as being exotic. The Prius is on the right way. Its drive system consists of a normal gasoline engine and an additional electric engine. This is fed by the gasoline engine by a generator and charges the connected batteries. At the same time, with each breaking the "discharged" energy is caught and used to fill up the accumulators of the electric engine. The Prius cannot only be driven in pure accumulator operation but also in mixed operation. By means of a sophisticated engine control system, the electric engine is used to mitigate rotation peaks and to keep the consumption curve low this way.

---

[158]   cf.

http://www.google.de/intl/de/corporate/green/energy/index.html 2008

Google's fleet goes even further by making most of the passenger cars plug-in capable. This means, that the accumulators were designed to be exchangeable and rechargeable and do not only concentrate on reusing breaking and engine power. Thus, employment as a purely electrical vehicle is also possible which is of high importance, especially in California. One of the most important effects of this measure is the fact that such cars become cheaper and cheaper with increasing age simply because energy becomes increasingly cleaner. With a CO_2 output reduced by 66%, this is probably the right approach. So Google consequently hit the right path. In any case, Google are not endangered of being accused of wasting energy on their shareholder meetings. In the objectives of the giant, even more ambitious projects can be found that exceed the normal dimension of ecological thinking of an IT company by far.[159]

Apart from the enormous wear of computer hardware, the global operation of their gigantic data processing centers also leads to big logistical problems. Servicing and maintaining a data processing center with several thousands of PCs without causing system failures is generally seen as a bit of magic. Google assessed that rightly at the beginning already and designed their computers much more intelligently than generally practiced. Thus, in a normal Google data processing center, between three and five PCs break down per day and have to be repaired or replaced. Furthermore, the demand for increasing performance has to be reconsidered daily. Not really astounding considering the flood of data and the growth of the Internet. The amount of information on the Internet doubles every four months. Consequently, there is enormous additional need for computers and staff. Today, Google's computers are so perfectly controlled that a breakdown is recognized completely automatically, analyzed and fixed. All that is made possible by Google's own software that controls, monitors and, if necessary, replaces every computer. Since all the data are always copied and saved several times, it is possible to exchange a broken computer simply by automatically switching on a new, up to then unused PC and controlling it via intelligent software technology. This PC takes the tasks of the old, defect computer then. The defect computer is switched off, the service personnel get a corresponding message and with the information the computer is either repaired or directly exchanged by a new one. With this highly efficient system they do not only achieve failure optimization but also save

---

[159] cf. http://www.google.org 2008

extreme amounts of energy due to the low number of employees and the timely deactivation of defect systems. This way, several millions of dollars are saved in the data processing centers alone every year.

Google's next coup is in the pipeline already and represents the most ambitious project the software giant can present. The vehicle to grid technology with which passenger cars cannot only produce their energy themselves to the greatest possible extent but also can put surplus energy back into the grid. California, in special, is known for its bad and frequently insufficient power supply. The idea to put temporarily surplus energy from the hybrid cars back into the grid, quasi to lend it, makes sense from this aspect in the first place. The details of this technology are not yet public but at this point you can safely say, too: Google are on the right way.

Practical Tips

- *The environmental consequences of all activities, also of "googling the Internet", mainly have to be regarded as a matter of the total responsibility of a company for securing the future in a sustainable way.*
- *Google's efforts for green energy supply prove that every company can contribute a big portion to the green business shift beyond their original business field.*
- *Everybody has to use the natural resources a hundred times better than today!*
- *From Google's permanent expansion of the product range, one thing can be derived in the first place: more than ever, service and handling quality are required in their entity instead of pure product responsibility to the successful sale!*
- *Profits should also be put in the maintenance and the expansion of the natural capital because they bring unexpected advantages in competition!*

Cisco's Green Dream

Whoever talks about the Internet, Silicon Valley or also about green IT today will hardly get around the company Cisco.

In 1984, Cisco was founded by the Stanford University scientist couple Leonard Bosack and Sandy Lerner with the objective to simplify the networking of computers. Exceptionally not in a garage but in their living room the two invented the technology with which Cisco grew up to be the most important and biggest global provider of network technology. In 1987, in the face of the growing competition, the couple decided to take up venture capital for the expansion of the company. But more than 70 venture capital providers simply declared them insane and missed the offered opportunity completely. Only Don Valentine, founder and shareholder of Sequoia Systems, realized how much profit could be made with network technologies in the future and advanced the couple capital amounting to 2.5 million dollars. With Apple and Oracle he had had the right sense already and his intuition was also right in this case. He provided the company with commercially-oriented managers and ensured clear structuring of the firm. The booming personal computer market also made the demand for networking rise rapidly and thus Cisco could increase their turnover from 1.5 million dollars to 27.5 million dollars between 1987 and 1989.[160]

In 1993, Cisco decided to expand their services and to concentrate not only on the business with routers. So-called end-to-end solutions, i.e. complete networks, were intended to guarantee Cisco a marketleading position with the networking of the upcoming Internet. The Internet boom in the middle of the 90s helped Cisco to increase their stock market value by 1.366% and made them the most precious company in the world for a short period of time.[161]

The considerable participation in the enforcement of a standard for data transfer on the Internet was one of the most important performances of their founding years. Here, the essential point is that it has to be made sure that all data that are sent to or via the Internet reach the recipient unchanged. This has always been achieved, to put it simple, by splitting up the information to be sent into data packets. Each of these data packets receives additional information about the sender, the recipient, data size and a check sum that is calculated from the binary codes of the sent characters. This data head is sent together with the data packet and the check sum is calculated again after receipt of the data. If these two values are the same, transfer was successful. But this transport control is only a small part of the Internet protocol, abbreviated IP. An essential component is the dispatch from the sender to the recipient. In order to reach a recipient on the Internet directly, one needs a clear mapping of every computer. This takes place in the form of IP numbers and a so-

[160] cf. Cisco Company Profile www.cisco.com 2008
[161] cf. boerseonline.de 2004

called subnet number. This form of numbering and classification resulted in every computer in the global network being able to be addressed directly. A company with 100 computers receives a circle of numbers with a subnet number range and can spread these computers all over the world. If you want to address and connect the computer directly, IP and subnet number are sufficient to establish a clearly defined connection.[162] The whole system is similar to the telephone system where we work with prefix and dial numbers. The determination of this standard is mostly attributed to the efforts made by Cisco. But from the foundation of the company on, the development and construction of intelligent networks on the Internet has been their most important task. For example, most of the broadband connections, so-called backbones, are controlled by Cisco routers today. Routers work as a kind of switching center when data is transferred via a network. With the big telecommunication companies like Deutsche Telekom, for example, the backbone describes those places where a great number of data cables come together and are further dispensed then.[163] Here, the routers act as a kind of track switch. Data that sent via the network are checked by routers whether they are to be forwarded or get access to the data lines behind the router. Meanwhile, routers have become indispensable helpers, too. They control data transfer, a task about which today users do not have to worry about any longer because it simply works and does not need to be serviced. Once put into operation and set to the respective IP number, these little aids render their services without even being noticed. Without Cisco's routers, the speed that can be realized in the global network today would be unimaginable because in these unimpressive boxes, apart from sturdy hardware, there also is a great portion of intelligence, the Internetwork-Operating-System (IOS). This software, originally invented by Bill Yeager already in 1980, was licensed when Cisco was founded, and has been continuously developed to this today as you can read in Cisco's story of success. [164] This software for routers and switches permits the communication of networks independently from the used network protocols. Up to the point when switches became affordable for companies, computers normally were connected with each other in series connections. Of course, this lead to extreme losses in speed because partly

[162] cf. http://www.ieee.org/portal/site 1999
[163] cf. www.wikipedia.com search Router 2004
[164] cf. www.cisco.de 2008

the distance a data packet had to cover could be very long. In addition, every computer in the network had to check whether the data were sent to it and then either forward or catch them. Today's networks mostly have a star distribution. A switch/router is connected with a central computer (server) and from this respectively one line leads to the single computers in the network. The IOS in the switch decides where the data goes. This allows for absolutely targeted dispatch. This is an inestimable advantage for speed and especially data security. It reduces the possibility of data interception by a manifold.

Thus, Cisco have been playing an outstanding pioneering role from the beginning of the Internet on. The company permanently expands this leading position and thus Cisco is the unchallenged number one if it is about the topic network and Internet still today.

In the year 1985, Cisco, as the first company, built in the above described data packet filters into their routers. These represent the basis for all the firewalls used today because a firewall does not do anything else but checking whether the data are really destined for the computer(s) connected behind the router.

As the head of this quiet giant with 61,000 staff worldwide, John T. Chambers has been acting since 1995. In 2007 Cisco had the highest turnover ever. The company produced a turnover of 34.9 billion dollars and could report profit amounting to 7.8 billion dollars. [165] In the beginning of the 90s, the mass product router already considerably reduced the efforts for the establishment of a network. From the point of view of environment technology, above all, the PVC coated cables play a crucial role in networks. Since all networks and their components are regulated by norms in order to guarantee trouble-free communication amongst each other, in the course of the years more and more functions and devices have been connected with each other with one and the same cable. In the area of research this can be attributed to Cisco's pioneering role to a great extent. In the 90s already, network cables for computers and telephone were the same. Thus the efforts for wiring could be drastically reduced for the first time. Since 1963, the standardization of protocols and specifications has been the liability of the IEEE (Institute of Electrical and Electronics Engineers), with 380,000 thousand members the biggest professional association of engineers.[166] In 1997, the IEEE also

[165] cf. Company's Business Data of Cisco Germany
[166] cf. www.ieee.org 2000

passed the first version of the IEEE 802.11 and thus defined the basis for the back then newly upcoming WLAN (Wireless Local Network). Since their foundation, Cisco has been considerably participating in the developments and definitions. With the bundling of information carriers like computers and telephones in one cable, the requirements at routers and switches increased too. This opened completely new fields of application to Cisco. Cisco was the first provider developing a complete strategy for the integration of data, speech and video within the same network infrastructure and thus paved the way for multimedia applications like video conferencing and unified messaging. With new systems like content delivery networking, a network architecture for faster transfer of contents, Cisco SAFE, the strategy for safe E-business, the IP+optical strategy for the integration of IP and optical networks as well as with the wireless products for the wireless connection of companies, the network specialist is close at the pulse of the time. Technological and strategic alliances with partner companies ensure perfect cooperation of the products and excellent quality.[167] With all these products the market for trouble-free connection of multi-media services like e-mail, video conferences, telephone transmission, image transfer and the connection with film data was opened.

All these developments are important cornerstones for energy saving and climate protection. Because today's global network would not be possible without these technologies. Just from the WLAN routers that have become a mass product, completely new possibilities and freedom have resulted for the end user helping him to save devices, raw materials and thus energy to an increasing extent. Today, establishing an intelligent home network for telephone, computer, music, radio, film and TV is no longer magic and enters the private households more and more frequently. If the private individual has avoided pulling cables because it was complicated and expensive, completely new possibilities have opened since the introduction of WLAN. This does not only save costs for cables and devices but thanks to the technology are getting easier, the jungle of electronic devices in households becomes smaller and smaller. If formerly telephone, answering machine, radio, TV, computer, video recorder or DVD player, CD player, satellite receiver plus amplifier were necessary to cover all the multi-media services, partly even two- or three-fold, thanks to the WLAN technology this can be reduced to the central

---

[167] cf. Cisco Corp. Company profile www.cisco.com

employment of an Internet-capable computer with satellite card, a telephone, a TV and amplifier. The computer takes every desired radio channel of the world into the living room; the integrated satellite card provides trouble-free TV reception and records every broadcast, if desired. In addition, it also is the storage place for the domestic music collection and can transmit it comfortably, in the same way as images and telephone, to every room of the flat via WLAN. Nowadays, the telephone mostly connects free of charge, also via the Internet, the most far-flung corner of the Earth with the domestic living room and in case of absence the computer records incoming calls simple, quick and for free no additional devices, no tapes, CD's, DVDs or cassettes. This saves power and reduces CO_2 emission because the then needed cable spaghetti with its entire heat output alone played a considerable role in our energy household in summary.[168]

Today, this nice new multi-media world connects us, as a matter of course, with all the media worldwide. But again this is just the beginning of the next step to global networking that offers even more different saving potentials in addition. The consequences of climate change, environment protection and energy saving enter the private households. At present still just with new buildings but surely also more and more in flats, the network connection of all power consumers via the Internet will play an increasing role. Here, the most important factor still is the heating of a house. Up to now, intelligent systems were designed to reduce or increase the temperature at defined points of time. But this shall become a part of the past soon. As soon as all power consumers are intelligently interconnected, which means that they can communicate with each other, it will be possible to break out of this up to now rigid temperature control. In order to realize that, routers are also necessary which are able to communicate with a heating system or a TV set, too.

The nice new future, once adjusted to heating, can look like that then: via the power circuit and a centrally positioned router, all power-consuming devices communicate with the domestic PC. In the computer, peak times or temperature reduction or increase are predefined. In case the family comes back home earlier than fixed in the scheme, they can give the order to raise the temperature earlier via mobile phone. This can already be technically realized. But the intelligent house of the future even goes further than that. If normally temperature is lowered at 11 p.m.

---

[168] cf. podcasts cisco Expo April 2008

because the family is already sleeping then, the system will then be able to recognize whether, for example, TV is still running and that it would thus be too early to make the family freeze just because they are still watching a movie. In the same way, room temperatures could be controlled individually by means of simple scanning with body heat sensors. Thus, suitable temperature can be selected for each individual room. Electrical blinds depending on the position of the sun, coupled with the habit profile of the residents, automatic time control for the washing machine so that you can take the ready washing out of the device when you come back home, activating the oven via mobile phone or initiating the recording of a TV broadcast via the mobile, the possibilities of saving energy in this area are great and the technical possibilities have not been exhausted by far. But here, too, these innovations only work if the entire networking can be realized cheaply and with low effort. Elaborate, wired home networks are already offered but due to the high costs rarely find their way to the user.

Regarding the topic "House of the Future" Cisco themselves write: "The possibility that soon houses and their technical devices can be completely connected and controlled via one single remote control have not been dreams of the future for a long time already. Apart from electricity, gas and water, the Internet will become a part of the basic supply of private households within a short period of time. Professional all-day life, family organization and housekeeping will become much easier by that. The central control of heating system and illumination, video monitoring and image telephone, online banking, multimedia in the living room, administrative matters done via the Internet and download of music files are the first step of a kind of global networking the vision of which was the impulse for the foundation of Cisco. Quality of life, leisure time habits and the way of learning and working will permanently improve with the Internet revolution. With the realization of all the possibilities arising from the Internet economy, Cisco systems will play the leading role and thus continue writing their story of success." Here they have recognized the possibilities and the needs at an early stage, too.[169]

On the part of the company it is primarily about computer networking and, even if not new, video conferencing that is gaining importance only now. On their company platform, Cisco expressly confess

---

[169] cf. http://www.cisco.com/web/DE/uinfo/erfolg_home.html

to green IT and see starting points for massive energy savings, especially in the field of video conferencing. For example, the Media-Saturn GmbH announced at this year's Cisco Expo in Berlin that they were able to reduce traveling costs by 30 to 40% due to the employment of 16 TelePresence systems.[170] By means of this form of communication, air trips to Russia alone could be reduced by more than 50% with this form of communication. The company prognoses the re-financing of the purchased systems after 1.5 years already. The topic centralization gains completely new importance due to today's modern forms of video conferencing systems. For example, UniCredit with 170,000 staff worldwide announced at the Cisco Expo that they will save about five million kilowatt-hours of IT-related energy due to the ongoing establishment of a completely interconnected IT architecture. This corresponds with savings of 89%.[171]

Thanks to the Internet and, above all, thanks to the area-wide available broadband connection, participants in a video conference can be faded-in in life-size and pin sharp via corresponding monitors or screens in real time. Body language and gesture, the most important elements in conferences, are transmitted closely to the other participants and data and facts, e.g. from a computer, can be faded into the conference image at any time. Here, language and image quality are so high that after a short period of time they make the participants forget that it is "just" a virtual conference. Such time and thus energy saving solutions are made possible by the intelligent usage of the Internet as the basis for the exchange of data. If in the beginning just text information could be transmitted, nowadays any kind of information is sent in real time, i.e. without time delay, around the globe.

Based on all these new technologies and, above all, the acceptance by the companies and users, the Internet becomes more and more the pioneer in solving the present energy and climate problems, simply by the fact that services can be bundled and "real" traffic from A to B can be replaced by the virtual traffic.

Practical Tips

---

[170] the modern form of video-conferencing
[171] cf. podcasts cisco Expo April 2008

- *Innovative technology applications have to correspond with the upcoming environment and climate protection requirements to a much larger extent!*
- *The technological realizations of networking solutions correspond with the biological-natural models to a special extent and should be used for environment and climate protection in a more consequent way.*
- *From the point of view of costs as well as environment, more and more companies search more consequent usage possibilities of the networking potential of modern IT and e.g. increase the amount of home office jobs.*
- *Further changes of the basic technologies for the creation of energy efficiency and wealth are required in all companies and households by expanding networking.*

Making More of Green Stuff: The IMEAS Formula of Success

Which general conclusions can be drawn from going green of the companies from Silicon Valley and the above described case studies? First, it becomes clear that the turn to completely different conduct with the natural capital takes place much faster than expected by most of the people. Over years, especially the USA have been lagging behind the international agreements for more climate protection and blocked new state regulations wherever they could. This inverses at a speed that internationally will be a big surprise for some countries and many companies. The political following wind is provided by Barack Obama's mantra-like citation: "Yes, we can." Likewise the first pre-election decision for a black candidate for presidency is already unanimously classified as "historic" by all the media today, a historic change in usage of the natural capital and in the awareness of the Americans pro environment and climate protection is happening now not really perceived by many people yet.

The formula of success is very easy:

	Ideas	For "going green" or other innovations
+	**Money**	Venture capital or other forms of financing
+	**Experience**	Experience, training
+	**Activity**	Maker's qualities, energy,

		entrepreneurship
=	**Sustainable Success**	Long lasting success

The acronym of the first five letters of these to be connected core requirements results in IMEAS, a formula of success after which many new foundations managed to break through and will be followed by many others. Without sustainable ideas one will not find capital providers who, in turn, bet on the experience in the market and the technical area, on the skills and the active maker's qualities of the founders for sustainable success. The case studies from the previous sections prove that very clearly and are all based on this connection of sustainable ideas that seems to be so easy, startup capital, know-how, entrepreneur's commitment with absolute will of success, even against the strongest resistance.

The following table shows further examples:

Table 8: IMEAS examples

Idea	Money	Experience	Acting Entrepreneur	Success
Graphical Application Software	VC	Carnegie Mellon University	Charles Geschke and John Warnock	Adobe Systems
Medicaments Delivery Technologies	VC	University of Montevideo, University of Rochester	Alejandro Zaffaroni	ALZA
Integrated Circuits (Inventor)	$2.5 m VC	Massachusetts Institute of Technology	Robert N. Noyce	AMD; Intel (Co-founder)
PersonalComputer/ HomeComputer	VC	ElectronicsExpert Knowledge	Steve Jobs and Steve Wozniak	Apple Computers

Atari Game	$500	Utah and Stanford University	Nolan Bushnell	Atari Games and Computers
Microcontrollers (Chips)	$23,000	Unknown	George Perlegos	Atmel
Internet Router	VC	Stanford University	Sandy Lerner and Leonard Bosack	Cisco
Transistoren	VC	Electronics Engineer	William Shockley	Fairchild Semiconductor
Triode (Audion)	$250	Yale University	Lee De Forest and Cyril Elwell	Federal Telegraph Company, Palo Alto
Publication of legal Documents on the Internet	VC	Standford University	Martin Roscheisen et al.	Findlaw (1. Company Foundation by Roscheisen)
Image Processing for Laymen	VC	California State University	L. George Klaus	Frame Technology
Audio oscillator	$538	Stanford University	William Redington Hewlett and David Packard	Hewlett & Packard
Hard Drives		University of	Reynold	IBM/General Products

Data Storage		Minnesota	Johnson	Division (GPD)
Moore's Law (Doubling of the amount of electron. assembly parts in an integrated circuit every 24 months)	$2,500,00 0 VC	University of Berkely and California Institute of Technology	Gordon E. Moore	Intel (Semicond uctor industry) (Co-founder)
Integrated Control Systems		Carnegie Mellon University	Nathan Zommer	Ixys
Roll Film	$40,000	Evening Courses at Commercial School	George Eastman	Kodak
Vacuum Pipe		Stanford University	Charles Litton	Litton Engineerin g Laboratorie s
Solar Collector on Pressure Basis	$48,000,0 00	Stanford University	Martin Roscheisen	Nanosolar
InternetBrowse r (Browser Mosaic)	VC	Illinois University	Marc Andreessen	Netscape Communic ation Corporatio n amongst others
Electronic Trade	Unknown	Columbia	Harry Saal	Network General

		University		
IC Technology (Processors for game consoles)	Unknown	Scientists and Electrical Engineers from Fairchild	David Allisin, David James, Lionel Kattner and Mark Weisenberg	Philipps Semiconductors (Signetics)
Animations and Films	Unknown	Unknown	Steve Jobs	Pixar-Studios; then Walt Disney Studios
Scalable Chip Technologies	VC	Stanford University	Michael Farmwald and Mark Horowitz	Rambus Inc.
Complex, Stateof-the –art projects (Construction of the neo computer firms)	Unknown	Builder	Onslow Rudolph	Rudolph & Stetten
PC "Unix OS"	Unknown	Stanford University	Andreas von Bechtolsheim	Sun Microsystems
Klystron Tube/Radar	Unknown	Stanford University	Russel and Sigurd Varian	Varian Associates (Co-founder)
Microwave	Unknown	Physics	William	Varian

Electronics (Klystron)		Professorship at Stanford University	Webster Hansen	Associates (Co-founder)
Elektron Tube (Helitron)	Unknown	Stanford University (electrical engineering professor)	Dean A. Watkins	Watkins-Johnson Company
Digital Circuits	Unknown	Stanford University	Bill Jarvis, Peter Lacy and Duane Dunwoodie	Wiltron Company
Video Portal	VC	Indiana University, Illinois University, Stanford University	Chad Hurley, Steve Chen and Jawed Karim	YouTube

Source: John McLaughlin, The Making of Silicon Valley. A One Hundred Year Renaissance, Published by Santa Clara Valley Historical Association, First Edition, Palo Alto 1995 ;John McLaughlin, Leigh Weimers, Ward Winslow, Silicon Valley: 110 Year Renaissance. Published by Santa Clara Valley Historical Association, Second Edition, Palo Alto 2008

Although in his guidebook "The Silicon Valley Way" (Discover the Secrets of America's Fastest Growing Companies, Prima Publishing, Rocklin 1997) Elton B. Sherwin names seven questions of success, in principle they can all be attributed to the above stated core questions of the IMEAS formula.

According to Sherwin, the seven core questions of every business plan comprise:
- What is the product?
- Who are the customers?
- Who will sell it?

- How many people will sell it?
- How much will it cost to design and build it?
- How high will the selling price be?
- When will the business leave the loss area?

Regarding that, W.K Müller-Scholz states in "Inside Silicon Valley" that every new founder has to make all efforts to formulate his business idea as simply as possible in one sentence: "The concept of the one who needs more space is too complicated. He will not only have difficulties in finding investors or partners with the business idea. Later, on the market, an unclear concept will not have a chance, too."[172]

For the business plan the following construction is said to promise success:

Cover sheet (project name, author, address, telephone, e-mail address, date)

1. Content
2. Financing Plan
3. Product/Service
4. Market/Customer
5. Marketing
6. Competitors
7. Management Team
8. Partner(s)
9. Time Schedule
10. Appendix, e.g. photos
11. Executive Summary (as in introduction)

In all, 30 pages should not be exceeded. In many cases the pressure to make it short is considered as decisive for success.

On the other hand, practical experience shows that especially that often is hard to do. One can understand that at the example of the market for bioplastics that is just globally emerging under the impression of the high mineral oil prices.

The market for bioplastics is enormous and there is a variety of new application areas from packaging materials to work materials with new and improved usage qualities. In the medium and in the long term there are excellent opportunities in production and processing of chemical

---

[172] Ibid., p. 67

products of renewable raw materials to sustainably develop the traditionally strong farming sector of the USA together with the chemical industry. Compared with the usage potentials estimated for 2010 by the expert work group "Renewable Raw Materials" from the EU Commission, with polymers only 5% are being used in the EU at present.[173] Renewable raw materials offer considerable innovation potential, now and for the post mineral oil era. In the medium term it can be assumed that the prices for bio and mass plastics will approach each other, especially considering that there are already open speculations that the price for mineral oil will increase to 150 to 170 US dollars per barrel (159 liters) and furthermore up to 250 US dollars in the medium term. Connected with that is the expansion of the production capacities while the common plastics will continue to become more expensive due to the increasing oil price. Compared with the year 2002, a price increase of 40% could be noticed until 2005 already.[174]

Experts from European Bioplastics are of the opinion that bio plastics could reach a market share of about 2% (approx. 1 million t) until 2010 and of 10% (approx. 4 million t) until 2020.[175] The "RRM Working Group Industry" that shall work out the political frame conditions for the "European Climate Change Programme" got similar results.

There are huge information deficits in end customer circles as well as amongst plastic manufacturers. Estimates assume that companies are at a five to ten-year old information level and thus are skeptical towards the technical performance profile and processing qualities of bioplastics. Frequently, this information gap towards novelties is a crucial innovation obstacle and becomes blatantly clear with the example of bioplastics. The positive thing is, that bioplastics can be processed with almost all common machines with just a few modifications. Negative experience from the last years can be smoothed out by increasing improvements.

With bioplastics, in the first place, there is a deficit in marketing measures and often enough there is faulty information. Frequently, the startups neither have the personnel nor the economic equipment to initiate a corresponding demand attraction. In general, up to now there are merely market researches regarding the consumer acceptance of bio

---

[173] cf. Memorandum Renewable raw materials, 10250/04, Brussels, June 17, 2004
[174] European Plastics, 2005
[175] cf. Käb 2005

plastics. When can the general shift of mineral oil based plastics to those made of renewable raw materials be expected under these conditions?

Especially the venture capitalists from Silicon Valley and worldwide had a convincing answer to this question.

The future is clean-green that is where chemical industry, politics and science are of one opinion. All leading chemical companies see biotechnology as the key technology for the 21st century. Main reason for that are the increasing mineral oil prices. Mineral oil is not only the most important energy carrier but also the most frequently used chemical raw material. The companies want to free themselves from this dependence. They bet on renewable raw materials, i.e. plants, as carbon source.

By 2030, one quarter of the organic basic materials is to be produced from renewable raw materials this is the ambitious objective of the American chemical industry. In Germany, only 10% stem from regenerative sources until now.[176]

The development of bioplastics is in full swing. Partly, high technical quantities are already used in packaging industry or die cast parts of bio plastics are employed for the automotive industry.

The development of bio refineries will be "the key for the access to integrated production of food, feedstuff, chemicals, work materials, commodities and combustibles on the basis of biological raw materials of the future."[177]

Bioplastics can be processed to a vast quantity of products with all common methods of plastic technology. Here, the process parameters of the processing machine have to be adapted to the specifications of the respective polymer. This can normally be done without higher effort. Today, machine and plant constructors also occupy with the processing of bioplastics in their plants. They are searching for optimization possibilities. Therefore, several plant manufacturers have organized themselves in the association European Bioplastics. With support by the EU Commission, the development of a European Platform for Sustainable Chemistry (SusChem) was pushed on that initiated the European Associations of the Chemical and Bioindustry CEFIC[178] and EuropaBio (European Association for Bioindustries, www.europabio.org). The GDCh

---

176

http://www.scinexx.de/index.php?cmd=focus_detail&f_id=337&rang=1
[177] National Research Council, USA, 2000,19
[178] European Chemical Industry Council, www.cefic.be

(Association of German Chemists, www.gdch.de) fixed the establishment of industrial bioprocesses in their Strategic Search Agenda (SRA). Amongst others, bio refineries are made a topic as new refineries for the efficient usage of biomass.[179] In a vision of this platform it is assumed that the share of renewable raw materials could amount to up to 30% of the raw material basis of the chemical industry until the year 2025. [180]

On an international level, the USA and Canada have a pioneering role. In the topic field »Biobased Products and Biorefineries« they have established clearly structured objectives and support guidelines. With collaboration of the local chemical industry, the USA aim at a market share of 45% until the year 2030. In other countries, the materialistic usage is frequently listed within superior categories like "Renewable Energy" or "Green House Gas Emission Reduction" (GHG) (according to Biorefinery 2006). In the USA, the National Research Council (NRC) expects that until 2020 about 25% of the organic base materials (base value 1994) and 10% of the oils and fuels that are presently based on fossil raw materials could be changed to a biological raw material basis and predominantly be produced by means of biorefinery technologies.[181] It is expected that thus in future the national own needs for organic base materials of the USA can be covered up to 90% and the need for organic oils and fuels up to 50%. [182] The objectives are ambitious because biorefineries still are in an early research and development stadium. The industry-controlled "Biomass Technical Advisory Committee" (BTAC) has concretized realization goals for the areas bioenergy, biofuels and bioproducts in a graduated scheme until the year 2030.

In all, it becomes obvious that plastics of renewable raw materials offer great innovation potential but demand the reestablishment of R/D capacities, investments in new and modified plants as well as considerable market introduction efforts with accompanying new norms, media campaigns and legal frame conditions for their realization.

Substituting single petrochemical-based basic materials with already existing applications, i.e. markets by chemically/application-technically "similar" substances on the basis of renewable raw materials, promises relatively "quick" success (e.g. sunflower-based polyol for the production

---

[179] Biorefinery 2006b, S. 8; www.suschem.org
[180] Biorefinery 2006
[181] Biorefinery 2006
[182] NRC et al. 2000, according Biorefinery 2006b

of polyurethane foams). However, in parallel the entire change of the petrochemical-oriented organic chemistry on family tree suitable substances of renewable raw materials has to be pressed ahead *already now*. The most important factor for the intensity with which the chemical industry will occupy with renewable raw materials for the production of chemical raw materials is at present as well as in the medium and short term the development of the oil price.

This short excursion to the innovation field of bioplastics alone shows that there are many big new possibilities to integrate green innovations successfully on the market. But this development must never be at the expense of the nutrition basis of humans but has to use the manifold other innovative possibilities of nature. First hunger revolts and uproars show how heavily this global balance can be destroyed if sweet corn or other foodstuff has to be bought in order to produce biofuel from it. The chance of going green has to be used in general and taken by company founders in the whole world.

Practical Tips

- *Successful company founders in the whole world use the IMEAS formula. Here, the practical energy, i.e. the practical pro environment activity, becomes more and more important!*
- *It always pays to practically evaluate and compare the activity ratio pro environment and climate protection. For that, even simple methods and instrument like the energy savings per work place or department are sufficient!*
- *In order to increase the activities for more green-tech, even little promoting financings pay!*
- *Successful company founders train persuading capital providers by means of clear, simple models instead of comprehensive charts and presentations!*
- *Everybody is well-advised to attentively watch the emergence of startups and their story of success in his business field!*

4. Entrepreneurship following Silicon Valley Pattern

For Green Tech Innovations from Childhood On

The "Tech Challenge" is one of the outstanding annual education events in the USA. Like "Jugend forscht" in Germany, young people work in small teams in order to solve the real problems of our times with new technologies and fun. The Tech gives all young people in Silicon Valley the feeling of having the chance to produce big inventions. The objective of this event, to motivate and inspire to puzzle and to fiddle about, was achieved in this region with this event. However, in contrast to our practices, not only the best solutions are awarded a price but also the most spectacular flops. One can also learn from mistakes and thus build up a corresponding foundation culture on time. The Tech Challenge is open for all children from the 5th to the 12th year. In spring 2008, the Tech Challenge addressed the topic clean drinking water. Since one out of two people do not have permanent access to drinking water, the task was to design a device that is driven by the river in order to correspondingly provide water for the water tanks of a village. Here, prices for the best overall solution, for the way of operating but also for the most resources-saving ideas were awarded.

In 2008 about 11,000 juveniles around Silicon Valley participated in this creative competition in order to find the most innovative solutions for real problems. In the last 20 years mainly global engineering questions were the center. Here, the fascination of exploring space often made the juveniles enthusiastic.

That they reoriented towards ecological problems now, speaks for itself. The competition takes place over several months in which the team goes through all the heights and depths of a development process, from the brainstorming to the development of ideas to the realization and testing of the method or the developed solutions.[183]

In this process, the teams are supported by the Tech Museum of Innovation and several sponsors and successful companies like e.g. Intel, Yahoo, SAP, Symantec, IBM and AMD.

The Tech Museum of Innovation in San Jose, the capital of Silicon Valley, inspires innovators by means of interactive exhibitions, theme galleries and with its Hackworth Imax ® Dome Theater and many singular museum programs. In exhibitions, scientists actually occupy with

---

[183] http://techchallenge.thetech.org/about.cfm

the latest trends and developments of science. In the exhibition area "Life Tech" visitors can gain experience how machines keep us alive and explore technologies that expand our natural capabilities. At the same time, the debate about the ethical evaluation of the employment of latest bio-technological innovations is not neglected. Furthermore, exhibitions about "Genetics" or "Transparent Bodies" offer pupils and students new and exciting education impulses and, above all, incentives to take part. By means of latest audio-visual methods, up-to-date knowledge is transferred in a vivid, reproducible and exciting way. As the first completely virtual human body, the "Visible Human" was generated from 1878 single images. With touch screens, different views can be projected and animations can be generated. Even in "Second Life" The Tech shows presence and calls for activity.

Similar adventures are also offered by the MIT Museum in Harvard that also promotes interactivity and creativity and motivates to take part or imitate. Big research institutions make intensive efforts to transfer their research successes to the young generation and to promote the best juniors in their very early years already.

There, mathematics play an important role as a frequently not directly visible power.[184]

In our digital era, many things have received a numeric expression. Whether music, films or photos everything is composed of numbers. Even alphabetic characters are represented by numbers. Only by mathematics many achievements of today's life, especially of technology, became possible. Whether computer, TV set, MP3 devices, biomedical apparatuses, navigation devices, ticket machines they all are possible because of mathematics only. The Internet search engines like Google are also based on mathematical algorithms.

But also complex flows of goods and finances could not be realized without mathematics. If you think of the influences of computerization on our every day life in the first place, represented in the flows of the ubiquitous[185] and pervasive computing[186] as well as the tendencies towards the electronic upgrading of our environment in the sense of

---

[184] Lossau, Norbert: Alles ist Zahl (It's all figures). – In: Die Welt, 25/03/.2008.(leading article)
[185] Omnipresent computer supported information processing in everyday life of humans
[186] Penetration of objects and infrastructures with microelectronics

151

"Ambient intelligence" then it becomes clear that in future life will not be controllable without mathematics. [187] Especially security models supporting persons and goods equipped with radio chips also need well-programmed processes and instructions. At the same time, many people face the high and increasing importance of mathematics for well-being and progress with lack of comprehension and ignorance. But also the educationists essentially contribute to that because quite often they do not manage to give the pupils concrete examples from every day life for the basics of complex numbers of functions. Someone who just practices scales in the music lessons without ever listening to a symphony or a song would give up his studies, e.g. of an instrument, very soon. However, while many people enjoy music there are surely just few who can enjoy nice mathematics.

In order to provoke higher awareness of mathematics and, above all, more enthusiasm in Germany, the year 2008 was declared the "Year of Mathematics". At numerous events, the organizers try to approach "dry" mathematics to the people and to include an increasing number of environmental topics at the same time. Without mathematically-talented spirits the competition of the future, be it in the battle against dangerous viruses, the development of new technologies for climate protection or the development of new energy technologies would not be possible.

Many associations, like the German Association for environmental Education (DGU), the Foundation for environmental Education in Europe (F.E.E) promote environmental education in childhood already. The objective is the pedagogically and scientifically founded occupation with the natural, the social and the cultivated environment.

In America and Australia there are, as a matter of course, spontaneous actions for tidying up the beach or planting trees that you acquire on the Internet. If you have the time, you go there. If only five people follow a call, everybody does more, if 100 people come, everybody has less to do. But all this takes place spontaneously and in a relaxed way. Up to now, such actions have been completely unknown in Germany. Except for the nationwide removal of leaves in front of the own door in autumn! In Germany, bureaucratic filling out of engagement declarations prevails, especially in the long term. But who wants to enroll himself for all Sundays of a year. Spontaneous actions would find the approval of

---

[187] Intelligent surroundings – equipped with computers and micro electronics

more people. At Greenpeace, practical training of less than one year is not even possible. In the USA and Australia, the environmental organizations are thankful for any kind of help, even if it is possible for three months only.[188]

Of course, the potential of the early interactive arousal of interest was also recognized by German companies and governmental education institutions. Private companies are particularly active with the promotion of education. An exceptionally successful example for this is the "IdeenPark. Zukunft Technik entdecken". In the year 2004 this initiative was initiated by the technology group "ThyssenKrupp" that invested 10 million euros in the park of ideas. More than 120 partners from science, economy, politics, media and sports participated in the realization in the year 2008 alone. Daimler, Bosch, Voith, Microsoft Germany or Carl Zeiss AG, just to name a few. Anyway, not one single company logo can be seen on the fair area even the one of the organizer is missing. "We do not want to advertise the companies but the professions that we will need very urgently in the years to come", a spokesman explains. "Every big concern depends on well-trained junior staff but if not more juveniles decide for professions in the field of natural sciences or mathematics, the current standard can hardly be kept up."[189]

250,000 visitors used this innovative education offer already. More than 3000 men and women were occupied with the organization of the big event.

In general, the motivation of the initiators, especially of the economy, is to make young people enthusiastic about innovations and the future of technology in order to give long-lasting incentives for education and job selection and thus to ensure qualified junior staff.

Thousands of children and adults poured into the halls of the Stuttgart Fair Area. Complete kindergarten groups traveled there, pupils came followed by parents, grandmas and granddads. Entrance was free and some halls so full that rigorous regulators periodically had to keep the public in check in front of the entrance. Compared with the "normal

---

[188] cf. Talk with the MTV-host, Nina Eichinger, The Tietjen and Dibaba, NDR3, May 30, 2008

[189]

http://www.derwesten.de/nachrichten/waz/2008/5/21/news4842747
8/detail.html Request of April 4th, 2008

153

school day" many regretted that they do not even closely get such exciting nerve food there.

In the year 2008, with the Ideen-Park at the area of the Fair in Stuttgart, Thyssen-Krupp created a unique technology adventure world for children, young adults and families. In seven living areas of our planet initiators, partners and visitors were looking for answers to the challenges of the world of tomorrow. The topics ranged from the interior of the Earth, the icy world of the poles, glowing deserts, pulsing cities, the depths of the oceans to the endlessly wide space.

With creativity and natural curiosity, discoveries and inventions could be made autonomously. Exciting workshops, experiments, shows and exhibits invited to do that. The objective was to open a completely new perspective of technology and environment and to prove how much fun that can be. About 500 engineers, researchers, tinkerers and students who answered questions and invited to become a constructor oneself guaranteed special experience.

Another main emphasis was SchlauLoPolis, the education paradise for curious children and juveniles. In the center were creative learning offers by partners from all over Germany. Even preschool children had the possibility to research with playful experiments guided by committed pedagogues. Juveniles learnt how to program computers, pupils' laboratories, workshops and competitions transferred fun with technique. In an own district of SchlauLoPolis, orientation and advise for the technical professional training were offered. Furthermore, parents and their children could go to the family unit and also solve tricky problems at entertainment events like "1, 2 oder 3" or the ARD quiz "Kopfball". Every day, Thomas Gottschalk and prominent guests presented amazing experiments in the show "Days of Innovation".

In addition, for the first time in Germany, in the year 2008, the "Studentische Ideenwettbewerb Generation-D. Ideen für Deutschland". "Gemeinsam anpacken" was brought into being by the Bayrische Elite-Akademie (Munich), Allianz SE, Süddeutsche Zeitung and Stiftung Marktwirtschaft. Climate and environment also belonged to the 3 main topics. The objective is to propose projects against the destruction of our natural fundaments of life, to initiate local changes in order to use the bases of the Earth for our economies in a better and more responsible way, to promote economic growth in big and small companies in order to create new jobs but protect resources at the same time. A central concern was thinking about a way in which the big climate objectives from Kyoto and Bali can be put into practice by every individual. At present, the first Germany-wide generation is present at German academies. The competition wants to transfer pioneering spirit, promote ideas regarding topics like sustainability in order to pack a livable future packet for Germany.[190]

This proves that also in Germany there are some activities in the field of early training of more innovation spirit for sustainable fitness for the future. The fact, that at many schools environment and climate protection are not yet topical shows how much remains to be done.[191] Single companies advocate climate lessons at schools, tendency rising.

The establishment of new curricula in the Federal Republic of Germany in 2005 offered the opportunity to include the topic of environmental problems in them. If in the beginning there was merely enough material available, in the meantime numerous publications have been published. Meanwhile, in higher classes, they execute bigger units as interdisciplinary projects. Regarding the occupation with environment topics in lessons the following has to be stated:

1. Not only reasons and consequences of the acting of the society should be discussed but also protecting measures and the conflicts resulting from them
2. The curricula should stipulate interdisciplinary discussion.
3. Experiments and fieldwork have to be planned-in more often than they hitherto were.
4. The suitability of single topics for the different age levels has to be inspected in more detail.
5. Too often, geography is taught by a non-geographer.[192] Here, the question shall be allowed what the qualification of the other teachers regarding environment and climate protection is like.

---

[190] http://www.gemeinsam-anpacken.de/profil/index.php Aufruf vom 04.04.2008

[191] cf www.ghs-flein.hn.bw.schule.de/umweltfr.htm Request from April 8, 2008

[192] This is espcecially applicable for the handling of go-scientific environmental problems cf. also Hagel, Jürgen: Geowissenschaftliche Umweltund Zukunftsprobleme im heutigen Schulunterricht.(Gep-scientific environmental and future problems in todays´ school classes) Berlin, Heidelberg: Springer, 2005

The "Arbeitsgemeinschaft Naturund Umweltbildung ANU" [193] summarized the variety of this education sector in a publication.

In the USA and especially in California and Silicon Valley much is done for the environmental information of the children and all the citizens, even without formal lessons. Books like "Green, Greener, Greenest" – A Practical Guide to Making Eco-Smart Choices a Part of Your Life" by Lori Bongiorno[194], a former Business Week journalist, are offered as bestsellers at a 20% lower price in order to reach even more readers. The same applies to Peter Barns' Citizen's Guide "Climate Solutions. What Works, What Doesn`t, and Why"[195] Without wanting to overrate such books or the numerous other flyers, ads in magazines or practical tips for more environmental acting, they support the change in consciousness and are worth being pointed out in so far as they hardly played a role in the USA years ago.

Today, pro-environment activity starts in kindergartens and schools and includes the universities. The main objective is to connect the still wide gap between data, information and knowledge abundance with much more environmentally-oriented acting on the one hand. Frequently, they talk about a knowledge-action-gap[196] that persists from the early years of education to the job activities. The companies suffer enormous damage because of the big difference between the abundance of information and practically usable and applicable knowledge. The earlier the young people realize themselves how important actionoriented knowledge and learning are, the better. In companies, this plays a

---

[193] ANU (Hrsg.): Natürlich. Nachhaltig. Mit Umweltbildung auf dem Weg in die Zukunft. (Natural. Sustainable. On the way to the future with envirnmental education) 32 S. ANU-administrative office, c/o Internationalpark Unteres Odertal, Criewen, Park 3, Schloss, D-16303 Schwedt

[194] Bongiorno, Lori: Green, Greener, Greenest. – New-York: Perigee Trade, 2008

[195] Chelsea Green Publishing Company, 2008

[196] cf. Knowing-Dowing-Gap = gap between generation of knowledge in the system of science to the transfer to the economic system as well as the realisation as value-generating application

success-deciding role.[197] Therefore, they put so much emphasis on training learning competences. In theory, they are divided into four steps.[198] Consequently, every higher learning level includes the total of those underneath. The ability of self-reflection (self-evolution), i.e. learning at level 3, includes the conscious acting on the previous learning steps. The entire process of evolutionary learning embraces:

1. Unknowing incompetence
2. Knowing incompetence
3. Knowing competence
4. Unknowing competence

There, the most important step is the conscious perception respectively realization of the own incompetence (step 2). The individual realization of the own weaknesses required both sensitiveness directed at the inside (mentally) and to the outside (socially) and is precondition for the acceptance of challenges and taking of chances. If entrepreneurial learning is absent in this process, i.e. there is no change and no gain of competence, the level of self-evolution cannot be reached. Only learning level 3 enables an all-over development of competences and consequently it is the key to the auto-poise[199] of creative entrepreneurship. The application of this thesis to this problem of the gap between knowledge and acting permits the statement that due to the impossibility of knowledge transfer to "untrained" an application of new knowledge can take place faster and more profitably by the academic entrepreneur, as you can see from the example of the successful Google-Stanford students. The scientist himself has to go through the processes of evolutionary, entrepreneurial learning, the development of ability consciousness and

---

[197] cf. Davenport, T.H./Prusak, L.: Working Knowledge: How Organisations manage what they know, Boston, 1998 and Pfeffer, J./Sutton, R.I.: The Knowing-Doing Gap – How Smart Companies Turn Knowledge into Action, Boston/Mass., 1999.)

[198] cf. Röpke

[199] Autopoiesis respectively autopoiese (classical Greek. ατός, "self", und ποιέω, "create") = process of self-creation and self-maintenance of a system, characteristic organization feature of living beings respectively living systems, term marked by the Chilean neuro-biologist Humberto Maturana.

push through his scientific new combinations on the market himself (or participate at least).[200]

Practical Tips
- *The earlier forming of eco competence is started, the more successfully environmental consciousness and competence develop.*
- *Learning must be fun! The new green learning offers many chances for that if the start is made as easy as possible: For example, how can everybody save water?*
- *Success in learning should be acknowledged and awarded. Even the littlest are proud of their certificates and you can safely take back home what you own black on white!*
- *One can also learn from mistakes, thus a culture should be developed for that!*
- *Being aware of the on incompetence helps managers, in special!*

Elite Academics with Entrepreneur Talent

The training of elites belongs to those buzzwords that internationally heat up the discussions in different ways. While in the USA they hardly discuss about elite training from the kindergarten age on already and children learn Chinese even at the age of 3, in Germany they still heavily philosophize about the risks of elite training. First gentle approaches like the support of elite universities show that something is happening in order to stand the international pace. Who wants to have a leading position in the sharpened innovation competition needs the best-trained people. At the beginning of July 2008, the German Science and Humanities Council "mercilessly criticized" the academies, teaching in particular.[201] The miserable situation was everything but elitist. "Teachers at all kinds of academies as teaching persons are mostly autodidacts, they teach on

---

[200] cf. Röpke; J.: Lernen in der unternehmerischen Wissensgesellschaft: Von der Inputlogik zur Selbstevolution (Learning in the entrepreneurial knowledge society: from input logics to self-evolution), in: Klemmer, P. et al. (editor), Liberale Grundrisse einer zukunftsfähigen Gesellschaft (Liberal outline of a society fit for the future), Baden-Baden, 1998, p. 140
[201] cf. Schonungslose Kritik an der Lage der Hochschulen (Merciless criticism at the situation of the academies), Frankfurter Allgemeine Zeitung, /.July, 2008, p.4

the basis of experience and without regulated professional feedback.[202] "The improvement potential ranges from the qualification of the professors to the equipment of rooms to the teaching materials and libraries and the supervision quota per professor. Professors mostly regard teaching as inconvenient obligation and as not very useful for prestige respectively acceptance. There is no question of elite teaching. In the schools there are just a few classes for the support of gifted children. Frequently, the universities do not even know their best students.[203]

The term elite (lat. "eligere" = select) describes pioneers in the most different fields. Thereby, "elite" can be widely diversified, in power and leader elites, education and performance elites, creativity elites, value elites, status elites, responsibility elites etc. The term elite does not define lordliness, arrogance or overestimation of the own capabilities but real pioneer and example roles the 3V (Vorbild, Verpflichtung, Verantwortung example, obligation, responsibility). But at present there is a huge gap between standard and requirement, especially in management. An expected example effect is often opposed by the reality of privates taking advantages.

Globally, one assumes that there are 2% highly gifted people, another 8% are strongly under-challenged by school. Due to the lack in promotion, about 15% develop to school losers. That equals an enormous waste of potential. The support of elite and gifted has to involve both, the ones and the others in the process.

For that purpose, with the Berlin School Law, in February 2004 a novelty was released saying that pupils with special talents and high cognitive skills likewise those with considerable learning problems, have a legal right to receive special support (§4 section 3, clause 1 SchulG.)[204] Offering special support offers for highly-gifted in mathematics-natural science network schools are also a part of that. Until the school year

---

[202] Friedmann, Jan; Kaiser, Simone;Verbeet, Markus: Forschung und Leere, (Research and Emptiness) in: Der Spiegel, 28, 2008, p. 52

[203] cf. Dieter Frey: Elite. Chancen und Gefahren.(Elite. Chances and Dangers) – Nov. 2007, Department Psychology, Ludwig-Maximilians-University Munich, Academic leader of the Bavarian elite academy

[204] cf. Senate administration for education, youth, and sports. The Senator. In a letter to all educational schools of Berlin Edit. Ms Kröner, http://www.berlin.de/imperia/md/content/sen-bildung/ Request from March 12, 2008

2005/2006, comparable support concepts were realized in the area of foreign languages and bilingualism exclusively.

In education, it is generally important to offer possibilities for a flexible selection through all age levels as well as full-time schools. At the same time, every pupil should have the right to be individually supported as it is offered in the K12 program,[205] for example. Here, children are supported in a very special way, also with mathematical and scientific or other talents. Exemplary is a 6-year old American who established his own foundation in order to support people in distress. He organizes numerous aid projects. Both Bush and Clinton congratulated him to his commitment.[206] On the basis of the flexible virtual and blended-learning concept he can learn in his early years already how to organize himself, to gain knowledge according to his rhythm and his skills and attend to the global problems of the Earth. Of course, new media offer special mechanisms in order to check performances regularly, to repeat or skip them. At present, this is hardly possible at "normal" schools, except for certain electronic studying programs that enrich the lessons to an increasing degree. If one inspects the growing challenges regarding mobility and flexibility, it is astounding that hitherto there are no "remote schools" at discussion in the future concepts for education. It is time that compulsory education is dropped in Germany and gives way to a different kind of educational obligation as it is already common in many other countries. In the USA there are almost two million children and juveniles who learn without school. [207] This does neither give reasons for pauperization in the social structure of relationships nor can lack of interaction with children of the same age be concluded from that. Much more, missing constraint to learn as well as space and time limitations open new ways for more motivation, creativity and self-responsibility.

At present, such challenges regarding transparent, understandable, standardized and nonetheless individual ratings exist in education systems in Germany as well as internationally. Frequently, the talents of children remain undetected because in the schools there are no general

---

205 See www.k12.com

206http://www.k12.com/promotions/family_spotlight_the_bonner_famil y Request of April 4th, 2008

207 http://www.d-perspektive.de/loesungen/bildung/schulpflichtueberwinden-teil-2.html Request of May 5th, 2008

160

test systems for "talent assessment" apart from the common performance ratings and the social ratings by means of assessment of the level of participation and behavior.

Regarding the contents, a more clearly turn away from the facts towards more knowledge, values and decision-making and responsibility becomes necessary. Irrespective some weaknesses, in Germany there already is a series of examples for the promotion of elites like e.g. the newly established categories of elite universities, the promotion of elite by the DFG in the form of research groups, special research areas and priority programs. In the research centers, elite support takes place by organizing scholarships and awards. In many firms, elites are promoted as high potentials although the really creative ones do not receive the necessary acceptance.

In the year 2004, the Institute of Higher Education of the Shanghai Jiao Tong University established a ranking list of all the universities in the world. Amongst the first ten there were American academies only. Exceptions are the English elite universities Oxford and Cambridge. Amongst the first 50 academies there are 35 American and only one German academy, the TU Munich. At the end of the 19th century this used to be completely different. Then the German academies belonged to the export highlights. The German University was the model for the reform of the US-American universities, e.g. the foundation of Johns Hopkins in Baltimore. It based on Humboldt's doctrines and theories and targeted the unification of teaching and research in the first place. Only good researchers are capable of transferring even most recent scientific findings to the students. The German academy also served as an example for the reforms of Harvard and the University of Chicago. For the best of American elites the academic stay at German academies was a compulsory "must".

Exemplary names for that are W.E.B. Dubois (studies in Berlin), William James (studies at Wundt in Leipzig), Talcott Parsons (Heidelberg). For a long time, due to the outstanding position of chemical research and realization of results in practice, German was a compulsory language for American chemists.

Despite lacking funding and the need for reforms at German academies, Karl Ulrich Mayer, Professor for Sociology at the Yale University, Director of the Center for Research on Social Inequalities and the Life Course (CiQLE) and Director at the Max-Planck-Institute für Bildungsforschung in Berlin sees their potential.[208]

At present, in the USA, there are 4182 academies, amongst them 544 universities with promotion study courses. 120 American academies are regarded as excellent research universities. Most of the American students are enlisted at academies that are rather worse than the average of the German academies from the academic point of view.

Mayer regards it as negative that many professors are "less qualified" because they did not produce more research results than their dissertation. Teaching is also made by "adjunct professors" and student tutors. Many events at the big academies are rather mass events with examinations according to the book and little contact between teaching body and students.

The financial equipment of the 20 30 top universities in the USA is enormous. For example, Yale disposes of assets amounting to 11 billion dollars. Thus it is possible, as the best football clubs do, to recruit the best top scientists. These only have few teaching obligations and search for themselves the best students in the world. Even if the first semesters of Yale students are not very different from those of students in Berlin, these even are technically better and broader trained, from the Yale students more performance is demanded on a long-term basis and the support by the professors is higher. The German students have excellent chances to study at the best American universities if they would only apply.[209]

A fiercely discussed topic of education in Germany is the tuition fees. While here protests take place at the universities, in America tuition fees are a part of the common sense, even if they have been enormously increasing in the recent years, as the following example shows.

On the international level, e.g. at the Graduate School of Business of the Stanford University, they calculate with the following cost scheme per year (specifications in US $) plus studies travel costs of minimally 1,500 to 4,000 US $ per stay abroad.

Table 9: Stanford MBA Program 2008

---

[208] Mayer, Karl Ulrich: Schatten auf der Elite. Amerikas Spitzenunis haben Schwächen, die Deutschland nicht kopieren sollte. (Shadows on the Elite. Americas top universities have weaknessess that Germany should not copy.) – In: Der Tagesspiegel, November 12, 2004.
[209] Mayer dito

Exemplary calculation for the budget of the first year of studies in US dollars				
(9 months=academic year) September 2008 June 2009				
Cost Type	Single living on the campus	Single not living on the campus	Married living on the campus	Married not living on the campus
Tuition Fee	48,921	48,921	48,921	48,921
Pocket money + side costs	19,932	22,602	28,116	31,923
Week Zero Expense	634	708	861	967
Books & Materials	1,869	1,869	1,869	1,869
Course Fees	1,845	1,845	1,845	1,845
Transport	864	1,818	2,679	3,624
Health Insurance	2,259	2,259	2,259	2,259
Total	**76,324**	**80,022**	**86,550**	**91,408**

(Source:) Stanford Graduate School of Business, Stanford MBA Program, Tuition & Expenses, 2008/2009, p.1)

Tuition fees, without compensating scholarships that grand the talented financial compensation und thus correspond with the performance principle, are indispensable. A generous and well-functioning scholarship system also has to work when, for example, a college year, be it at a private college or a university, meanwhile amounts to almost 40,000 US dollars per year. If the elite training becomes a privilege of the economic elite only, then the number achievements will also sink in the perspective.

From the psychological point of view, elite training is partly seen critically since it is not always fun in innovations and pleasure in discovering things that drive the young people. The increasing pressure to be taken by a top university frequently leads to strong stress and failure experiences that have to be compensated by additional trainers in leisure time at high costs. Like in the coaching in the German law studies, the American students prepare for the SAT tests and applications. This leads to socially selective distortions with the selection. In addition, the privileged treatment of formers, like e.g. President Bush's children, do not always play a positive role. Such methods are generally a scandal for institutions working according to the performance principle. The values of sponsoring, lobbying, of the alumni networks must not become a contradiction to the performance maxims of the universities. 14% of the Yale undergraduates are children from Yale graduates. The role of college sport at many academies and the dependence of the alumni connected therewith can also be considered dubious. A football coach often earns a manifold of what a University president gets. Good sportsmen are preferred with recruiting and even in examinations they do not hesitate to render "university help".

It seems to be amazing that the equipment of the professors at top universities is frequently lower than at most of the German universities. But this does only refer to the general basic equipment concerning secretariat, helpers or employees. More abundant resources can only be referred to with corresponding means by third parties. But this is very similar with the practices with junior professors that have also been introduced in Germany lately. These normally have not put a secretariat at their disposal or just shared. Helpers and employees can only be recruited from additional means by third parties.

In the USA, the financings by the industry often cannot be compared with German financing aids. For example, according to his personal statement, Chris Sommerville from Berkeley University just received a 500 million US dollars research order for new biofuels by the industry in spring 2008. German academy professors can dream of that because here three decimal places less are even regarded as an outstanding, excellent result.

Of course, this raises the question in how far the ambivalent ratio between excellence in research, teachings and industrial realization can be kept in Europe and especially in Germany in the long run. On a continuing basis there will not be any top results without top conditions in science and research, education and further training, especially in those green fields of innovation from which new industries develop. In essence,

164

it is about the development of a new type of entrepreneur the academically trained entrepreneur.

The scientific entrepreneur himself becomes the enforcer of the new combinations generated in science within the economic system. He owns the same evolution capacities in the scientific system as the inventive and the innovative scientist but he is also directly connectable with the system economy. He has the capacity to operate in both subsystems. Etzkowitz names this type "entrepreneurial scientist" and in this connection he talks about "entrepreneurial university acting as a generator of spin-off firms."[210]

The causal factors for scientific entrepreneurship are the three components:

- Capabilities
- Motivation and
- Rights to motivate[211]

The latter factor sounds a bit surprising but due to the German authorityship it definitely has to be taken seriously. In many cases, the entrepreneurial activities of professors are highly limited and the university legislation of the Landers forbids economical activities. On the other hand, many students complain that their too busy professors do not have enough time for them due to their additional businesses.

In specialized literature in connection with the role of outstanding personalities in the sense of scientific and/or entrepreneurial personalities they point at the increasing importance of incorporation teams opposed to single individuals.[212] Without referring to a joint source,

---

[210] Comp. 546 Viale, R./Etzkowitz, H.: Third academic revolution: Polyvalent knowledge; the DNA of the triple Helix, Theme Paper, 5th Triple Helix Conference, Turin, Milano, 2005, p. 10

[211] Cf.. Röpke, J.: Transforming Knowledge into Action – The Knowing-doing Gap and the Entrepreneurial University, Bandung/Marburg, 2003, p. 2

[212] Cf. own composition, data taken from Mellewigt, T./Späth, J. F.: Entrepreneurial teams – A survey of German and US empirical studies, in: Albach, H./Pinkwart, A. (Editor): Zeitschrift für Betriebswirtschaft, Ergänzungsheft 5/2002, Gründungsund Überlebenschancen von Familienunternehmen, Wiesbaden, 2002, p.110

a great number of qualitative studies define incorporation teams by means of three factors:[213]
According to them, characteristics of foundation teams are:

1. Two or more natural persons who found a new independent company together.
2. Financial participation by each partner in the company (no matter, how high).
3. The partners have direct responsibility for the company and for its objectives, planning and control.

If you take this definition as a basis, capital providers, secret partners or other legal persons are not a part of the incorporation team. Although the specified definition cannot be named a standard, it is the one that can be found the most frequently.[214]

Empirical studies executed regarding the emergence of team incorporations mainly try to answer the two following questions:
How high is the share of team incorporations relating to the total number of newly founded companies?
Can a general tendency towards team incorporations be observed?

The results regarding the proportion of team incorporations of the total number of foundations vary strongly. For example, literature gives values between 8% and 81%. That does not legitimate a reasonable

---

[213] cf among other Ensley, M.D./Carland, J.W./Carland, J.C.: The Effect of Entrepreneurial Team Skill; Heterogeneity and functional Diversity on New Venture Performance, in: Journal of Business (Mellewigt, T./Späth, J. F.: Entrepreneurial teams – A survey of German and US empirical studies, in: Albach, H./Pinkwart, A. (Hrsg.): Magazine for business economics, Supplementary issue 5/2002, Gründungsund Überlebenschancen von Familienunternehmen, (Founding and survival chances of family companies) Wiesbaden, 2002, p. 118-119

[214] For example, Kirchoff / Klandt / Winand name the factor full time profession in addition (Cf. Kirchoff, S. / Klandt, H./ Winand, U.: Unternehmerische Partnerschaft: Ein Erfolgsfaktor, in: Böhling, D. / Nathusius, K.: Unternehmerische Partnerschaften: Beiträge zu Unternehmensgründungen im Team, Stuttgart, 1994), while Ucbasaran et al. do not consider the factor power of direction as important (cf.. Ucbasaran, D. et al.: The Dynamics of Entrepreneurial teams, in: Frontiers of Entrepreneurship research2001, in: Proceedings of the Twenty-first Annual Entrepreneurship Research Conference, Babson Park, 2001).

conclusion. Due to the enormous bondage of new knowledge respectively technologies to persons, entrepreneurial own activity of the scientist is compulsory for closing the commonly bemoaned gap between knowledge and acting.

The especially fast growing domestic economies in globalization like China and India have also realized that and massively support the formation of university-based companies. In China, the URE's (University Run Enterprises), i.e. companies that are founded and run directly by the academy, play an important role. More than 5000 were already listed in China's S&T[215] index. This fact advocates the dynamics of growth.

If you inspect the university system in the United States, it is apparent that the positioning of academies takes place by the intense competition amongst each other. They compete about the best students and professors in the first place. A big share of the financing of academies is made by so-called foundation funds. These funds are managed by professional funds managers and are not bound to certain investments. With his fund, David Swensen, head of the foundation fund of the University of Yale, achieved an average annual return of 17% in the last ten years. In 2005, the average of all university foundation funds amounted to 9.3% and thus still clearly above the average development of the stock market index S&P 500 (6.3%).[216] "Here, the structural junction between economy and science is controlled by civil service law, bureaucracy, ethics, prosecutors, risk aversion, technology consequences evaluators, lawyers, advisers and target objectives but not by those who could do it themselves. [...] Universities give away billions because they cannot (may, want, cannot) put their knowledge and the carriers of their competences into the innovation systems. And they moan and moan. And they beg for handouts from their political masters. They sit on bags of money without knowing or using it. They dispose of rich resources but refuse to recombine them. They look for salvation in resource optimization and controlling (i.e. management, not entrepreneurship). Doing the wrong things right. Result: static efficiency, dynamic

---

215 S&T – Science & Technology

216 cf. Kuls, N.: Wie amerikanische Universitäten Milliarden verdienen (How American Universities earn billions), URL: www.faz.net, October 26th, 2006, request October 27th, 2006.

(Schumpeter's) inefficiency."[217] But the natural-scientific, more research-intensive specialized areas depend on means from third parties due to financial misery. But in parallel there are also some private academies in Germany.[218]

In the course of the Lisbon strategy (3% R&E portion in the GDP until 2010) the Federal Government initiated the so-called high-tech strategy.[219] Until 2009, another 6 billion euros shall be invested in research and development. At a first glance, this is pure input logic. If you then watch the effective share that shall flow in the support of new, small and medium-sized companies, in 2006 that were about 80 million that are in addition distributed via complicated application procedures, it becomes clear how serious politics are with their support of the innovation power of new foundations and SMEs.[220]

Practical Tips:

- *Give demanding tasks to the youngest already and forget the discussion about excessive demands!*
- *As a company, invest in the best minds!*
- *Get actively and regularly involved in the discussions about the further studying programs of the academies and do not be afraid of big titles!*

---

[217] Röpke,J./Xia, Y.: Reisen in die Zukunft kapitalistischer Systeme; Grundzüge einer daoistischen Kinetik wirtschaftlicher Entwicklung, (Journey into the future of capitalisitc systems; Basics of daoistic kinetics of economic development) Marburg, 2007, p. 222)

[218] cf. Interview with Winnacker, E-L.: Den Universitäten fehlt das Geld, (Universities are lacking the money) Handelsblatt, October 9th, 2006, p.2.

[219] Goal that Germany will become one of the nations with the most research and innovation of the world

[220] cf. BMBF: Neue Impulse für Innovation und Wachstum, 6 Milliarden Euro-Programm für Forschung und Entwicklung, (New impulses for innovation and growth, 6 billion Euro program for research and development) Report of the German government, Bonn/Berlin, 2006, p. 1, 10 ff. 691 Cf. Horn, K.: Bildung am Reißbrett, (Education at the drawing board) Frankfurter Allgemeine Zeitung, March 10, 2003, p. 11, Chapter 6: Unternehmertum in der Universität – Modell und Vision 2050 (Entrepreneurship in the Universiy Model and Vision 2050).

- *Compare the debate about tuition fees of 500 euros per seme ster here with the fees of about 50 000 dollars at elite univer sities in the USA!*
- *Help highly-gifted with scholarships!*

Sponsors from the Grass Roots to Stanford's Going Green

In 1891, after their only son died at the age of 15, Jane and Leland Stanford founded the university that was named after them in order to do something for the benefit of other children.

After their family had become very rich in the years of the "gold rush" and the construction of the transcontinental railway connection, they saw their money invested in the best and most sustainable way here. They donated the ground, more than 8000 acres,[221] of their Palo Alto Ranch that was originally used for horse breeding and training.

Interesting for us is Stanford's unofficial motto: "Die Luft der Freiheit weht." but in German, not in English "The wind of freedom blows". This quotation stems from Ulrich von Hutten, a well-known humanist of the 16th century. This motto was even taken into the university seal.

Since its foundation, sponsoring has played a crucial role for Stanford University. Thereby, single individuals, organizations and companies support in the form of money, non-cash or services. Even though science sponsoring is of quite new origin. The companies from private economy or even single persons support research projects without orienting them at concrete results as it is the case with externally funded research. The Institut zur Zukunft der Arbeit (Institute for the Future of Work) is considered a pioneer in Germany.

Name-sponsoring, as it was exemplified by the Stanford University, was and still is rather unusual in Germany and still very young. The private International University Bremen, since 2007 named Jacobs University Bremen, is a popular example. With a record donation of 200 million euros it followed in Harvard's footsteps. But not everybody involved was happy with this change of name.

In practice, the control of the success of sponsoring measures is mainly restricted to the registration of the media feedback. One acts on the assumption that it is sufficient if the target group is aware of the sponsor as such. But reality is much more complex: sponsors follow

---

[221] 1 a. (acre) = 4.046.87 m2 ; 3 acres are a bit more than one hectare (a square of 100 m × 100 m).

169

different targets (e. g. transferring the image of the sponsored to the own brand, gaining reputation, connect the brand with characteristic emotions of the respective event). These targets have to be taken into consideration with the control of success (i. e. target-performance comparison). Consequently, systematic objective planning is a necessary condition: Companies shall focus on concrete targets that they want to achieve with sponsoring. Furthermore, precondition for control of success is that the success can be quantified. For that purpose, several measuring instruments have been developed already (e. g. sponsormeter of the European Sponsoring Market, sponsoring-navigator of the TU Dresden). According to these approaches sponsorship is considered successful, if with the target group an effect corresponding with the company's objective can be measured. For example, if the company is rated as well-known, sympathetic, singular etc. In doing so, measuring of success should be based on a control group approach: the values measured with the visitors of the sponsored event are compared with those from a reference group that has not experienced the sponsoring. With the help of statistical methods it can now be determined which characteristics (e. g. kind of appearance, integration of the sponsoring, selection of the sponsored) decide whether sponsoring is successful or not. With the help of this approach, the chair for marketing at the TU Dresden could identify the success factors of sponsoring in the scope of a study of numerous sponsoring measures.

For example, every year the medical faculty in Stanford (School of Medicine) receives grants amounting to more than 300 million for research, teaching as well as patients' care from sponsors.

From that, they developed the "Disease Management" program. The Stanford Patients' Education Research Center developed programs for people with chronic diseases, including arthritis and HIV/AIDS. This program was adopted by more than 500 organizations in 17 countries and 40 states.

In Stanford, more than 4,500 externally sponsored projects with a total budget of 1,058 billion US dollars in the period from 2007 -2008 extended the research budget. This included the Stanford Linear Accelerator Center (SLAC) for the U.S. Department of Energy. The SLAC is one of the internationally leading research institutions.

The linear accelerator[222] is 3 km long and able to accelerate electrons respectively positrons to up to 50 GeV. It is about 10 m under the earth and crosses the expressway "Interstate 280". The experimental possibilities of high-energy physics[223] connected therewith and the synchrotron radiation is used by more than 3000 guest scientists from universities, laboratories and the industry, and thus enriches the work of the SLAC.40 Highly-trained and award winners, whether physicians, engineers, computer specialists and other experts decorate the chronicles of Stanford. Three Nobel Prices for physics were brought about from research at the SLAC.

In addition, the klystron was partly developed a the SLAC, a component for the reinforcement of micro waves In the 1980s, the conference rooms of the institute served as a meeting point for pioneers of the home computer revolution. Here, they also hosted the first web site of the USA, the interface of the database SPIRES.

Today's president of Stanford, John Hennessy, initiated a university-wide program in October 2006 in order to search for solutions for the currently biggest global challenges. There, it is about both, the creation of a future leading elite and strengthening of Stanford's academic excellence. In order to follow this objective, the university started "The Stanford Challenge", a five-year fundraising program over 4.3 billion dollars. These contributions are justified because the complexity of social and scientific challenges has been rising enormously in the last decades. Universities are predestined for that and Stanford in particular because of their entrepreneurial tradition and their innovative pioneer's spirit.

The Stanford challenges are composed of three components:

- 1.4 billion dollars for multi-disciplinary initiatives, amongst those three transformative (redesigned) initiatives around groundbreaking progresses in the fields of human health, friendliness to the environment and international peace and safety

---

[222] Linear Accelerator or Linac = a kind of particle accelerator, electrically charged particles (e. g. electrons, protons, positrons or ions) can be accelerated on a straight track
[223] High energy physics = Structure of small and smallest particles and elementary particles and their interaction. It is a collective term for particle physics and high energy heavy ions physics

- 1.17 billion dollars for initiatives for the improvement of the K-12 education. K-12 is a leading program for the transfer of individualized single lessons for learners from the kindergarten to the high school, through all states by means of exhibitions, researches and special performances.
- 1.725 billion dollars for the reinforcement of the core offers of the Stanford University.

Multi-disciplinary projects can be initiated over all 7 Standford schools and numerous institutes already. In detail, it is about focusing the research cooperation crossways the campus and furthermore on special problems. SUNet, Stanford's university network, helps with that. It includes more than 150,000 computers. About 6000 are active every day. More than 9.5 terabytes of information are exchanged between SUNet and the Internet every day. Stanford has 40,000 e-mail accounts. Not long ago, the Stanford graduates Jerry Yang and Akiko Yamazaki showed what performances successful entrepreneurs are ready for. They donated to the university more than 50 million dollars for the construction of the so-called Y2E2 building, colloquially used for Yang and Yamazaki Environment and Energy Building. In the special edition "Sustainable Stanford" of March 4th, 2008 that was handed to all visitors at this occasion it says: "The building shows how Stanford is pioneering energy-efficient ways of operating a university campus". Yahoo's co-founder Yang and his wife do not expect any service in return for that. Yang was born in Taiwan and grew up in San Francisco's Bay area. He did his bachelor and master in electrical engineering until 1990. During his doctorate studies in the same discipline he acted as Yahoo's co-founder in 1994. Since 2005 he has also been collaborating in the Stanford Board of Trustees for a 5-year period. His wife Yamazaki grew up in Costa Rica and completed her bachelor degree in Stanford in 1990 also, but in industrial engineering. This impressing generosity is looking for imitators in Germany. Because except for Hasso Plattner, co-founder of SAP, who supports a privately financed institute at the University of Potsdam, there are only few examples from the high-tech sector, except for single foundation professorships. In addition to the already mentioned 50 million, Yang und Yamazaki donated another 5 million US dollars for a new learning and knowledge center of the Stanford School of Medicine and announced another 20 million with the project objectives to be announced later on.[224]

---

[224] cf. Sustainable Stanford, March 4, 2008, p. 8

Over the years, the two have already initiated and co-financed other projects, from education programs to research centers like the Asia Pacific Research Center, the Stanford Japan Center and the Jasper Ridge Biological Preserve. They supported new establishments of professorships and co-financed the running campaign for the improvement of undergraduate education.

In the new Y2E2 building, for which other sponsors also donated money, multi-disciplinary research at difficult environmental problems, a main theme of the Stanford Challenge, shall be promoted in the first place.

Practical Tips

- *Germany's tradition in academy sponsoring has to be intensified and calls for new and inventive ideas. Participating in their design is exceptionally profitable for the future and the improvement of environment and health protection!*
- *Even small contributions by sponsors can be very helpful because at schools and academies there frequently is a lack of elementary things like ink for printers or books for the library!*
- *Use sponsoring for science in order to save taxes!* Check actively, how green business teaching and research topics are positioned at academies and how they are put into practice! Help with sponsoring and your requirements!

Alumni and Network Activities

In the USA, alumni associations have a long tradition. But also in Germany such initiatives have been springing up like mushrooms since the 90s. The word alumni stems from the Latin language and means pupil (alumnus). Nowadays, this names the former members of an academy, whether students or scientific personnel. On the one hand, the goal is to promote the contact of the alumni amongst each other and to achieve strong permanent networking. On the other hand, they want to keep up the contact with the scientific institution. Of course, the bonding from the financial point of view and with regard at lobbying, especially with private institutions, plays a considerable role, too. Academies are proud to be able to show reputable personalities on their alumni lists. This contributes considerably to a good reputation of the institution. In many cases, the graduates are included in university rankings; they help to win new students and junior scientists, to practically increase the attractiveness of the studies by mentoring partners but also with interesting practical trainings in industry, economy, service in general.

Here, the immaterial support is in the fore. The practical realization of the activities of the alumni can be highly varying there. While institutions "torture" themselves with regular newsletters, others offer their members regular meetings with people from the same year, trips, and discussion clubs.

At present, the Technical University of Munich disposes of an alumni database with currently 12,000 entries.[225] The connection of Alumni & Career Service is a poster child for the quality of the training at the same time.

In Stanford and many other universities a big portion of the total academy financing stems from donations of the graduates. They are invested in funds. Often, their professional performance is impressive and is used again for start-ups and participations in companies. In Germany, due to the very inflexible budget law of the academies, even small deviations of project costs are almost completely excluded and participations in company foundations impossible. The participation model of the academies in patents and inventions of professors and scientists, as well as employees that is already stipulated by legislation is subject to the respective employee's invention law. Whoever experienced the bureaucratic procedure connected with that will avoid participation models with academies as organs of the public law at all costs. This hampering impact of legislation on incorporations out of public academies is obvious. But nothing changes, they rather talk about the necessity of the connection of theory and practice and keeping up contact with graduates.

That in Germany such activities are still relatively young is shown by repeatedly emerging indications of missing network structures and common grounds offering incentives and motivation and achieve bonds between the graduates of the same institution. The precondition of "Social Networking" is definitely more than just a formal structure. As far as alumni from the same courses, e.g. international general corporate communication and international information management (Uni Hildesheim) organize in regulars' tables and exchange job offers at the same time and initiate projects together, alumni movements bear a higher

---

[225] http://inhalt.berufsstart.monster.de/2046_de_p1.asp Request of May 12th, 2008

chance of success. But in Germany some time will have to go by until a pride develops that can be compared with American academies. Because an alumni association requires commitment of the organizers, design of web sites, conception of events, contributions for newsletters of high quality.

In turn, with private academies, a difference to American approaches can hardly be detected. The culture of sponsoring, the financial investment in education and a certain elite thinking connect in a different manner. Here, you will rarely find students who "just" want to bridge periods or study "by the way". Most of the young people are strongly career-orientated and this remains the same, even after their studies. They definitely estimate the value of networks for the further professional path of life.

Stanford alumni are spread all over the world. Stanford clubs exist in Europe alone.

Everywhere at American academies they put special emphasis on cooperation, the early learning of "networking". A great number of activities are connected with this systematically maintained network of relationships. Therefore, the research of social networks is paid high attention to.

Amongst others, ethnology, social-psychology, communication sciences, computer physics and theory of games research social networks. Here, e.g. multiplexity, network density and many other things play a role. The proceedings developed there can be used for the webometric (control and measuring of the linking of Internet sites) research of the Internet. It becomes obvious that the structures of social networks often generate small-world-networks in which the maximum distance between single units is surprisingly low.

The small-world-experiment of the US-American psychologist Stanley Milgram of 1967 became popular: 300 participants from the middle west of the USA in the experiment should send a parcel to a target person in the surroundings of Boston. In doing so, they were only allowed to transfer the object directly to known persons. If the recipient was unknown to the participant in the experiment, he handed the consignment over to a known person, hoping that this would possibly know the target person.

In this process, Milgram discovered that normally 6 intermediate stations are sufficient in order to deliver the parcel from the sender to the recipient. From that he developed the theory that the members of a social network are in contact with each other via six junction points ("six degrees of separation").

Global social networks as they develop in the form of online communities by using social software have not yet been sufficiently studied with respect at their sociological, cultural and political consequences. In turn, there already exist numerous studies about the economical and user-specific aspects. For peace research, for example, it would be important to know, whether such global social networks rather tend to develop new concepts of the enemy (e.g. towards minorities) or whether they rather serve peace because interest-guided, pretended reasons of the rulers for hostility can be quickly revealed and invalidated by the worldwide exchange of information. In each case, global social networks come along with hitherto unknown momentum of opinion forming of the world public.

In Europe, with 9.6 million people, the British use the Web 2.0-typical social networking web sites the most. According to an estimation of the information provider *Datamonitor,* until 2012, with 27 million people, almost half of all British will use services like e.g. Facebook or MySpace. Datamonitor attributes this to the fact that the British have been in front up to now due to the offers normally being started with English versions. According to Datamonitor, people especially appreciate that they are able to make contact and to keep up relationships from their homes. Even if mainly younger people were behind the growing amount of users, also many older users would add to them. With 8.9 million people, the French represent the second-biggest user-group of the social networking offers, the Germans follow with 8.6 million on rank three in April 2008 then. In Germany, the study predicts 21.7 users until the year 2012. Spain, positioned at place four, only had 2.9 million users in spring 2008. In total, 41.7 million Europeans were registered with social networking web sites, in four years it should be 107 million according to Datamonitor. The second worldwide study regarding the brand affinity of juveniles, executed by the community operator Habbo, comes to a conclusion that outlines the language problem. The remarkable result: 40% of the about 60,000 questioned teens from 31 countries do not regard social networks as important part of their online activities. According to the Global Habbo Youth Survey one of the main reasons for that is that many of the communities are directed towards the English language.

Colloquially, networkers are people who actively build up and expand a relationship network.[226] By means of "networking" persons actively expand their meshwork of relationships in order to inform themselves. Independently of the services, sometimes it also serves to promote career or obtain other advantages. In this context, "networking" can also be meant deprecatingly. Terms like cronyism, insider deals or old boys' network are synonyms for that. Here, in the first place, it is about the constructive side of networking that provides advantages for everybody.

Practical Tips

- *Keep up lifelong contact with your education institutions and co-students and feel obliged towards young students!*
- *You can learn much from the pride of being alumni of a famous academy and conclude for the improvement of the reputation!*
- *Actively help actively to provide the academies with a better international reputation!*
- *Do not let yourself be infected by the general concerns towards graduates!*
- *Build-up an own alumni network with your academy!*

Innovation Hubs by Implementation of Knowledge in Company Foundations

Stanford's entrepreneurial spirit brought about a vast amount of very successful companies. More than 3000 firms developed know-how and expertise in the field of high technology. Thereby, Frederick Terman is also named the "academic architect" of Silicon Valley. He acted as the chancellor of the university from 1955-1965. With the establishment of a partnership between the university and the industry he considerably contributed to making the start of the companies' high-tech revolution possible. Furthermore, Terman encouraged the students to entrepreneurship and in California he created possibilities to offer Stanford engineering graduates continuous further training programs for the regional companies. For this purpose, the University Industrial Park was brought into being, too. Companies like Hewlett-Packard could grow roots there. Terman initiated a corporate culture from which all academic directions profit yet today.

---

[226] Also called "social network".

177

Everybody is aware of the fact that knowledge-based company foundations can only be successful if they can take place almost seamlessly from academic environment. In Silicon Valley, the Tec Museum in San Jose provides the proof for that. As with the Walk of Fame in Hollywood at Sunset Boulevard you can find the palms of important sponsors, innovators and the tech-founders on CDs. In the Tech Innovation Museum in San Jose, there is this extraordinary appraisal of those who did or still do something concrete for the business location, the region and, of course, the Tec itself. The handprints of big sponsors and innovators serve, in a big image wall on CD-similar discs with short explanations, as rolls of honor. First, the attentive visitor is a bit startled because normally one expects the heads. Then he comprehends that in the innovation process resolute practical acting is more important than just a head alone, even if it is most brilliant. As companies of the superlative and living evidence for the outstanding importance of connection of incorporators with the academies, Adobe, Google, Apple, eBay, or HP can be found within a radius of 20 miles.

In all, by emphasizing the hand traces of the innovators, emphasis is put again and again on the practical importance of pushing through innovations, the connection with entrepreneurship. Finally, the market introduction of novelties is crucial for structural changes. The Federal Government is of the same opinion if it emphasizes that finally the market results are the mirror of the technological and thus also the scientific efficiency of a country.

"In the first place, there are the inventions of new technologies, the introduction of new products on the market and the diffusion of new technologies in the economy (innovations). Finally, these are the direct determinants of the technological efficiency. In the medium term, it is important that the innovation-oriented structural change advances by the realization of new ideas in the form of new incorporations in the technology-oriented industries of the economy and by complete renewals of the production range of established companies."[227]

What Germany's real situation is in this respect can be taken from the following table:

---

227 BMBF: Report to the technologic capability of Germany 2006, Bonn/Berlin, 2006, p. 17

Table 10: Total Entrepreneurial Activity (TEA) Ranked by Country[228]

Country	Average%	2006%	2005%	2004%	2003%
Peru	40.3	40.2		40.3	
Uganda	31.6			31.6	
Ecuador	27.2			27.2	
Venezuela	26.2		25.0		27.3
Colombia	22.5	22.5			
Philippines	20.4	20.4			
Indonesia	19.3	19.3			
Jamaica	18.7	20.3	17.0		
Jordan	18.3			18.3	
Thailand	18.3	15.2	20.7		18.9
New Zealand	16.2		17.6	14.7	
South Korea	14.5				14.5
India	14.2	10.4			17.9
China	14.0	16.2	13.7		12.0
Uruguay	12.6	12.6			
Iceland	12.5	11.3.		13.6	
Chile	12.2	9.2	11.1		16.3
Brazil	12.2	11.7	11.3.	13.5	
Australia	12.1	12.0	10.9	13.4	
United States	11.2	10.0	12.4	11.3.	
Malaysia	11.1	11.1			
Argentina	10.8	10.2	9.5	12.8	
Poland	8.8			8.8	
Canada	8.4	7.1	9.3.	8.9	
Norway	8.4	9.1	9.2	7.0	
Czech Republic	7.9	7.9			
Mexico	7.9	5.3	5.9		12.4

228

http://www.internationalentrepreneurship.com/total_entrepreneur_acti vity.as p, Request from June 8th, 2008

Ireland	7.6	7.4		7.7	
Greece	6.7	7.9	6.5	5.8	
Switzerland	6.7		6.1		7.3
Latvia	6.6	6.6	6.6		
Israel	6.6			6.6	
Croatia	6.1	8.6	6.1	3.7	
United Kingdom	6.1	5.8	6.2.	6.3.	
Turkey	6.1	6.1			
Spain	6.1	7.3	5.7	5.2	
Singapore	5.9	4.9	7.2	5.7	
Austria	5.3		5.3		
France	5.3	4.4	5.4	6.0	
South Africa	5.3	5.3	5.1	5.4	
Denmark	5.1	5.3	4.8	5.3	
Netherlands	5.0	5.4	4.4	5.1	
Finland	4.8	5.0	5.0	4.4	
Germany	4.7	4.2	5.4	4.5	
Taiwan	4.3				4.3
Hungary	4.1	6.0	1.9	4.3	
Portugal	4.0			4.0	
Italy	3.9	3.5		4.3	
Slovenia	3.9	4.6	4.4	2.6	
Sweden	3.7	3.5	4.0	3.7	
Russia	3.7	4.9			2.5
UAE	3.7	3.7			
Belgium	3.4	2.7	3.9	3.5	
Hong Kong	3.0			3.0	
Japan	2.2	2.9	2.2	1.5	

The table shows how many people out of 100 adults at the age between 16 and 64 years are active as entrepreneurs. The average of all countries is 8.4% in 2005, in South America an over average percentage of 16.6%, in North America 11.1%. With 5.4%, the EU ranks far below and with 4.7% Germany is even below the European average.

Germany has been in the back range for years and there is no real change visible. That is proved by numerous other international studies. The Global Entrepreneurship Monitor (GEM) provides more detailed information.[229]

GEM is the globally biggest empirical inquiry regarding entrepreneurship. Since 1999, more than 60 countries have been participating in it. Thereby, the GEM research is targeted at 3 main objectives:

- To measure the differences in the early stages of entrepreneurial activities between the countries.
- To reveal factors causing the amount of entrepreneurial activities and
- To transport frame conditions, e.g. in the political environment, to the entrepreneurial activities.

What are the most important fields of innovation for green business company foundations? The result from numerous analyses shows that the following areas are considered to have special chances:[230]

1. Solar energy and applications
2. Wind energy and other renewable energy solutions
3. Biofuel and bio materials
4. Green buildings and green design
5. Clean transport possibilities, clean cars and personal mobility
6. Changes of infrastructure
7. Mobile applications and green IT
8. Water filtration and clean water technologies

Section 9 of the book "Clean-tech Revolution" is particularly remarkable. It is named "Create your own Silicon Valley".[231] As the only German region "Sun City" in Freiburg is highlighted. The Fraunhofer Institut für Solar Energie Systeme located here is specially mentioned as Europe's biggest solar research organization and refers again to the intermeshing of science and company foundation. But also the fact that

---

[229] cf. www.gemconsortium.org/ Request from June 12, 2008
[230] cf. R Pernick, C. Wilder, The Clean Tech Revolution. The next big Growth and Investment Opportunity, Harper Collins Pub., New York 2007
[231] cf. Ibid, p.237

Freiburg is the only city with a solar guide for the region, published in German and English, is paid attention to.

The support of research and development for cleaner green-tech foundations is mandatory and exists with practically every successful company. In their ratings, even with cities, the ranking agency SustainLane from San Francisco event takes into account whether they have at least one university or a renowned research institute in the so-called "knowledge base". [232]

The new companies from the above-mentioned innovation fields that have to be observed particularly intensively according to investigations by Pernick and Wilder, belong to the eight areas:

Table 11: New green-tech companies

Solar Energy		
Company	City	<URL>
Applied Materials	Santa Clara California	www.appliedmaterials.com
Miasolé	Santa Clara California	www.miasole.com
MMA Renewable V entures	San Francisco California	www.mmarenewablesventures.com
Nanosolar	Palo Alto California	www.nanosolar.com
Q-Cells	Thalheim Germany	www.q-cells.com
REC	Hovik Norwegen	www.scanwafer.com
Sharp	OsakaJapan	www.shgarp.co.jp
SunEdison	Baltimore Maryland	www.sunedison.com
SunPowwer	Sunnyvale California	www.sunpowercorp.com
Suntech Power	Wuxi Jiangsu China	www.suntech-power.com
Wind Energy		

---

[232] Ibid. p. 243

Acciona	Pamplona Spain	www.acciona.com
Austin Energy	Austin Texas	www.austinenergy.com
FPL Group	Juno Beach Florida	www.fpl.com
Gamesa	Madrid Spain	www.gamesa.es
General Electric	Fairfield Connecticut	www.ge.com
Horizon Wind Energy	Houston Texas	www.horizonwind.com
Iberdrola	Bilbao Spain	www.iberdrola.com
Southwest Windpower	Flagstaff Arizona	www.windenergy.com
Suzlon Energy	Pune India	www.suzlon.com
Vestas Wind Systems	Randers Denmark	www.vestas.com
Biofuels / Biomaterials		
Archer Daniels Midland	Decatur Illionois	www.admworld.com
Cilion	Menlo Park California	www.cilion.com
Diversa	San Diego California	www.diversa.com
DuPont	Wilmington Delaware	www.dupont.com
Imperium Renewables	Seattle Washington	www.imperiumrenewables.com
Iogen	Ottawa Canada	www.iogen.ca
NatureWorks LLC	Minneapolis Minnesota	www.natureworksllc.com
Novozymes	Begswaerd Denmark	www.novozymes.com
Toyota	Toyota City Japan	www.toyota.com

Green Building Technology		
Aspen Aerogels	Northborough Massachusetts	www.aerogel.com
Clarum Homes	Palo Alto California	www.clarum.com
Cree	Durham North Carolina	www.cree.com
The Durst Organization	New York	www.durst.org
Interface Engineering	Portland Oregon	www.interfceengineering.com
Ortech	Braeside Victoria Australia	www.orgtech.com.au
PanaHome	Osaka Japan	www.panahome.jp/english
Rinnai	Nagoya Japan	www.rinnai.co.jp
Turner Construction	New York	www.turnerconstruction.com
WalmartStores	Bentonville Arkansas	www.walmartstores.com
Personal Transportation		
CalCArs	Palo Alto California	www.calcars.org
Chery	Wuhu China	www.cheryglobal.com
EEStor	Cedar Park Texas	www.eestor.com
General Motors	Detroit	www.gm.com
Honda	Tokyo Japan	www.honda.com
REV A	Electric Car Bangalore India	www.revaindia.com
Tesla Motors	San Carlos California	www.teslamotors,com
Toyota	Toyota City	www.toyota.com

	Japan	
Valence Technology	Austin Texas	www.valence.com
Vectrix	Newport Rhode Island	www.vectrix.com
Green Energy		
BPL Global	Pittsburgh Pennsylvania	www.bplglobal.net
Comverge	East Hanover New Jersey	www.comverge.com
CURRENT Communicati ons	Germantown Maryland	www.current.net
Eneroc.com	NOC Boston	www.enernoc.com
Electric Power Research Institute	Palo AltoCalifornia	www.epri.com
GridPoint	Washington D.C.	www.gridpoint.com
Hunt Technologies	Pequout Lakes Minnesota	www.huntechnologies.com
IBM	Armonk New York	www.ibm.com
Itron	Liberty Lake Washington	www.itron.com
SmartSynch	Jackson Mississipi	www.samrtsynch.com
Mobile Technologie s		
3M	Minneapolis	www.3m.com
A123	Watertown Massachusetts	www.a123systems.com
ECD Ovonics	Rochester Hills Michigan	www.ovonic.com
Jadoo Power	Foilsom	www.jadoopower.com

Systems	California	
Konarka	Lowell Massachusetts	www.konarka.com
Mechanical Technology	Albany New York	www.mechtec.com
Noble Energy Solar Technologies	Hyderabad India	www.solarnest.net
SkyBuilt Power	AirlingtonVirginia	www.skybuilt.com
Smart Fuell Cell Germany	Brunnthal	www.smartfuellcell.de
Soldius	Veendam Niederlande	www.solius.com
Water Filtration Systems		
AqWise	Herzliya Israel	www.aqwise.com
Christ Water Technology Group	Mondsee Austria	www.christwater.com
eMembrane	Providence Rhode Island	www.ememnrane.com
Energy Recovery	Sanleandro CA	www.energy-recovery.com
GE Water & Process Technologies	Trevose Pennsylvania	www.gewater.com
Hyflux	Singapore	www.hyflux.com
NEwater	Singapore	www.pub.gov.sg
Siemens	Munich Germany	www.siemens.com
WaterHealth International	Lake Forest California	www.waterhealth.com
YSI	Yellow Springs Ohio	www.ysi.com

In the list there are only three German companies and in one domain of the industrial base Germany, the automotive industry, not a single one. Many of the green-tech companies named here have been almost unknown up to now or just to insiders. New German incorporations are missing. One more time, this proves the need for stronger scientifically-founded entrepreneurship for environment and climate protection. However, the research universities for that are also missing here in Germany and cannot be developed out of the old structures without new foundations.

5. Reorientation of Academic Education towards Sustainability

The Green League Sets Benchmarks

Internationally, there are numerous efforts to evaluate the activities of the academies in the field of environment and climate protection, i.e. sustainability. In contrast to our own points of view, German academies do not perform too well but rather range amongst "also-ran". According to the Association of University Leaders for a Sustainable Future[233] the following countries are particularly highlighted, for example:

Table 12: Green Universities[234]

Country	No. of "green" Universities
Australia	12
Germany	0
Finland	1
Hong Kong	2
India	2
Ireland	1
Japan	1
Canada	11
Mexico	1
New Zeeland	1

---

[233] cf.www.ulsf.org./resouces.html Request of January 24th, 2008
[234] Association of University Leaders for a Sustainable Future, in: www.ulsf.org./resources.html.; Request of January 18th, 2008
187

Portugal	1
Spain.	2
Great Britain	4
USA	92
Total	**131**

The lack of European universities in this list is remarkable. Countries like France, Italy and Germany remain as unmentioned as China. But under the patronage of the Ministry for Education of the People's Republic of China there is an exchange between the Berlin Humboldt University and 21 "Chinese key universities".[235]

Amongst the Chinese universities participating in the exchange there also was the Shanxi University, Taiyuan (SXU). It was founded in 1902 in the southwest of Beijing as one of the three universities financed by the Chinese Government. The SXU developed to an internationally renowned university. According to their own specifications they specifically occupy with the fields of arts, sciences, medicine, engineering/technique and law. Today, the SXU is an important teaching and research institution where 19,913 students are enlisted at present. It counts amongst China's 60 top universities and gained the title "the green university". In the year 2004, there were 1683 public and about 1000 private academies, which also handle the topic of green-tech to an increasing extent. This can already be noticed in numerous areas of life, like e.g. in food research.[236]

Japan's academy system is also remarkable. There are 716 universities three quarters of which are private academies. These private academies that all claim higher tuition fees than the governmental ones are fiercely fought about, and are considered the ticket for an ensured professional career. In 2005, almost 51.5% of the gymnasium graduates decided for attending an academy. Seen globally, this is record level. But this must not hide the fact that only 0.8% of these graduates did their doctorate after that. This can be attributed to the professional situation. In Japan, a bachelor is completely sufficient for a professional career. Thus, promotion is interesting for the academic career only. A ranking

---

[235] cf China Campus Berlin 2002, in: http://www.china-campus.de/unis/ index.php; Request from July 4, 2008
[236] Source: http://www.uwm.edu/Dept/CIE/studyabroad/programs/ShanxiUniversi ty China.htmRequest of July 4th, 2008

system of the American Institute for Scientific Information (ISI) evaluates the number of publications and quotations of the Japanese academies and research institutes. This quotation index differentiates between academies and expert fields. If you take the global data as a basis, Japan has considerably improved its position in the last years. In 1981, Japan still ranked at position 4 behind the USA, Germany and Great Britain. Germany was overtaken in 1988 already and in 1998 Japan achieved rank 2 in the world ranking list with 73,000 scientific publications.[237] The number alone is amazing considering the fact that Japan has 127 million citizens.

In 2001, the Japanese Ministry for Education proposed a model for strengthening the state-financed "top 30" universities that are listed as "world class universities" and put their main emphasis on the areas science and technology. Basis of the ranking became the factors promotion of research, mentioning in publications, degree of difficulty of the entrance examinations and the reputation of the university. As the best three universities, the state-operated universities of Tokyo, Kyoto and Osaka are named in the list. But the privately financed universities that are very different from their profiles remain unconsidered. However, without doubt some of them, like Waseda and Keio, belong on the list of Japan's "world class universities".[238]

Today, the "Ranking of the World Universities", for the first time published in 2003 by the University of Shanghai, is regarded the globally most important ranking. Here, the first ranks have been occupied by American universities for years. Amongst the top 20 alone there are 17 American academies (Harvard holds position 1 with 100 points, Stanford position 2 with 73.7 points and Berkley position 3) At least, Cambridge University still reaches position 4 and Oxford position 10. Far behind at position 53 there is the Ludwig-Maximilians-Universität (LMU) Munich and at position 56 the TU Munich. Both academies are counted amongst the best academies in Germany, too. Furthermore, amongst the best one hundred "world class universities", there are Heidelberg, Göttingen, Freiburg and Bonn. The Berlin Humboldt-Universität and Freie Universität were not taken into consideration because of internal reasons

---

[237] Source:
http://www.internationalekooperation.de/de/laenderinfo21964.htm
Request of July 4th, 2008
[238] Source: www.nigelward.com/top30.html Request of July 9th, 2008

that did not really contribute to their positive outer appearance. This ranking, too, included state-financed schools only and "going-green" was not asked for.[239]

On the World Summit for sustainable Development in Johannesburg (WSSD), the "Global Higher Education for Sustainability Partnership" (GHESP) was founded as official partnership. Founders of this partnership are the International Association of Universities (IAU), the Association of University Leaders for a Sustainable Future (ULSF), the COPERNICUS-CAMPUS as well as the UNESCO. Main objective of this partnership is the coordination of "education for a sustainable development" on the global academy sector. Basis of the GHESP is the "Lüneburg Declaration on Higher Education for Sustainable Development" that was passed in Lüneburg (Germany) in 2001. It expresses the obligation of universities to make a contribution to sustainable development. The objectives of GHESP are the distribution of implementation strategies for the consideration of sustainable development in the academies, the exchange and further development of best practice examples, the evaluation of hitherto taken measures and the conclusion of recommendations for the further development of academic education for sustainable development.[240]

Particularly great efforts for the ranking of environmental activities of the academies are made in England as it is shown by the "Green League" evaluation that is common there.

---

[239] Source:
http://www.spiegel.de/unispiegel/studium/0,1518,512066,00.html
Request of March 14th, 2008
[240] www.unesco.org/iau/sd/rtf/sd_dluneburg.rtf Request from March 12, 2008

Rank	University	Publicly available environmental policy	Full time environmental staff	Comprehensive environmental audit	Green travel plan	Fairtrade University status	% total energy from renewables	% waste recycled	Carbon emissions per head (Kg CO2e)	Final Score (max. 50)
1	Leeds Metropolitan						85%	36%	636	48
2	Plymouth						7%	40%	501	46
3	Hertfordshire						16%	31%	553	44
4	Glamorgan						64%	32%	579	43
5	Gloucestershire						36%	6%	242	42
5	Oxford Brookes						34%	—	376	42
5	Queen's, Belfast						17%	17%	1,091	42
8	Anglia Ruskin						6%	14%	460	40
8	Cambridge						22%	29%	2,349	40
8	Edinburgh						25%	26%	1,868	40
8	Leeds						0%	33%	1,252	40
8	Portsmouth						0%	27%	722	40
8	Sheffield Hallam						2%	10%	476	40
8	St Andrews						30%	22%	1,896	40
8	University of the West of England, Bristol						—	29%	522	40

Figure 7: Best British Universities according to Green League Evaluation

At present, a comparable ranking of German academies is missing completely. The Federal Parliament took up the understanding of new educational requirements formulated in the Agenda 21 and worded objectives for the realization. For the academic sector, they mainly highlight need for research in "sustainable consumption and life styles as well as sustainable economizing and global interconnections" as well as environmental education research. In addition to a reference to the required alternation of study guidelines, regarding the knowledge transfer function they refer to the orientation framework "Bildung für eine nachhaltige Entwicklung" (Education for sustainable development) of the Bund-Länder-Kommission of 1998.[241]

In all, the global significance of German academies in the field of green-tech still is relatively low. Even though there are numerous approaches and initiatives to conduct corresponding researches. For example, a project promotion fund for students' projects that focus on environment and sustainability at the BTU Cottbus. A first solar project was put into operation at the beginning of 2007. In the light of the global situation this is a start. But in any case it is sufficient to cover and fix the need for research and, above all, the will to think sustainably.

With this, the efforts on federal and Lander level shall no way be disregarded. But in international comparison unavoidably one comes to the conclusion that Germany will miss the bus if drastic and instant

---

[241] BLK, 2000.

changes are not introduced. For example, the *Berliner Zeitung* titled in their issue of July 8th, 2008 "Overcrowded lecture halls, ancient equipment". This described the general situation of the German academies to the point. In order to make Germany and its universities competitive and supporting pillars as suppliers for research and science, corresponding equipment and the right attitude are needed in the first place. Urge and eagerness for research can only develop where students do not have to crowd in the lecture halls, and where adequate supervision by the professors is ensured. Hannah Blum from the head of division committee of the Berlin Humboldt-University expresses that as follows: "Doctrines are just consumed but one does not research anymore."[242]

These conditions, amongst others provoked by the introduction of the bachelor concept, are one part of the problems German academies have to deal with. How should an academy teach environmental consciousness and sustainability if they cannot exemplify that? If energy saving is not practiced in a conscious and clearly visible way?

For example, the University of Cottbus shows the way in the right direction with its "Referat für umweltgerechte Entwicklung (RUGE)" (Report for environmental development). This paper defines saving measures and effective methods for the improvement of the environment at academies to the implementation of an environment management system for academies.

But the most essential point should be that the connection academy economy is not yet mature enough. The "Excellence initiative" that has to be praised from the approach is still in its infancy although it was started in 2006 already. This initiative by state and Landers shall promote outstanding researches and finally ensure international acknowledgement in this segment. But hitherto results are still owed. As Martin Spiewak formulated so nicely at academics.de, up to now no excellence cluster has lead to scientific results, none of the nine honored elite universities has taken up the competition with Harvard and Oxford. Still, their presidents are mainly occupied with personnel discussions and building applications.[243]

---

[242] Source Berliner Zeitung No. 158 dated June 8, 2008

[243]

http://www.academics.de/wissenschaft/die_exzellenzinitiative_ein_harte r_we ttbewerb_um_ gelder_und_prestige_30779.html Request of July, 12th, 2008

Although there are topic groups in the so-called excellence clusters that deal with the topic of climate change, there is just one excellence cluster that really seems to deserve the name green-tech, namely the one at the university of Aachen with their study "Maßgeschneiderte Kraftstoffe aus Biomasse." (Tailor-made fuels of biomass). In the light of the approved list of 37 excellence clusters this clearly is not enough. [244]

Even in the CHE research ranking that explores the best conditions for scientists in research there are just the classic disciplines like machine building, informatics or similar on the list. Thus, Michael Kanellos, reputable journalist for cnet.com, did not only attest Germany a leading role in solar technology but also seriously warns that Europe was definitely in the position to game away the leading role in green technology.[245]

Today, America's academies clearly show how this change can be executed. More and more academies establish special courses of study that exclusively deal with green-tech and are considerably supported by the economy. Such direct financial support of the universities by the economy could give another impetus towards Germany and greentech.

In their orientation framework "Bildung für eine nachhaltige Entwicklung" of 1998, the Bund-Länder-Kommission für Bildungsplanung und Forschungsförderung (BLK) classifies the basic principle of sustainable development at academies in five tasks, independently from the type of academy:

- For solving problems, inter-disciplinarity shall be promoted by also referring to cultural, social-political and economic-scientific disciplines besides nature- and technology-scientific disciplines.
- Environmental education in teaching needs to be founded by research. "Ecological future research" is named as target perspective here, researching the "feedback effects of human acting on natural systems on the one hand but at the same time

---

[244] Deutsche Forschungsgemeinschaft, List of supported Excellence Clusters
http://www.dfg.de/forschungsfoerderung/koordinierte_program/exzelle nziniti ative/exzellenzcluster/liste/exc_gesamt.html Request of July, 12th, 2008
[245] http://news.cnet.com/How-green-could-make-Europe-a-tech-power/201011392_3-6235385. html?hhTest=1&tag=nw.4 Request from April 14, 2008

also the feedback effects on the human society resulting from the changes of the natural systems"

- Sustainable development requires systematical knowledge and research transfer between academies, economy, communities and citizens, the development of networks in research and teaching as well as the establishment of partnerships.
- Academies as technical and administrative enterprises have to design their own resources consumption and the material flows exhausted by them more efficiently under the basic principle of sustainable development.
- The demands of education for sustainable development require permanent further training of the academy personnel in the sense of environmentally friendly academy management. At the BLK congress "Zukunft lernen und gestalten; Bildung für eine nachhaltige Entwicklung" in 2001, Seybold/Winkelmann already state that comprehensive changes are required for the educational sector.

Consequently, the center of the further changing process has to be the question how such a reform of academic education can contribute to sustainable development. There, the authors see five essential starting points for changes, namely in the areas of inter-disciplinarity and plurality, globalization by intercultural collaboration (generation of networks), knowledge transfer and life-long learning, participation and trans-disciplinarity as well as self-obligation. Even the German Parliament regularly deals with the progresses of education for sustainable development.[246]

But obviously these political initiatives and activities only take effect very slowly. Curricula, examination forms and methods do not approximately meet the requirements of the new actual challenges, let alone those of 2020 to 2050. The federal structures of the education system have additional effect until, for example, the UN decade "Education for sustainable development 2005 to 2014" is put into practice everywhere or green-tech is firmly anchored in the classic curricula.

Looking back at John Doerr's speech (see p. 58), the statement of his 15-year old daughter Mary should make everybody think. In a discussion about global warming she said to her father: "Your generation has caused

---

[246] cf. Deutsche Bundestag Drucksache 15/6012 of October 10th, 2005

the problem, now it is up to you to solve it." A responsibility that everybody has to face consciously.

One can only agree with this statement and most people are of the same opinion. Today, massive changes have to be initiated in order to solve the upcoming challenges, to manage to do groundbreaking leaps as it was the case with the dot-coms back then, so that everybody can benefit from that. With the dot-coms, many things were neglected that will have to be made up for with the dot-greens now. Nobody doubts the qualities of German research. But the marketing and the economic use of these inventions still leaves space for improvements.

In order to keep up a leading role in the field of green business, private academies are needed that completely specialize on this topic. Be it by privately sponsored institutes like, for example, the Hasso Plattner Institute at the Uni of Potsdam or completely private universities.

The necessity of such a private university can be explained in a simple way:

In economic practice, research and teaching, the global need for managers and experts with knowledge about latest environment technologies and the climate rises disproportionately. To an increasing extent, in the USA, India and China as well as in the Gulf region, the "going green" trend follows strong economic, social as well as regulatory pressure, not so much eco-ideological arguments as frequently in Europe.

In the globally leading business schools the new challenges to education and further training are thought by means of integration of environment and climate topics as well as by special master courses, based on already present technical specializations. (e.g. Presidio School of Management SF).

In order to develop a European green university in further development steps from that, a new type of academy, e.g. in the first step a green master school supported by the environmental industry, trade and service companies, especially the energy and water industry, has to be created.

Profile of a Green Business Training

Starting from international studies and requirements by the industry in Germany, in the scope of the training of industrial engineers, the already above mentioned clean technologies should be the central point of education and further training as well as for strengthening company foundations:

195

- Solar energy and applications
- Wind energy and other renewable energy solutions
- Biofuel and biomaterials
- Green buildings and green design
- Green design
- Changes of the infrastructure
- Mobile applications and green IT
- Water filtration and clean water technologies

In concordance with the industry the first studying years could comprehend the following topic areas:

- Sustainability strategies under special observation of climate, environment and noise protection, of renewable energies, traffic and building alternatives.
- Environmental protection and environmental hygiene for humans, animals and ecosystems (keeping clean of air, water and soil)
- Eco-intelligent and eco-efficient product and technology development incl. material circuits and disposal.
- Risk assessment and pollutants safety in chemical and biological processes including test procedures and standardization.
- De-carbonization and emissions trading as well as management and controlling of the observance of the climate and environment protection norms.
- Sustainable innovation and environment management for companies in the scope of supply chain management.
- Media ecology and sustainable future-capable event management.

Likewise in the Stanford pattern, direct networking and collaboration with the big companies should take place. Such networking provides advantages to all network partners. The companies could deliver guiding information, relieve their own researches or push them in terms of emphasis. The question of the employees of tomorrow would reduce itself drastically because one learns to know and appreciate them beforehand already. An advance in time can definitely still be achieved if reaction takes place instantly.

Application of Modern Teaching and Practicing Methods and E-Learning

Of course, studying at a green master school should also provide incentives in other areas.

1. Interactive teaching, in which the active participation of the studying with intellectual, physical, ethic and intuitive challenges is assumed at a high level. Embedded goal-oriented entrepreneurial and social activity has more motivating and sustainable effect than the frequently still dominating ex-cathedra teaching method. At the same time, be means of interactive course works, a high level of self-developed activities opposed to authority-oriented instructions shall be achieved. In this sense, co-creation of the courses of study is assumed in which a series of modules and basic knowledge subjects are carefully structured and modeled, others are developed together during the process.

2. System-thinking and practice-oriented approach. Here it is particularly about the understanding for the complex interrelationships between technical, economical, social and ecological activities as well as problems. By means of system- and process-oriented thinking, the limits of long-year narrow technique-specific opinions should be overcome and interdisciplinary ways of thinking and working should be trained. In this process, it has to become clear that a high portion of today's environmental problems developed by reason of the one-sided technique-specific approaches during the last 150 years.

3. Development of Creativity and Communication Competence The studying should be made capable of finding new and unexpected solutions on their own and simultaneously receive deep understanding for innovation-theoretical foundations of the preparation, enforcement and distribution of eco-induced changes. As a result of the master studies, if possible, every graduate should develop concrete practice-oriented models and venture plans for innovative product solutions that have real chances to be put into practice and ideally lead to real incorporations.

4. Environmental problems always have global character, even if they occur locally in the beginning. For example, CO_2 input has no borders. Hence it follows that the new type of academy has to be directed towards internationality from the beginning and that it

includes operations abroad as well as international project work. The students have to learn a new way of global thinking and solving problems and be able to practice that.

5. Experience teaches that apart from theoretical fundamentals, the practical competence to solve problems and entrepreneurial acting deserve much more attention in the first place. It is not sufficient just to develop concepts or knowledge, much more emphasis has to be put on realization competence. In China, they are seriously working on examining practical skills on top of theoretical knowledge. We would be well-advised if we did not miss but determine this new trend.

From the beginning, all possibilities of the employment of latest and environmentally friendly learning aids, based on e-learning, mobile learning, blended learning, should be used. Such a private academy should not suffer from out-of-date means of learning, computers from the late 80s or missing supervision. Economy-oriented development could set new impulses here and is compulsory from today's point of view.

Ways to Support Sustainable Development at German Academies

CO_2 reduction or effective, sustainable measures for the increase of energy efficiency have to be accepted as socially relevant topics by the universities. But pro-active tendencies and "prompt" reactions for handling the challenges to teaching and research connected therewith are definitely missing. Implicitly a problem that has to be solved is the result even if many German academies have been including an increasing amount of activities for sustainability in the canon of their efforts for the social development over years.

More than fifteen years after the Rio conference[247] generally binding and accepted strategies for a way that has to be taken jointly for the solution of the task that concerns the entire society, the educational sector especially in the environment of the academies towards sustainable and sustainability transferring education politics are still missing. The processes and structures required for that are present in

---

[247] United Nations UN-Dok. A/CONF.151/26 (Vol. I-III), Report of the United Nations Conference on Environment and Development (Rio de Janeiro, 3-14 June 1992), New York, August 1992

rudiments rather continuous, integrative concepts that are jointly borne by the academies are missing.

The current development rather shows the trend towards individualization: the academies behave like lone warriors with the goal to ensure the public budgets for their own activities instead of exchange about more or less successful measures in association with likeminded people und to make the target a homogenization of the programs for the promotion of sustainability. Especially under this aspect it becomes obvious that the educational politics of the Federal Republic of Germany show considerable deficits: instead of promoting inter-disciplinarity and joint research activities, lone warriorship is pushed consequently and finally a high amount of redundant activities is accepted. All that at the expense of a needed (and possible!) process landscape that shows effective and efficient communication about definitely present good examples with the objective of structured recording, further development and joint realization.

The direct reaction of politics and economy can be found in the contempt and/or undervaluation of the academy potential in the environment of sustainable development. In doing so, informative opening of the academies is compulsory: after the motto "you cannot communicate enough" it is high time to communicate the right things in order not to lose connection. Because hitherto, in international comparison, there still is a lack of exiting new messages about top performances from the environment of German academies, although performances are rendered on a very high level. But although foreign countries are definitely interested in "sustainable" German academy activities, frequently the degree of popularity is a problem.

From the academy location Germany, in particular, clear impulses in the scope of educational politics marked by sustainability are expected. In the absence of academy politics that coordinate and support joint use of resources and due to the lack of structures that can be used for that, compared with centrally controlled approaches like e.g. in Great Britain (see above), the efforts regarding sustainability appear to be rather helpless the outer presentation suffers from that in particular.

Apart from consequent support of success-promising juniors there is also a lack of central coordination of all academy projects and measures with focus on topics like research, cooperation possibilities, inter-disciplinarity and the public relations connected therewith with the target to free the performance providers (but also the juniors) from their isolation and finally show perspectives that stop a migration of this extraordinarily important circle of people to foreign countries.

In principle, the entire current educational system has to be rethought. It is not sufficient to introduce innovation markets for scientists and students and wanting to stimulate the labor market this way[248] it is much more important to promote the exchange of information between academies and companies by preparation of a comprehensive knowledge management and transfer system that also meets the political requirements of the labor market. This requires clearly more flexible, academy-political and simultaneously enterprise-oriented education management and "loads of courage" to put it into practice because many academies still struggle very hard with modernization and innovation.

The following theses for a new educational concept summarize what the academies, the economy, what Germany needs today in order to be competitive yet tomorrow.

- Sustainability in research and teaching requires categorical rethinking in academic education and in this context the prior processes on the educational sector.
- Innovations not only on the academy sector are driven by the implicit interdisciplinary aspect of a sustainable development.
- Sustainable development requires clearly better usage of academic networks and strategic alliances as well as clearly more efficient and more effective planning and usage of synergy effects, even exceeding the borders of the campus. The sustainability of academic education cannot be ensured in a solo attempt.
- Without "external" incentives, advice and support in change management the academies will struggle to meet the requirements of sustainable development. They have become time-critical already today and are endangered to lose connection in the international environment.
- Sustainability in research and teaching acts as driving force pointing at clear changes in educational politics of the academies and other educational providers as well as technology and knowledge transfer to the companies.
- Sustainable economic growth is indissolubly coupled with sustainable educational growth.

---

[248] UNI 21; BMBF 2004

- Sustainable educational growth does not only require quality controlled projecting but also needs multi-layer horizontal and vertical controlling of the process environment of educational politics.

The term "Green Business School" can generate a simple "trademark" for a quality-assured process that can support the German academies in making their contribution to a sustainable development in a better and more creative way.

6. Summary

The current situation with weekly increases in fuel prices, rising food prices and permanently increasing electricity and gas costs as well as inflationary tendencies in many areas changes the common consciousness at high speed. One feels shifted back to the times of the first oil crises with driving prohibitions and tends to compare the present mood with that. But the really grave differences make it clear very quickly that it is really the beginning of a new era now. The dearer raw materials, especially the fossil fuels and above all the drastic alarming signals of climate change cannot be rationalized away any longer. Playing the facts down like back then is no longer possible today.

This becomes particularly obvious at the example of the change in the USA described in this book. If the USA had always been considered as the biggest ignorant in terms of climate change and attention in environmental questions, the new gold rush mood for green-tech in the United States will now intoxicate all the other countries. The comparison with the dot-com wave at the end of the last millennium clearly showed how strongly innovations can be unleashed if the economic interest is high enough. In this connection the fact that the dot-com era was also accompanied by collapsing companies plays a sad but from the geopolitical point of view rather minor role because the enormous technological progress on the Internet sector stands against that. A demonization of the dot-com phase would ignore the skyrocketing development in the field of high-tech. Now there is more at stake than just economical profits. At stake is survival under the conditions of the rapidly progressing climate change.

If countries like the USA unleash a really unparalleled catch-up race, one can be sure that they will come up with results very soon. That

201

especially the USA is predominantly focused in this book has got to do with exactly this unleashing of highest power in critical situations. Without envy one has to appreciate that the USA sometimes start a bit belated but the more vehemently then.

The dot-com era gifted all countries with a countless number of technological innovations. Without this high, PCs might have entered every day life of many people to this extent years later only. Life without the omnipresent Internet is very hard to imagine today. The mobile phone in its present form would still live a shadowy existence and films on DVD or digital satellite reception would still be in their infancy. Entire professional fields have developed from the basic technologies of this time. That exactly will happen with other progresses in the field of green-tech and much more comprehensively than many think today.

For many years, Germany has been said to be leading in the development of renewable energies. But Germany could lose this leadership position very soon if instant and un-bureaucratic action does not take place. In the middle of June 2008, the media received the message that the USA will catch up with Germany as operators of wind power wheels in the course of this year already. In Silicon Valley, with nanosolar, a completely new solar technology develops at the same time that shall only cost a few dollars per watt then. Such messages are the more surprising since the USA's activities in this field have taken place very half-heartedly up to now. The calls of the government and surely also the upcoming US elections and, above all, entrepreneurial activities, effect a rapid change in consciousness. Thus, it is not surprising that an US oil billionaire invests 10 billion dollars in a wind park in Texas.[249]

Although Germany has been attributing high significance to the topic of renewable energies for a long time already, the influence of politics on innovation processes appears to be too volatile. One example for that is the biodiesel industry. First they create incentives and tax relieves, then they are revoked or partly suspended or corrected in essential frame conditions from the point of view of the changed prices for food. The press releases by the Biodiesel Association regarding that are very clear.[250]

---

[249] Source: Berliner Zeitung and
http://www.energieverbraucher.de/index.php?itid=706&st_id=706&cont ent_news_detail=7175&back_cont_id=706 Request of 23rd of May, 2008
[250] cf. for example www.biokraftstoffverband.de Request of June 6th, 2008

The insolvency of the "Biodiesel Industries AG" that was in detail commented in press releases as an example has deterrent effect on investors and is directly linked with the lack of political trustworthiness and reliability. If governmental regulations and frame conditions change according to the political mood instead of the objective global requirements, green-tech investors get unsure and this kind of sense of departure that was so typical for the dot-coms is missing completely. However, regarding dependency on regulatory policies, the newly developing dot-greens are completely different from the dot-coms. International and national laws, norms and restrictions have crucial influence on the activities in the new green business. The ongoing discussion about safe, industry-political energy supply outlines that very clearly. While with the dot-coms the influence of the entrepreneurs and the capital providers shaped the development in the first place, on the environmental sector politicians always intervened with laws and regulations. The entrepreneur and holder of the German Environment Award (Deutscher Umweltpreis), Hermann Josef Schulte from HJS, declared on the occasion of a symposium in the Deutsche Bundesstifung Umwelt in Osnabrück (Federal German Environment Foundation) in summer 2008 his catalytic converters and particle filters being "political products" for which there would be no market without national or international environment regulations. The achievement of market attraction is accelerated to the greatest extent when more and more consumers realize that environmental products are frequently good for their own health at the same time. In order to spark off innovation streams in a faster and more sustainable way, the connection between environment and health protection has to be emphasized much more clearly. Another multi-billion deal will result from that if more creativity and entrepreneurial spirit can be deployed.

While other countries, for example, approach the development of new enterprises from universities in a simple and un-bureaucratic way, sometimes even playfully, Germany still follows strict norms and regulations and has numerous interdictions and regulations for scientists on the public sector. This hampers entrepreneurship. In the field of educational institutions, in particular, the seemingly endless chaos of regulations is disturbing. Although it is compulsory to promote innovations in the academies, free of financial shortage and long-term approval processes. If you wanted to wait until all possible occurrences are regulated by the state and anchored in laws and resolutions, it could happen that the new wave of "green technologies" passes by Germany although many developments were tackled very early as pilots here.

Germany has to act instantly and become active now and that is meant in the literal sense. The pain barrier with energy prices is reached, now the increases in costs of living reach dimensions that hardly leave space for other private consumption. Now, sense of departure is propagated everywhere and the time has come to play out and force our technological capabilities. Now it is not just about economic consciousness, but about a new type of green market bearing the chance of profiling Germany remaining a technologically leading country. That in doing so one also uses the experience of other nations does not have to be considered a negative bandwagon effect.

By means of the examples from Silicon Valley given in this book, it should have become clear how important interaction between education and economy is. Companies like Google had never come into being if the desire to research and try out had not been supported at the academy already. Never would a company have become so big if there had not been a direct connection between the academies and the venture capital providers.

The moment when fears resulting from the negative experience with the dot-coms are dropped, promotion of new innovative developments is possible. German enterprises should become even more aware of the importance of the academies and their possibilities and support them to a higher extent in their own interest. There, recruiting future staff is an aspect that will take place much more targeted due to the mobilization and support of the will to research with the students. This should become the central interest of the companies. To an increased extent, established companies should see themselves also as partners of the junior entrepreneurs because both parties can only benefit from the innovation potential and the synergies on the green-tech sector.

In this field of innovation for green-tech anchoring the new brand label "dot-green" seems to be worth considering in order to transmit the interconnection of innovation, sustainable fitness for the future and economic growth already from the name on an international level.

If managers from German companies deal with the topic of "green technology" to an increasing extent and consequently anchor their findings in their company philosophy respectively marketing strategy, this will surely have positive effect on the global acceptance and the long-term growth of German companies. But for that integration of the academies into the development of new technologies has to be increased by a manifold.

Apart from the companies, venture capital providers and private investors are challenged in the first place. Better support of incorporators in the field of green technologies and simplified grant guidelines for loans would support many innovative company foundations that frequently fail because of formalities today. Massive support in the management of young companies supports the investment security of the venture capital providers in addition. Giving up their inapproachability would lead to more collaboration between venture capital providers and academies and junior entrepreneurs and thus to the promotion of innovative developments and implementations on the market.

On the part of the academies, of course, measures are required, too. Easy access for students to economy and the venture capital firms surely would support the desire to research of the studying much more. The global importance of the green technologies should be made transparent for the students at the academies already. Because green technology promises the highest increase rates worldwide. A clear commitment of the German academies could constructively influence the will to cooperate with the technology companies. For that, a lead organization had to be founded, like e.g. a private "green university" connected with a process of permanent auditing of all academies regarding their contribution to mastering climate change and their own "going green". Academies that cannot execute such environment-oriented quality assurance would have to have the possibility to resort to the capabilities of external cooperation partners and to actively search international exchange.

Finally, of course, the commitment of politics remains an important aspect. Politics must stop just composing recommendations and long-term guidelines of dubious stability with regard at the next elections. Targeted measures and concrete support for the field of green-tech should take place now, not in a graduated plan until 2012. Because climate change and green-tech are not buzzwords for the next federal or state election but require long-term obligations and measures exceeding the election periods. Green-tech environment strategies should be sustainably integrated into our economic system and become as normal as e.g. waste separation. In his latest guidebook "Unterwegs zu einem ökologischen Wirtschaftswunder" (On the way to an ecological economic miracle) Maximilian Gege has worked out many precious facts and recommendations.

Germany should not only pay lip services, but start to make climate protection and green-tech development topic number one. In the education system, in particular, instant acting is indispensable. Only if politics give the corresponding signal, companies will be ready to intensify their efforts.

In other countries, collaboration of educational providers and the economy has been much more pronounced for a long time already. Supporting a private green master school and university can be an additional marketing instrument for many companies and accelerate technological innovations by a manifold. The experiences from the dot-com period, in special, should motivate not to leave the pioneer role to the USA another time. Because Germany is and remains a country with excellent visionaries, developers, and companies. All that is needed in order to stabilize the position of a high-tech nation for green-tech is development, resulting from innovative education politics and interweaving collaboration between inventors, incorporators, capital providers and, in the first place, young and enthusiast people.

With this widely arched range the book on hand intends to provide incentives how the activities for climate and environment protection can be increased on several levels.

No matter whether entrepreneur, environment protector or private individual everybody will also find practical advice here in order to increase his personal activity quota for our climate, all in the sense of Goethe's Faust:

> "The Spirit helps me! I have it now, intact. And firmly write: 'In the Beginning was the Act!'"
> (Faust in Goethe, Faust 1236/37)

Index

www.ingramcontent.com/pod-product-compliance
Lightning Source LLC
Chambersburg PA
CBHW060550200326
41521CB00007B/544